A Chinese Beggars' Den

A Chinese Beggars' Den

Poverty
and Mobility
in an Underclass
Community

DAVID C. SCHAK

UNIVERSITY OF PITTSBURGH PRESS

Published by the University of Pittsburgh Press, Pittsburgh, Pa., 15260
Copyright © 1988, University of Pittsburgh Press
All rights reserved
Feffer and Simons, Inc., London
Manufactured in the United States of America

Library of Congress Cataloging-in-Publication Data
Schak, David C.
    A Chinese beggars' den.

    Bibliography: p. 237.
    Includes index.
    1. Beggars—China—Case studies.   Poor—
China—Case studies.   I. Title
HV4610.A4S33 1988   305.5'69   87-16191
ISBN 0-8229-3822-7

This book is
dedicated to Wolfram Eberhard, teacher and friend,
and to the memory of James C. Jackson
who left us too soon.

Contents

Illustrations

TABLES

CHARTS

Acknowledgments

I OWE A DEBT of gratitude to a number of persons and organizations for assistance with the preparation of this book and the financing of the research that went into it. The initial field research was made possible by a grant from the Joint Committee on Contemporary China of the American Council of Learned Societies and the Social Science Research Council. Subsequent research trips were financed by the Research Sub-committee of the School of Modern Asian Studies, Griffith University, Brisbane, Australia.

Several persons—Steve Tobias, Stevan Harrell, Lawrence Criss-man, Bruce Jacobs, James L. Watson, Rubie Watson, T'ang Mei-chun, Liu Ts'ui-jung, and Hsiao Hsin-huang discussed the research with me, read parts or all of the manuscript, made helpful suggestions, and gave encouragement during the research and writing. Professor Liao Lung-li, Department of Sociology, National Taiwan University, was a friend, advisor, and sponsor during my stays in Taiwan. Iek-a, the former subdistrict head, gave much of his time and shared with me his knowl-edge both of the Beggars and of Taiwan society. Philip Baity, Hideo Suzuki, and Reiko Atsumi assisted with some translations. Lindy Mark and Richard Basham provided secondary references. The residents of Liong-hiat gave me their friendship and trust. Janne Quagliata pre-pared the manuscript, Darren Gale drew the map, and Hu Kuo-t'ai wrote the Chinese characters in the list of terms.

Finally to my wife Cordia Chu, who has assisted me for so long and in so many ways, Doh-jie, doh-jie.

Liong-hiat: Layout, Households, and Residents

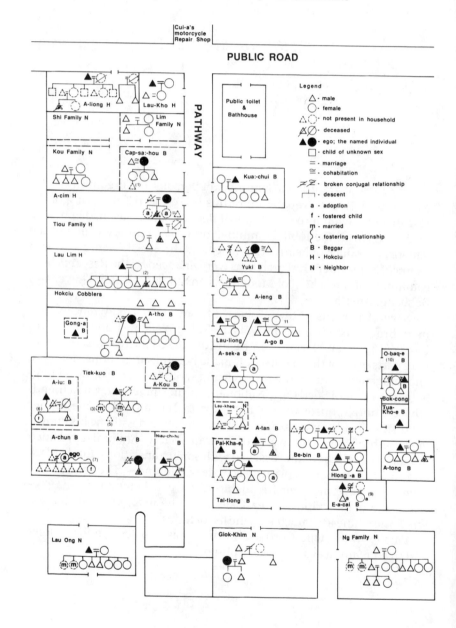

Notes

For all these relationships, see chap. 6 and charts 1–4.

1. This child was not living with his mother but was being cared for by Tiek-kou's relatives in rural Lotung. He later returned to his mother after she married.

2. This son was adopted out to A-liong's daughter.

3. Married to A-tan.

4. Married to Niau-chi-hi:.

5. This child was not living with his mother but was being cared for by Tiek-kou's relatives in rural Lotong. He returned to his mother's care after she married.

6. These children were the offspring of two deceased beggars and were being cared for by A-iu:.

7. This girl was the daughter of a deceased beggar and was cared for by A-chun.

8. This boy was formally adopted out to A-iu: as a descendant, but he lived with and was reared by his natural parents.

9. These are children born to A-pui-a but were adopted by E-a-cai after his relationship with A-pui-a ended.

10. O-baq-e was not a resident of Liong-hiat when fieldwork began in 1973.

A Chinese Beggars' Den

CHAPTER ONE

Introduction

THIS BOOK IS a study of mendicancy in the Chinese cultural tradition and a study of poverty. As a study of mendicancy it examines a number of questions: Who becomes a beggar and why? How do beggars ply their trade? How are they organized and led? What sorts of social relationships do they develop in both kin and nonkin spheres? How do other people conceive of beggars, and why do they give alms to them? In what ways is begging legitimate in the folk view and according to the formal-legal system? And how do beggars adapt to different social, political, and economic situations?

As a study of poverty, the book explores the social life of a poor, highly stigmatized group and the ways in which they finally lift themselves out of their lowly position to a more respectable, orthodox, and prosperous style of life. It looks at the social and cultural compromises they must make in order to acquire descendants, to secure allies, and to survive. It analyzes how they see their life chances and what they do to improve on them. Finally, it looks at the ramifications of this research for theories of poverty, particularly those of Oscar Lewis, Anthony Leeds, and Chaim Waxman.

Data for the book come from both primary and secondary sources. The latter consist of historical and early ethnographic materials, travelers' reports, folklore, and popular magazine articles, and they represent, for the most part, the premodern period and the early twentieth century. The former are data collected in the course of field research among a group I will refer to below as the Liong-hiat Beggars in the periods November 1973 to August 1974, December 1977 to January 1978, and December 1980.

A number of themes and questions run through the book. First,

3

beggars are a subgroup of the poor. Many aspects of their social and economic life reflect this. They expand kinship networks by manipulating real ties and creating fictive ones. Their sexual and "marital" relationships, while not conforming to the professed norms of the outside society, do manifest an order and a logic; moreover, the degree of deviation the beggar community will tolerate is limited. Their level of living, though not necessarily their incomes, is similar to that of other people in the Taipei area. A high percentage of family and household members earn money. In doing so, they must make a choice between legitimate and poorly remunerated activities and illegitimate but usually more lucrative ones, and they often take high risks to gain a better income or achieve mobility.

Second, like other poor people, beggars are creative, innovative, and adaptable. The change in their legal position from legitimate in premodern times to illegitimate in modern times, and a corresponding change in official reaction to them from acceptance and toleration to restriction and suppression dictated a change in the tactics used to get alms. No longer could they openly extort or make an undue nuisance of themselves. Instead they have had to use less obtrusive means. There have also been changes in their organization, especially the means available to the beggar chief to lead and govern them. Without the backing of the state and resultant right to use force, and the ability to monopolize the right to beg in a territory, the chief has had to use the carrot rather than the stick to attract followers. Moreover, begging itself is an adaptation. It is a way to get a living when one can do nothing else, and it is an activity to cease when a more attractive alternative presents itself. The Liong-hiat Beggars, in the degree to which many have been able to achieve upward mobility, have shown themselves remarkably able to take advantage of changes in the opportunity structure in Taiwan brought about through economic development.

Third, beggars are a severely stigmatized group. Social realities belie the number of positive aspects to the image of beggars in the Chinese cultural tradition. Even some persons who view beggars with pity and sympathy also look down on them. The stigma suffered by the Liong-hiat Beggars has left deep emotional scars upon them, especially the younger generation. On the other hand, it has been a powerful motivating force in their quest to leave begging and other stigmatized aspects of the community—gambling, adultery, and failure to marry—behind them.

Fourth, the term *beggar* and its Chinese equivalents are quite nebulous in the way they are used by both Chinese and Westerners who have written on the subject, despite the fact that in both languages the equivalent words have a relatively clear primary denotation. Thus, in what follows, one will see references to "beggars" who work, entertain, perform services, extort, coerce, steal, and even rob. The explanation for this is that many of those who begged in the primary sense—beseeching alms—also did other things to make a living. The loose usage reflects the wide variety of economic activities engaged in by those who, at least part of the time, begged for a living.

To get a perspective on the changes in begging and in the lives of individual beggars, comparisons are made over three time periods. The earliest is the premodern. The little that is known about beggars from this period comes from historical and early ethnographic materials, travelers' reports, and folklore. Because of the scarcity and lack of specificity in these accounts, differences in practice over time and place have largely had to be ignored. However, from these data we learn that beggars were legally accepted and were organized into groups. Their leaders were frequently a part of what amounted to the local government hierarchy, and they had the backing of the state. Being legal, beggars in this period had relatively free rein in their choice of tactics, with the obvious exceptions that they could not break laws against such things as banditry, stealing, or arson. Although begging was regarded as a lowly undertaking, there were no legal restrictions on mobility out of begging such as there were on other low-status occupations. But aside from a few legends and folktales, virtually nothing is known about how common or possible it was for people who once begged to find a more respectable and prestigious way to make a living.

The second period is based on the initial term of field research on the Liong-hiat Beggars, 1973–74, and represents the way they were living then and had been living for the previous decade or so. The most important difference in conditions between this second period and the premodern period is that begging in Taiwan was now illegal and in some ways actively suppressed. This necessitated a change in both tactics and organization. No longer was the beggar chief officially linked to government. No longer did he have the backing of the state in controlling the beggars. No longer could he use force in his exercise of power over them. And no longer could beggars beg openly in the street or resort to forceful measures to extort alms.

The final period is based on subsequent fieldwork (1977–1978; 1980) and represents the changes that, although they had begun to happen several years earlier, had by then become quite evident. These changes were a weakening of the previously strong interpersonal ties and sense of community among the Beggars and a quickening of the pace of upward and outward mobility from begging to other lines of work. These changes were brought about by the rapid economic development in Taiwan in the 1960s and 1970s, which provided both jobs and a vision of the possibility of a livelihood outside mendicancy.

Theories of Poverty

Probably the most widely known of the theories of poverty is the so-called culture of poverty of Oscar Lewis. Though heavily criticized—some would say thoroughly discredited—it or similar ideas persist. Having used it initially only as a phrase (1959), Lewis gradually developed and explained the culture of poverty in a number of publications (1965, 1968). Essentially it is an attempt to explain poverty as a vicious cycle—why it seems to persist among certain populations and families. Lewis proposed a subculture composed of a number of behavioral traits supposedly characteristic of the poor. Initially these are responses to the impoverished conditions the poor are forced to endure, but over time they become a way of life passed down from one generation to the next, and they become a barrier to mobility out of poverty, a sort of low-level equilibrium trap. In his explanation of the failure of the poor to achieve mobility as due to what must be termed flaws in their value system, cognitive structures, and behavior patterns, Lewis' position is similar to that of a number of other writers: Miller (1958), Banfield (1968), Bernstein (1964), Rainwater (1960), and Sowell (1975). This position holds that the poor have a different subculture from that of the dominant classes, and it has been labeled "culturalist" (Waxman 1977).

The main critics of the culture of poverty have taken a "structuralist" (Waxman 1977) position; that is, the differences one finds in the behavior patterns of the poor are imposed on them as a result of their place in the social structure, and they do not have a separate subculture of their own but share the mainstream culture of their society (see e.g., Leeds 1971; Leacock 1971; Valentine 1968).

Waxman is critical of both positions. He cites a number of studies that show that there are, indeed, differences in the value systems and behavioral syndromes between the poor and the nonpoor; moreover, these differences, while they might initially have been adaptations to unfavorable conditions, appear to have become internalized (1977:51–56). His criticisms of the culturalist position are: 1) the internalization of values and cognitive structures does not mean that they cannot be changed when the perceived situation warrants it; and 2) the subculture of poverty, according to Lewis' own words, is not independent of the distribution system of the dominant culture of the society (ibid.:57–67).

Waxman regards these two positions as inadequate to explain persistent poverty, and he offers an alternative: that it is the stigma placed on the poor by the dominant classes that explains their poverty. After demonstrating the centuries-long Western tradition of stigmatizing the poor as lazy, morally depraved and of weak character, and (some) as being welfare cheats, he takes the position of Goffman (1963) that stigmatized persons, reacting to the attitudes of others toward them, redefine their "we." Whereas Goffman speaks of individuals, however, Waxman extends this to "*groups* of people [who] may collectively derive techniques of adjusting to their situations of stigma." They thus develop a subculture "which may persist as the result of internal pressures to retain the group's unique norms and values, or may persist as the result of outside pressure, that is, restrictions and barriers placed upon the minority group by the dominant group" (Waxman 1977:91; emphasis original).

This is not so damaging for homogeneous groups, which may develop an acceptable status-honor system of their own; but for a heterogeneous lower class, "there is little basis from which may be formed an alternative system of status-honor with which members of the lower class can identify. It is under these conditions that the reactions to the stigma of poverty are likely to result in a cluster of traits that have been described as the culture of poverty, which is not an independent culture nor a completely self-perpetuating subculture, but rather a quasiculture, *a dependent subculture,* in the sense that the persistence of the subculture is dependent upon the persistence of the stigma" (ibid.:92–93; emphasis original).

Waxman compares the situation of the poor and their reaction to it to Merton's self-fulfilling prophecy (1968) and asserts that the "self-perception and techniques of adjustment to the situation of stigma is internalized and most often . . . passed on intergenerationally through socialization" (Waxman 1977:94). Furthermore, these patterns of adjustment will continue to be transmitted so long as the poor continue to be stigmatized. However, this does not result in the poor having a complete cultural system of their own. They neither share the system of the dominant classes as posited by the structuralists nor develop one that is completely their own, as the culturalists claim.

Another set of observations about poverty are contained in the "underclass" literature, the primary example being Ken Auletta's book (1982). Auletta does not claim any sort of general explanation for poverty but says that it is caused by and persists as a result of a number of factors—race, the capitalist system, a different and sometimes self-destructive set of values, growing up in a poor home, personal habits, the failure to take advantage of educational opportunities, the middle-class orientation of secondary education, and the existence of a welfare safety net. None of these factors is a sufficient reason for persistent poverty, and the effects of each differ in importance in individual cases. The thrust of Auletta's book is that, of the twenty-five to twenty-nine million poor in the contemporary United States, something like nine million make up an underlcass, a category of people who not only are poor but have little chance to escape from poverty. Moreover, while it has always had its poor, the United States did not have an underclass until after World War II. However, that underclass now appears to be a permanent fixture.

The present study, while its main focus is on begging in Chinese society, is relevant to and has ramifications for the validity of these ideas, and they will be discussed further in the concluding chapter.

The Present Study

This study came about in connection with a project, which commenced in July 1973, to examine the applicability of Oscar Lewis' "culture of poverty" on low-income people in a Chinese cultural setting. The initial target population was a group of squatter households in Taipei City, but soon afterward, with the aid of the Taiwan Christian Service (*T'ai-wan Chi-tu-chiao Fu-li-hui*, hereafter TCS), a number of welfare recipient families (*p'in-min* or *p'in-hu*) were added. Several weeks later, the head of TCS, Mr. Chan Ssu-ts'ung, mentioned another area in which social workers from his organization were working. They initially learned of this area through a clinic they operated when they noticed that a large number of elderly, ill, and disabled people who came to them lived in one small neighborhood. They went to investigate and soon after began a larger-scale project there to improve the welfare, sanitation, and hygiene in the area. When Mr. Chan spoke about that neighborhood, he described it as inhabited by beggars and spoke in some detail of some of the more bizarre aspects of the community—the begging and the gambling, the sexual looseness, and the very crowded conditions in some homes, in which the whole family, teenage sons and daughters included, shared the same sleeping platform. He asked me if I would like to visit the area, and I naturally told him I would. We arranged a time, and one day he and some of his social workers took me out to the Liong-hiat community.

The first few times I visited Liong-hiat, I went with one of the TCS social workers. Initially I was to some degree identified with that organization. Being American, the nationality of many Christian ministers working in Taiwan, and given my acquaintance with the TCS social workers, this is not surprising despite the fact that I was introduced as a *phok-su*, a Ph.D., teaching at National Taiwan University and doing research on Chinese customs (*hong-siok sip-kuan*) in Taiwan. But over the first few months of research, my identity gradually changed from that of minister/social worker/dispenser of largesse to that of researcher. This came about because of several factors. First, TCS had completed most of what it had set out to do in Liong-hiat, and its levels of activity and presence in the community were decreasing. Second, I went to Liong-hiat more and more frequently, and I went on my own. Moreover, my questions were quite different from those of the social workers, and I did not participate in any of the TCS activities there. Finally, after visiting the area for about three months, I was asked twice for assistance of the nature given by TCS. One man, whose consort was terminally ill with uterine cancer, asked me to tell my "boss," meaning Mr. Chan, that he needed money for medical expenses. I told him that Mr. Chan was not my boss, that I had no official connection with him or his organization, and that I was simply a teacher and researcher. The next time I saw Miss Chang, the TCS social worker who had taken me to Liong-hiat, I mentioned the request to her, and she later spoke to the man, affirming what I had said about my role in Taiwan. Another man asked me to contact Miss Chang regarding a tuition grant for his son. I told him essentially the same thing, that I had no way to contact her myself but just saw her occasionally when I ran into her in Liong-hiat.

These two incidents, combined with the other factors, served to clarify my role to the residents, a role that they gradually accepted. The only other questions or suspicions they had about me were, first, why did I, as a Ph.D. and researcher, not work at the university as other scholars did; why did I come to them? Second, would I tell anything about them to a newspaper? In answer to the first question, I told them that one could not learn about the customs of the "old hundred surnames," the common people, from the professors and books at the university and that I wanted to observe and talk to them firsthand. They not only accepted this but actually seemed quite pleased that they were regarded as important. Their anxieties reflected in the second question were based on an incident that had occurred the previous year. Mr. Chan had taken some local officials and reporters out to Liong-hiat to shown them what TCS was doing there and to generate some publicity for the organization. One reporter, in a story that appeared in a major Taipei daily, focused instead on the sensational aspects of the community. The residents of Liong-hiat were both embarrassed and angered, and a few of the young men of the community reportedly went out looking for the reporter to "settle accounts." I told my informants that I had no connection with either reporters or newspapers, and when no stories appeared in any of the papers about them, they began to believe what I had said, and they trusted me with information about the community and individuals in it.

Liong-hiat

Liong-hiat is located in one of the suburbs adjoining Taipei but not within the boundaries of Taipei Shih (Taipei City). Liong-hiat itself is a pseudonym, not for the town in which the beggars' den is located but for the small neighborhood in which the beggars and a number of other families lived. At the time of the research, the general area was a zone in transition. It had previously been agricultural land (used for raising chickens); indeed two Liong-hiat families still made a part of their living growing *ieng-chai* (water convolvulus), and another two had pig sheds, where they kept up to ten pigs at a time. At the time of the research, however, the surrounding area was being developed. Smaller and larger roads were being built, and three- and four-story, blockhouse-style buildings, ubiquitous in greater Taipei, were going up all around Liong-hiat to house families, businesses, small factories, and workshops. The land on which much of Liong-hiat itself was located was privately owned. But it had been condemned by the government as a site for a public building to be built at some future date, and officially, no improvements were allowed on it. Thus the homes the beggars built, first by stealth and then with the unofficial permission of the local government, were squatter huts (*ui-ciong-kian-tiok*).

These homes were originally little more than tiny lean-tos, the barest form of shelter, but many were gradually improved to the state of being well constructed, relatively spacious, even comfortable homes. At the time I began doing research in the area, the larger houses were made of brick and concrete and had metal roofs. Several had two stories, and some had up to eight rooms, small but providing privacy from what was taking place in other parts of the house. The smaller homes were, by contrast, one- or two-room affairs. Some families lived in places as small as fifteen square meters, and single men lived in huts of only ten square meters. These dwellings were made of wood and had no windows and thus no source of ventilation or external light except the open door.

There was no natural boundary completely isolating Liong-hiat from all other neighbors, but it was discrete on two sides. A main road crossed in front of the community (see map, p. xii), on the other side of which were farmers' fields and two small buildings—a workshop for manufacturing ink, and a motorcycle repair shop. Both belonged to people living in Liong-hiat. On one side was a vacant lot that separated Liong-hiat from a row of recently constructed apartment buildings. At the rear and on the other side, homes of members of the Liong-hiat community blended in with those of other neighborhoods, a maze of narrow pathways separating and connecting them.

Two factors made Liong-hiat more or less separable as a community. First, there was a relatively wide L-shaped pathway, the one repaired by TCS, running down the center of the area, with another smaller path feeding into it. Those who lived in the community used the main pathway when leaving and returning to their homes. Outsiders did not. Second, the members of the community all cooperated to gain access to water. None had running water in his home, but one had a tap attached to the outside wall of his house. Community members got their water from him, attaching a hose to his tap to fill large cisterns inside their homes. The payment of the bill was coordinated by the beggar chief. Further, although quite incidently, those I included in the Liong-hiat community are members of an official neighborhood (lin),[1] of which the beggar chief is head. My definition of Liong-hiat differs only slightly from the group of families assisted by the TCS social workers; using the criteria I have already outlined, I have included a few families that they did not.

When I began research there late in 1973, the Liong-hiat community consisted of 37 households and had a population of 169, 78 of whom were adults. The community itself divides into three populations, the Beggars, the Hokciulang, and a residual category that I have called the Neighbors. (When capitalized, Beggars and Neighbors will refer to groups in Liong-hiat. Otherwise, the terms will have their conventional meanings.)

The Beggars, who are the main focus of the field research, are the largest of the three groups. Moreover, it is because of their activities—

begging, gambling, relative sexual looseness, and general behavior—that Liong-hiat has its reputation, not only as a beggars' den (*khit-ciaq-liau*) but also as a place that is *luan*, "chaotic" or "unorthodox." The Beggars make up twenty-four households[2] ranging in size from 1 to 12 members and totaling 101 persons, 46 of whom are adults.[3] At one time or another members of nineteen of these households begged; sixteen households relied on begging for at least part of their income in 1973. The five households in which no one begged are included as Beggars on sociological grounds. Two are kin to Beggar families, and another two had fictive kinship relations with Beggars. More important, their social networks and interaction patterns are inextricably interwoven with those of the Beggars. They form close friendships, chat with one another frequently, gamble together, eat and visit in one anothers' houses, go out drinking together, help one another out in mundane affairs as well as crises, and attend and assist in life-cycle ceremonies of others in the group. Further, they refer to other Beggars as "we" (*guan*) and to the Hokciuling, the Neighbors, and any others as "they" (*in*). This is not to say that there was an absence of contact and interaction between the Beggars and others in Liong-hiat—as is shown in chapter 4, there most certainly was not—but there was a palpable difference in the intensity and the moral and emotional content of the social relationships among the Beggars and between them and others.

In terms of speech group, with three exceptions, the Beggar households are all Hokkien Taiwanese. Most are from Juifang in northern Taiwan, Lotung in the northeast, or Changhua County in the south-central part of the island. The three non-Taiwanese are also speakers of Southern Min (Minnan), the language family to which Hokkien belongs, but they are immigrants, former army commandos, from the Chinese mainland. Two are from Swatow and the other from Tihua.

The Hokciulang, a Hokkien rendering of "people from Foochow," are households in which the heads[4] are all from Foochow. They all emigrated to Taiwan in the 1930s, and they all practice traditional Foochow crafts: making brushes, repairing shoes, making ink sticks and slabs for use with traditional Chinese brush pens, and beating gold leaf for setting into engraved stone.[5] They all speak Hokkien and in some cases Mandarin, but they also speak the Foochow dialect, their native language, which is not mutually intelligible with the other two. Morover, their native region is in a different cultural area from that of the Hokkien speakers, and, like others with a cultural minority self-identification, they have a strong affinity for one another. There are six Hokciu households in Liong-hiat containing twenty-eight individuals, sixteen of whom are adults. One of the households contains only an elderly widow, and another consists of three single male cobblers. Three of the Hokciu households were neighbors of the Beggars before they came to Liong-hiat. The others, tipped off about the available housing by other Hokciulang, moved there as vacancies opened up.[6]

The third population, the Neighbors, is not sociologically a group but is a residual category. There are seven Neighbor households. Two moved there in the early 1950s; one grows vegetables, and the other raises pigs. Attracted by the availability of cheap housing and/ or land and by the location of the area, convenient to local industry and to Taipei the other five came after the Beggars. Three households migrated from the south within the past seven years, renting land to grow vegetables and working as laborers in their slack time. The other two are longtime Taipei residents. One is an old widower living with his son who works as a furniture mover, and the other is a peddler. All except the widower, a Hakka, are Hokkien speakers. Their relationships with others in Liong-hiat vary, but in no case are they very intense.

Data for this book come from interviews and observations in the field and from a variety of written sources. Interviews, usually in the form of casual conversations, were conducted with people from all three populations within Liong-hiat. These provided a number of points of view on the Beggars' activities and life-style. Talking to non-Beggars was also helpful in that they were willing to talk about things the Beggars were at least initially reluctant to discuss. But after learning something about a certain Beggar, whether from a Beggar or a non-Beggar informant, I was able to check it out with others and was frequently able to parlay it into other information. Once it was known that I knew there were beggars there, for example, people became willing to say that they, their parents, or someone else begged, where they begged, how much they made, or how they went about begging. The more I could demonstrate that I knew, the more I was able to find out.

Two sources outside Liong-hiat were also important. Most valuable was a relationship I developed with Iek-a, a man who had been the head of the subdistrict (*li-chang*)[7] that included the Beggar community for almost twenty years. Although of a much higher socioeconomic status than the Beggars, he was a man with a spirit of noblesse oblige, reinforced by his identification with some aspects of Christianity. He attended Christian services with his wife and had great respect for the minister, but he was never baptized because he felt a man in his position vis-à-vis the community must be able to participate in certain customs—drinking, visiting teahouses, and going to folk-religion temples to burn incense. As their subdistrict head, he had been helpful to the Beggars in many ways, and he knew them well and was very well received by them. Moreover, although in a completely amateur fashion, he had taken an interest in them as beggars, and his insights into their society as well as their relationship to the outside world, though unsystematic, were nonetheless valuable to me in learning about the Beggar community. I was at first somewhat reluctant to trust some of the things he told me about the Beggars, but after checking them out with members of the community, I found them to be completely accurate. The other source consisted of friends and informants from Taipei, completely unrelated to the Beggars and often ignorant of their existence. Their thoughts and opinions were valuable in learning about how Chinese view beggars and what movitates them to give or not to give.

The written materials on Chinese beggars are quite varied. The authors, some Chinese, some foreign, include folklorists, ethnographers, historians, travelers, free-lance writers and journalists, missionaries, doctors, administrators, and what might loosely be called social welfare workers. Some references are only brief mentions or observations of beggars buried in works on other subjects. Others are chapters in books or articles specifically about beggars. The longest is an entire book, Shih Ch'ien's (1925) sociological study of Taiwan beggars he contacted through his Ai-ai Liao (now the Ai-ai Chiu-chi-yüan), a charitable organization he and his wife established both to aid beggars and to keep them off the streets. There is also an undated mimeograph report of several pages from the Ai-ai Chiu-chi-yüan (Ai-ai Report) recounting beggar activities in Taiwan and the work of that organization on their behalf. Many of the written sources are lacking in objectivity, the authors displaying a condescending attitude toward Chinese beggars and often toward Chinese in general. Some are unsystematic, either with a flair for reporting the stereotypic and the sensational or simply not specific in terms of number, frequency, or location. Finally, the reports, for such a large country as China, are too few. Given all these factors, there are obvious limitations to an attempt to develop a systematic, accurate picture of begging in premodern times.

There are also regrettable gaps in the field data. More hard information would have been desirable on economic matters—specifically how much the beggars made, how much the operators of the gambling dens made, how much people lost gambling, how people spent their money—and also on the role of the beggar chief and his outside contacts, his relationships with politicians, and his experience in settling disputes. I was unable to collect much of this information for two reasons: first, people were reluctant to talk about it because of its sensitive nature, and second, they often simply did not know; they did not keep track of how much they made or spent. Toward the end of the initial field study, three famiies kept a detailed budget of expenditures for a month. These records turned out to be as informative to them as they were to me.

Most of those living in Liong-hiat were native Hokkien speakers. Few of the adults or uneducated children in the area spoke Mandarin. I used both languages in the field, Mandarin when I could because I am much more fluent in it, but Hokkien when necessary. Most of the transliterations in the book reflect the Hokkien pronunciation, however, as that is the everyday language of the Beggars and for some terms it is the only language in which they make sense. The romanization systems used are modified Bodman (Bodman/Wu) for Hokkien and Wade-Giles for Mandarin. Terms are identified as to language in the index of Chinese terms.

In the sections of the book on Liong-hiat, frequent reference is made to individual beggars by name. To assist the reader there is an appendix consisting of a name list identifying all individuals referred to and a map on p. xii of Liong-hiat showing households and heads of households. The names listed are nicknames and pseudonyms. This reflects usage within the community. Virtually everyone there is referred to by nickname. For example, even children, although not his own, refer to Tiek-kou, the beggar chief, as Tiek-kou, not as Mr. So-and-so. When I initially referred to people using *Mr.* or *Mrs.* and a surname, I was often met with blank stares, particularly by the younger generation. No one used proper or formal names, and the children were often unaware of a person's surname.

Readers who know Hokkien will recognize that some of the nicknames are derogatory in nature. This is true, but so are the real nicknames of these people. These names often reflect something of the character or physical attributes of those who are tagged with them. Cap-sa:-hou, for example, although the name is pseudonym, is well described by it, and her actual nickname has a similar meaning, "dizzy" or "muddleheaded." Pai-kha-e ("crippled") is actually crippled, and his real nickname indicates this. Most of the nicknames, however, reflecting common practice, are the person's surname or a character of his given name preceded by "A-," or followed by "-a." As a prefix, "A-" is used with familiar versions of names, terms of address or reference, and kinship terms. As a suffix, "-a" is a diminutive and is used with names of both persons and things.

The first part of the book (chapters 2 and 3) deals with begging on a historical and general level. It discusses beggar organization, tactics and appeals of beggars in premodern times, their status and image in Chinese culture, and the values, ideas, and thoughts that contribute to the decision to give or not to give to them. With the exception of the last topic, on which earlier observers wrote very little, most of the data in these chapters come from secondary sources. The later chapters, 4–8, deal primarily with the Liong-hiat Beggars and are based mostly on field research in that community. The final chapter ties the two sections together, comments on the themes, and draws possible conclusions from the preceding materials.

CHAPTER TWO

Institutional Aspects

The Legitimacy and Organization of Beggars in Premodern China

BEGGING IN PREMODERN China was a legitimate if lowly occupation. On the level of the "old hundred surnames," people viewed begging either neutrally, as an activity not especially liked but nonetheless the only way to survive for those who took it up, or, in the case of Buddhists and Taoists, positively, as an ideal state of existence divorced from the desires and temptations of the material world. Beggars were also accepted by the government, as both objects of charity and objects of control. As objects of charity, beggars were treated much as were poor people. Central government policy toward the aid of the poor recognized two sorts of relief, public and private (Gamble and Burgess 1921:264). Direct government aid—public relief—was provided in the event of a disaster. Provisions from the "ever-normal" (public) granaries were distributed, and sometimes cash was also given to those in the affected area (see, e.g., ibid.:265–67). Such assistance, to the degree that it actually reached the needy, was no doubt valuable and probably reduced the number of people who might otherwise have temporarily taken to the road to beg.

But the problem of poverty was not restricted to times of disaster. Many people, because of physical disability or lack of property or position, were unable to support themselves even in normal times, and they were provided for under private relief statutes. These policies, which called for the maintenance of poorhouses, foundling homes, lepers' asylums, old age homes, and public cemeteries, varied from period to period and were administered at the local county (*hsien*) level. They were unevenly carried out for a number of rea-

17

sons. First, the central government itself provided no funds, although it did sometimes stipulate a revenue base to support the mandated charities. In the Sung, for example, monies were to come from the estates of the heirless, with any deficit to be made up from interest earnings of the ever-normal granaries (Hsü I-t'ang 1956:208). In the Ch'ing, funds were supposed to come from a tax imposed upon the salt merchants or from "the sale of lands and houses" (Gray 1878ii:48). However, the appropriate revenue base was often insufficient, and it was up to the local magistrate to make up for this either through his own contributions or by tapping the generosity of the local gentry and well-to-do commoners (Ch'ü 1962:161); they, in turn, were sometimes granted titles or posts as rewards (Hsü I-t'ang 1956:211–14). Second, magistrates were rotated about every three years. Thus, no matter how conscientious an official was—and some scored high in this regard (Ch'ü 1962:308)—there was no guarantee that a replacement would be so dedicated. Third, the official expectations of a magistrate were entirely unrealistic, and there were a number of factors that militated against good administration. The magistrates themselves were always outsiders in the district in which they served, and frequently they did not speak or even understand the local dialect. They brought only a skeleton staff with them and had to rely mostly on the more or less permanent body of local underlings who served in the *yamen* (county government). These factors, in combination with the short period of service in any locale, meant that it was extremely difficult for the best of magistrates to keep an eye on what was going on. Moreover, the *yamen* underlings earned the great bulk of their income on a fee for service basis, and they were notorious for their schemes and methods of squeezing the local population for their own benefit. Yet the magistrate had to delegate many tasks to them, including, often, such things as verifying reported charitable cases and administering relief funds. The result was that the underlings often lined their pockets, put their relatives on the relief rolls, and embezzled donations to those who were sick and could not come and collect them (Hsü I-t'ang 1956:210). Furthermore, the magistrates themselves were not infrequently corrupt. Thus a situation existed wherein, because of an insufficient revenue base and dishonesty in the administration of welfare in particular and government in general, the poor were inadequately provided for. This, without doubt, greatly increased the number of persons who felt compelled to turn to begging for a living.

Aside from the government itself, there was a number of sources of private charity in China. Corporate lineages and guilds frequently had funds to assist their indigent or otherwise needy members. Religious groups, especially Buddhist and Muslim, established a number of different sorts of charitable institutions. And many private individuals were very generous with their substance, contributing to both government and nongovernment charities.

Despite all this, welfare was insufficient to support all those in need. In face of this, another step the government took was to do nothing about beggars—simply to allow them to beg even when this took the form of coercion that was virtually impossible to resist. Thus Gray reports that in Kwangtung, because there were not enough asylums to house all the lepers, some anchorages were set aside for boats to accommodate them. If they had too little money to support themselves, they paddled their boats along the river to beg from the crews of other boats. Ten to twenty leper boats would together set upon one boat, almost forcing the sailors to contribute (1878ii:52–53). Macgowan speaks of beggars being "entitled to collect a fee on the occasion of a marriage" (1912:295), and after a detailed description of how they thoroughly disrupted the wedding ceremony of a family that refused to pay a sum deemed appropriate to their wealth, he states, "no law can touch for what they are doing [and] . . . they are careful to commit no act that shall bring their headman, who is responsible for their conduct, within the clutches of the law" (ibid.:297). The same license applied to their exacting money from shopkeepers or from those holding birthday celebrations or funerals. Macgowan refers to the former as "levying what is really a poor rate on the warehouses and shops of the town" (ibid.:295). This policy of simply allowing beggars to beg as a substitute for providing government support is consistent with the policy adopted toward banished criminals. Not only were they allowed to beg, but they were even issued with permits by the local mandarin (ibid.:299). Although there is no reference to beggars being so formally legitimated, what they did was quite permissible in the eyes of the authorities.

In short, beggars, as well as vagrants, vagabonds, and other poor and rootless elements who also begged from time to time, were legal in premodern China. Begging was not a crime (F. Liu 1936:99), and those who did it were not suppressed or hindered by the legal machinery of the state as long as they broke no law. This is in stark contrast to the treatment of their counterparts in preindustrial Europe. There one could not legally beg or be a beggar, and those deemed guilty were variously expelled, imprisoned, confined to their home area, or put into workhouses (Tuan 1979:188–94). In China it was only after foreign intervention into government affairs, in post-Boxer Peking and in the International Concession in Shanghai, for example, that begging became illegal, either in law or in fact, and was subject to police supression (Gamble and Burgess 1921:275–76; F. Liu 1936:102).

However, begging, though permitted, was controlled in China. Local magistrates appointed beggar chiefs for various areas within the cities (Macgowan 1912:293; Wang 1974:148; Doolittle 1865ii:260; Gee 1925:24), providing for indirect supervision of the beggar groups by the magistrate (Gray 1878ii:59). Their aim was by no means to stop begging altogether but to regulate and limit it. The chiefs would negotiate with local shopkeepers and with wealthy families holding private ceremonies to keep the beggars away in exchange for a fee. Proprietors of large and medium-size shops usually paid in advance in exchange for freedom from beggars for a period of several months to a year and were given some sort of symbol to hang above the door, a gourd or a piece of paper on which were written words to the effect that this "good man" had made his contribution to the welfare of the beggars and that the "good brethen"[1] should stay away. Anyone caught violating such an agreement was subject to severe punishment (see, e.g., Doolittle 1865ii:261). Proprietors of smaller shops who could not afford to pay in advance had to endure daily visits from beggars, who came to receive the one or two cash[2] considered rightfully theirs. Well-to-do families could also pay the chief to ensure that no beggars would come to disrupt a celebration or funeral at their home, and the chiefs would then post a beggar or two outside the front gate to keep their colleagues away (Wang 1974:150). Failure to pay a chief would, of course, have the opposite effect: the chief would then appoint beggars to beg at the shop or home (Gee 1925:20; Bennett 1931:216). Gray noted what is a remarkable example of vertical integration: beggar chiefs were not infrequently city watchmen or "proprietors of establishments where marriage chairs or funeral biers are kept for hire" (1878ii:60), just the right places to gather "intelligence" useful to the beggars.

Beggar chiefs could control the activities of those in their dens, and by granting the beggars exclusive right to beg in their territory of residence, the authorities, through the beggar chief, also achieved control over itinerants. Someone new to the area was required to pay a "courtesy call" on the beggar chief (Liu Hsü 1936:171), and to beg in that area, one needed to join the group itself (Gamble and Burgess 1921:274). Those desperate or foolish enough to attempt to beg in an area without the permission of the chief would be set upon and beaten by local beggars, who were only too happy to protect their monopoly (Matignon 1900:237; Wang 1974:152). In the event that the intruders were too strong, the chief would have to pay them off in order to protect the local shops and residents from them (Gee 1925:12–13).

I have found no evidence of such a scheme to protect those in rural areas, but in all probability they would not have been bothered so frequently or constantly as those in the cities. There were undoubtedly beggars who lived and found support in the towns and marketing centers, and there were also the local bullies and the gangs of bandits who were termed beggars by some writers (see, e.g., Hsiao 1960:455–62). However, the relative poverty of the peasants in all probability did not provide an adequate support base for a permanent contingent of beggars. Moule, in fact, states that beggars were found in the country-side "chiefly in the warm weather," and that they returned "to the great cities when winter [drew] near" (1902:123–24), probably because there they had access to free food from government and private soup kitchens (chou-ch'ang) (Gamble and Burgess 1921:276).

It appears that the beggar chief had an even wider responsibility toward the maintenance of social order than simply the control of beggar activities. According to Gee, together with the di-fong (local warder), he was charged with monitoring and reporting illegal activities in the area under his jurisdiction: "If a theft took place in the night, the di-fong was called to look into the matter, but if it took place during the day the Kha Doen (beggar chief) was called to clear up matters" (1925:24). This connection between the local warder and the beggar chief is substantiated elsewhere. Gray writes that "watchmen in charge of the streets of cities are also usually the heads of [beggar] guilds. This is . . . [because] . . . tradesmen consider such persons to be in a position to quell the disturbances which mendicants are sometimes disposed to create" (1878ii:60). Macgowan notes that the ti-pao (another term for "local warder") were always about when the "wandering criminals" were begging; "dressed like any ordinary coolie . . . smoking his long bamboo pipe, ready at a moment's notice to intervene (in the event that they tried to injure anyone), and drag them off to prison" (1912:299). Chu goes so far as to give the beggars themselves a role in maintaining social order. He recounts a legend told by Peking mendicants that the original beggars there were Manchu vagabonds who followed the Ch'ing rulers into the city and, in exchange for a protection fee, kept order on the streets. They were displaced from this function when the Japanese military, following the Boxer Uprising, set up a police force in the part of Peking they controlled; the Manchu court followed suit a short time later (1974:27).

Although the evidence does not all point in the same direction, it is quite likely that the beggar chief was not actually a beggar. Liu Hsü (1936:171) and the author of the Ai-ai Report state that the chief more or less worked his way up through the ranks and became a sort of primus inter pares, and Matignon says that he was elected by the universal suffrage of the city beggars (1900:236). However, others say that the chief was not a beggar himself but an ordinary citizen who volunteered for the position (Wang 1974:147), paid for it, or had it officially conferred upon him "as an act of benevolence . . . [because he] . . . had been sick and was unable to make ends meet, or . . . had met with certain reverses and was down and out financially" (Gee 1925:24). Considering the degree of interaction between the chief and his followers, it is most likely that the former was not himself a beggar; several report that the chief left the day-to-day running of the den to his assistant (who *was* a beggar), and Matignon states that he rarely showed himself among his subjects (1900:236). It is quite possible that the first in an ancestral line of chiefs might actually have been a beggar, but it is likely that the position of beggar chief was usually filled by the same sort of person who became a *yamen* runner or clerk, one from a lowly background looking for a fairly lucrative and secure position, albeit one that carried a low level of prestige. Although the position was not necessarily permanent (Wang 1974:147), on good behavior it could be held for life, and, like a franchise, it was both salable (Gee 1925:24) and inheritable (Doolittle 1865ii:261; Wang 1974:149). Thus in all probability the position passed from father to son.

Given such a position, it was expected that the beggar chief would achieve the desired result of control over the local beggars as well as any wandering elements, and there were consequences if he did not. Wang reports that in Taiwan, under Ch'ing law, a chief was held legally responsible for crimes committed by those in his charge (1974:154); Macgowan substantiates this for south China (1912:297). This being the case, it is not surprising that the chief had great power over the beggars to effect his will and to control them. Shih Ch'ien likens a chief's power to that of a king and states that the beggars must obey him absolutely (1925:12). Chu describes his power as "unsurpassed," stating that "none dare oppose him" (1974:27). Matignon calls him an autocrat and claims that in carrying out his legitimate duties, such as settling disputes, he is never interfered with by the police, and that he holds life-and-death power over the beggars (1900:236). Wang agrees, describing the chief-beggar relationship as one between "master and servant," and reporting that if one disobeys an order of the chief, he could expect punishment "to the extent that his eyes may be plucked out or his shinbone broken in two. . . . His flogging of the beggars is not regarded as strange; it is a common thing, even to the extent of beating one to death" (1974:148). Only the Ai-ai Report gives a different picture, stating that a chief was not a "tyrant who must be obeyed," but this source reports the situation in Taiwan under the Japanese, when the government had and exercised far greater control over local social order than did the Ch'ing authorities under the dynasty or any of the warlord regimes on mainland China, and it probably did not authorize a beggar chief to use physical force to control the beggars.

Aside from controlling the activities of beggars, the responsibility of the beggar chief included helping them to beg, looking after their welfare, and keeping order in the den. In regard to the first, a chief gathered information useful to the beggars—where and when an "unpaid for" celebration or funeral was to be held or where a new shop was about to open. He directed the beggars where and when to beg (Gee 1925:20, 25), assigning each a territory and making sure that no one encroached on the area of another (Gamble and Burgess 1921:274). He or his assistant took them out to beg each day and brought them home again in the evening, and he determined the amounts due from shopkeepers and wealthy families (Ai-ai Report). He sometimes represented the beggars to shopkeepers who did not pay periodic protection money, collecting the alms and dividing them up so that the shopkeeper did not have to deal with each beggar individually (Wang 1974:150; see also Bennett 1931:216). In Peking, at least, he taught them how to perform the arts, to sing, and to insert "lucky" lyrics into their songs (Liu Hsü 1936:174), and he also regulated the use of tactics depending on age, state of body and health, and other criteria. Some types were allowed to go from house to house whereas others had to beg on the streets; some could go from shop to shop whereas others had to beg in one spot: only one beggar was allowed on a street, never two, one working each side. Even the terms a beggar could use to address a potential giver were regulated: certain beggars were allowed to call people *ta-shu* (oldest of father's younger brothers) or *shen-tzu* (father's younger brother's wife) but never *lao-yeh* or *t'ai-t'ai* (honorable gentleman, honorable lady) (Liu Hsü 1936:176–79).

In terms of welfare, the chief provided beggars with housing, "simple, little rooms" according to Wang (1974:148), for which they paid him rent (Gray 1878ii:59). He also saw to the expenses of those who were sick and bought medicine for them, and he paid the funeral expenses of those who died (Liu Hsü 1936:171–172). For their part, the beggars had to obey the rules of the den (Gray 1878ii:59) and turn over a share of their take to the chief (Gamble and Burgess 1921:274).

Beggars' dens were corporate groups, the organization of which resembled that of a guild or lineage (Gray 1878ii:59, Gamble and Burgess 1921:274). In Taiwan dens, at least,[3] there was a patron deity, Li Thiq-kuai, "Iron-crutch Li," one of the Taoist Eight Immortals, and reportedly a beggar himself. His image was on the main altar of the den. New members paid fifteen cash to the chief, who then burned candles, incense, and ritual money as a sacrifice to Li (Wang 1974:152). The new member was then brought before the image and bowed to it (Shih Ch'ien 1925:16), much as a new bride is presented and bows to her husband's ancestral tablet. The beggars credited their success in getting alms to Li working through the givers, and they believed they would die without his protection (ibid.). They celebrated and made sacrifices to him on his birthday, the eighth day of the fourth lunar month (Wang 1974:152), and violaters of den rules (such as those who stole another's possessions or anothers man's woman), in addition to making recompense to the offended and to other members of the den, had to make sacrifices to Li and ask his forgiveness (Shih Ch'ien 1925:16).

The dens consisted of both single beggars and those in family situations, including children. Aside from the chief and possibly the assistant chief, the beggars were ranked according to age and called accordingly, *Lao-ta, Lao-erh, Lao-san*, "Eldest, Number Two, Number Three" (Liu Hsü 1936:171).

Several observers claim that there was a sort of communistic order within the dens. Matignon writes that all monies collected by the beggars were pooled and then distributed among the members of the den (1900:238). Wang states that the beggars all lived together in a house, although each family had its own stoves, utensils, and personal property (1974:152). Stott reports, however, that the food for the community she observed was prepared in two big kitchens and shared alike among the members of the den; moreover, each member was required to contribute a "minimum quantity of food and cash" to the common store (1927:831). There was also cooperation and mutual aid among the beggars. If one was ill or could not beg, others would sustain him, at least for a time (Wang 1974:152).

There is some question as to whether beggar groups were actually guilds. They are referred to as such by most Westerners who mention them (Gamble and Burgess 1921:274; Gray 1878ii:59–61; Martin 1900:79; Smith 1900:71; Gee 1925:2; Matignon 1900:236–38; Gernet 1962:99; Moule 1902:123), many of whom emphasize their strength or their ubiquity. However, neither Morse (1909) nor Burgess (1926), whose works on guilds are most authoritative, write of beggar guilds, the closest to them being the San Hwang Hui, a guild of blind persons who earned their living by singing and telling fortunes (Burgess 1926:17–18), activities often associated with begging. Moreover, Chinese writers, in referring to beggar groups, use words that denote a place (*kai-ch'ang, ch'i-kai-liao*) rather than an association (*hui*). Of the Westerners, only Stott gives a Chinese term, that being *t'ao-fan-hui*, "beggar's association" (1927:831). Others simply use the English term, *guild* (*gild*).

The Status and Conflicting Images of Beggars

In the information provided from folklore material and from literary and ethnographic sources, there emerge two opposing views of beggars in the Chinese cultural tradition. A negative view holds them to be lazy, scornful, "useless" creatures, lower even than gangsters or prostitutes. A positive one depicts them as pitiful beings, often connected in some way with positive supernatural beings and miracles; paragons of virtue and thus worthy of support; or strong, powerful knight-errant heroes who beg for their daily needs. The negative view comes mainly from ethnographic materials and field research and without doubt represents the majority view of beggars. The positive view is found more frequently in the folk literature materials but is also reflected in varying degrees in many informants' private interpretations.

Primary evidence of the low status of mendicants may be seen in the sorts of activities considered begging and the kinds of persons included in, or excluded from, the category "beggars." In the folk world view, not all who "beg" are beggars. The Liong-hiat Beggars exclude some activities from begging, giving them a higher prestige value, and exclude others—faking and strong-arm tactics, for example—in order to raise the status of those who do beg.

The most basic act of begging is to ask someone for food or money as charity or with no serious intention of repaying it. Such an act is called in Hokkien, the language of the Liong-hiat beggars, *pun-*

ci: (money) or *pun-png* (food).[4] But not everyone who asks for donations of food or money is a *khit-ciaq,* "beggar."[5]

For example, there are certain similarities between beggars and monks. Both are described as having no family to rely on (*bou ka kho kho*), and both go from shop to shop, sometimes from house to house, asking for money. But there the similarities end. Although monks who "beg" are called "beggar monks" (*khit-ciaq he-siu:*), they are not "beggars" (khit-ciaq). Moreover, a beggar *pun-ci:,* but a monk *hua-ian.* This term refers to the Buddhist nature of his act. Literally, *hua-ian* is to "transform destiny," to teach people to change (*hua*) the cause and result (*ian*), that is, their previous karma and their fate in the next life. It also denotes a bringing to fruition of one's Buddhist destiny by means of begging (*bo-hua*); begging is a way to rid oneself of one's earthly desires, a prerequisite to self-perfection, and it also provides an object of charity for others, who can gain merit by giving. Thus, although in some respects the deed is the same in both *hua-ian* and *pun-ci:,* the intent and purpose are different, and the two words cannot be used interchangeably.

But there is another difference between the "begging" of monks and of beggars. When beggars solicit alms, they dress in old, tattered, strange-looking rags, while monks dress in their normal religious garb, black robes and a black belt with a bag attached and hanging down in front. Moreover, the manner in which each asks for money is different. The beggar implores or entreats a passerby, and in the process he demeans himself, kneeling or sitting on the street or standing with his head bowed and his hand outstretched, placing himself both literally and figuratively below the potential giver. The monk, on the other hand, without a hint that there could be anything shameful or demeaning in what he is doing, stands erect in the door of a shop or home and extends a receptacle for money with one hand while ringing a small bell with the other. He need not say a word; his message is clearly understood. Furthermore, as a beggar's appeal is based on pity, he must continually empty his receptacle of all but a few small coins. The monk's appeal, on the other hand, is based on moral obligation; thus he displays a fuller receptacle in which there are several quite conspicuous large bills.

A second type of person who asks for money but is not usually considered a beggar is referred to by the Ai-ai Report as a *sin-su khit-ciaq,* a "gentry beggar." He is nicely dressed, well mannered, and well spoken, and he approaches an individual on the street, in a shop, or in a government office and asks for money on compassionate grounds—to help someone in his family who is in need of medical treatment or to make a trip home for which he does not have sufficient funds. Several informants described a variation of this type. He is an acquaintance of those whom he asks for money. Usually male, he is educated, perhaps a schoolmate of the donors, and, if not from a middle- or upper-middle-class background, he at least affects the appearance and demeanor of one who is.

However, these people do not work but instead sponge off friends, classmates, or people of substance over whom they can exert some sort of moral claim. An informant told of two such men, one a classmate, the other a former student. Neither would take up any job offers acquaintances arranged for them. One claimed that he was going to be a banker and frequently talked about how this or that bank was negotiating to hire him, but none ever did. These men managed a living by making periodic rounds of friends, acquaintances, schoolmates, relatives, and others, asking each for a bit of money, a "loan." They never asked for much, but, getting a small amount from each contact, they were able to maintain a standard of living that apparently was satisfactory to them. This pattern had persisted for about twenty-five years. My informant said that what distinguished these men was their persistence and their being thick-skinned (*bin-phe kau*). His wife had berated one of them one day when he came around for his handout, telling him that he should get a job. Undaunted, he listened patiently until she had finished and then, calmly, asked again for the money. This same individual would also stand outside the door for hours if she did not answer the bell, and if she did succeed in outwaiting him, he would simply return a few days later.

Another informant, whose father had been quite prominent in his home area near Foochow on the Chinese mainland, related how, in Taiwan, people would come to ask his father for help—financial assistance, introduction to employment, or other types of sponsorship. Sometimes their claim on this man was that they were distant relatives, but most frequently they were simply *t'ung-hsiang*, people from the same county. His father helped whenever he could because of the moral element in the claimed relationship, a feeling of noblesse oblige, the prestige he gained by being able and willing to help, and the potential embarrassment that could result from a refusal.[6]

Although such people were referred to as beggars in the Ai-ai Report, informants did not clearly classify them as such or their activities as begging because they did not affect the appearance and demeanor of beggars. Several described them as "not knowing shame" (*beq kian siau*), but because they did not plead, entreat, or appear dirty, poor, ragged, disheveled, or disabled, they were not regarded as beggars.

A third group who "begged" but were not considered beggars were refugees, people fleeing from some natural or man-made disaster and who had lost, at least temporarily, their means of livelihood. "Refugees beg for food," said an informant, "but that is only temporary. They have both self-respect and a skill. As soon as possible they will begin to earn their living again." Another informant remarked that although refugees might be dressed in ragged clothes and ask people for money or food, they were not beggars. They had home and kin. They needed some assistance, but only temporarily. He even insisted that what refugees did could not be referred to as *pun-ci:* or *pun-png*, begging.

Some people in China became temporary beggars on a fairly regular basis. Huntington writes of peasants from villages in Hopei whose fields were so small that they could grow only enough food to last nine to ten months of the year. Each year in autumn they would put aside enough grain to allow them to plant the next year's crop and to survive until it ripened. Then they consumed the remainder of their grain into the winter, and when it was exhausted, they sealed up the doors and windows of their houses and went out to beg for their survival, returning the following spring to plant their crops (1945:188–189). Ti reports a similar phenomenon he observed as he traveled throughout China as a Red Guard. Every once in a while he and his friends would encounter groups of people carrying a certificate signed by the chairman of the Assistance to Poor Peasants Committee of X Brigade, Y Commune, detailing the name, sex, age, and place of origin of the group leader, explaining why the people were begging—usually because of a bad harvest or other disaster—and urging readers of the certificate to "extend comradely concern and the spirit of mutual cooperation, and arrange satisfactorily for their food, shelter, and work" (1974:77).

Another type of "nonbeggar" is one who, while literally "asking" for it, actually demands money by means of threat, either direct or implied. Although such people are sometimes referred to as *khit-ciaq lo-mua:*, "beggar-gangsters" or *pa-to khit-ciaq*, "tyrant-beggars," many informants, both beggars and nonbeggars, denied that obtaining money in this manner was begging. Beggars, they said, never demanded money or threatened; they *kiu*, "beseeched." Only hoodlums *kha-iu*, "extorted." (However as will be shown in the next chapter, it is not uncommon to see extorters, bullies, and even bandits referred to as beggars.)

Finally, in popular Chinese literature one finds knights-errant (*wu-hsia*) who asked more commonly for a meal than for money. Again, they were not seen as beggars. Whereas beggars were power-less, bowing or prostrating themselves before the potential giver, the knight-errant was strong and asked for what he wanted as an equal. He did not beg because he could not make a living but because a living in a conventional manner was such a mundane affair, and he was concerned with more profound matters.

Aside from the types just described who ask for charity but are not considered beggars, there are also certain activities, often associated with mendicants, that are not regarded as begging in the normal sense of the word. Although Chinese researchers, when writing about Chi-nese beggars, include those who entertain by such means as singing, dancing, playing a musical instrument, telling stories, acting, or per-forming martial arts, many informants, especially the Beggars them-selves, do not classify these acts as *pun-ci:* even when a receptacle is passed around or set upon the ground in hopes that those watching will put money into it. Instead, they say, this is *be-gi,* "selling art or talent." According to informants, one does not give money to these people as a charity but as payment for a good, entertainment. And although they do not deny that many who earn a living this way are beggars, they rank them well above those who merely beg on the streets, and several sources indicate that their income is also substan-tially higher (Liu Hsü 1936:172; Wang 1974:150–51).

In a similar vein, it is a custom, called *tiau-lo-ce,* at Taiwan funer-als for some mourners to wait along the roadside for the procession to the grave site and to offer a sacrifice to the spirit of the deceased as the coffin passes by. The procession stops as it encounters such groups, and a member of the party gives each mourner a return gift (*hui-li*), either a piece of white silk or money (see Wu Tao-ying 1969:154) on behalf of the family of the deceased and in appreciation for sacrificing to their ancestor. Beggars take advantage of this cus-tom. They learn when funeral processions of wealthy individuals will be held and go en masse to sacrifice and receive their gift. But to the beggars and others, even the writer of the Ai-ai Report, this is not begging but *work,* a *cit-giap* (occupation); those who *tiau-lo-ce* are performing a valid service, sacrificing to the ancestors of another, and contributions to them are payments for it.

Two other conditions could exclude one from being a beggar.

One old woman in the Liong-hiat community, A-chun, lived a humble existence, getting her money from government and Christian welfare agencies, gambling, and occasional gifts from her sons. Once in a while, however, she would go to the homes of wealthy persons and ask them to "help her out a bit." But her neighbors did not regard her as a beggar because she did not go out often, and when she did, she went only to certain homes, not onto the streets to kneel and entreat passersby with an outstretched hand. In this case, selectivity and frequency, together with her style of asking for money, excluded her from being considered a beggar. However, in excluding her, the Beggar chief also reinforced the lowly status of "beggar," a label to avoid if at all possible.

Finally, Tiek-kou, the Liong-hiat Beggar chief, and several others made the stipulation that a true beggar was one who was unable to support himself because of his physical condition; he begged because he was unable to work (*bou kang-cok lieng-liek*). They expressly excluded those who faked injuries or handicaps, who "borrowed" children, who misrepresented themselves in any way, and whose purpose was to beg in order to avoid working. Such people, they insisted, were fakes. They were not beggars. They simply used tricks (*khi-phian chiu-tua:*) because they were too lazy to work. In making this distinction informants attempted to confer at least a little prestige on a lowly status position; real beggars may be at the bottom of the heap, but at least they are honest and truly in need.

Taking the elements just discussed, we have the following definition: a beggar is one who is in dire need and asks for goods as a charity or gift and who offers nothing tangible or intangible, in return. He does this voluntarily, in order to survive, not for religious or spiritual reasons. He is regarded as having no home or family, no property, and no skills by which he can earn a living. In appearance he is ragged and dirty, he looks poor, and he may be disabled. He must beg on a regular basis. He must ask for donations without threat or coercion, either direct or implied, and he must ask in a humble, lowly, self-deprecating manner. Such a definition would be quite impractical, however, as it is not adhered to in the literature on beggars, or even by the Liong-hiat Beggars themselves, among whose number were a few who, despite being quite able-bodied and capable of working, begged for a living and were referred to throughout the Liong-hiat community as beggars. Nonetheless, our definition and the reasons behind it do give an insight into some of the ideas about beggars in the Chinese cultural tradition, and they also indicate the low status of those who make their living that way.

There are a number of reasons why beggars are looked down upon or viewed negatively. They are regarded as repulsive, unpleasant to be around, and even contagious or contaminating. They are described by informants and in the literature as being dirty, smelly, ragged, disheveled, and diseased. In the folk literature,[7] there are many instances of beggars having leprosy, scabies, or running sores. Others in the stories are asked to clean the sores, perhaps to suck the pus (a more defiling and contaminating substance even than feces) from them. The purpose of this ordeal or test of faith is to demonstrate that the giver is a truly compassionate individual who is willing to transcend the world and his cares for self (Eberhard 1965:131–32; Wu Tao-ying 1969:404–05). Statements from informants support this defiling image of beggars. One said that she was afraid to be touched by "dirty beggars," and another said that his grandmother always fed the beggars who came to her door, but she never took a beggar's own bowl into the house to fill it. She considered it too dirty, too potentially contaminating. Instead she gave him a bowl of her own and told him to keep it; she did not want it back in the house after the "dirty beggar" had used it.

Other informants mentioned the potential contamination of beggars with regard to food. One said that even if a beggar had the money to pay, a restaurant owner would not want him in his place, and neither would the patrons. Beggars were simply too dirty, smelly, and ragged, too unpleasant to be around. Another informant confirmed this, saying that a beggar could never get a job as a cook. People would not want to eat food prepared by such a person. One of the men in the Liong-hiat Beggar group was a good cook, but although he was not a beggar himself, he had been unable to find work cooking because of his association with beggars. Moreover, according to one informant, business at the noodle shop just outside Liong-hiat, which is run by one of the Hokciu families living there, has suffered because beggars frequent the place.

Another reason for the low status of beggars is that they are seen as inadequate (be-sai). Traditional China can be seen as a Spencerian world—as the Chinese express it, a "man-eat-man world." There is ample literature on the predatory nature of traditional Chinese society, of lineages bullying other lineages (Watson 1975:23) and even swallowing up weaker ones (Freedman 1958: chap. 13), of local bullies taking advantage of others (Smith 1900:216–17), and even of hungry ghosts (spirits of those who have no heirs on earth to make sacrifices, thus to feed them) bullying the spirits of the poor but not those of wealthier families (A. Wolf 1974a:170). Beggars can be regarded as unable to survive in this world for several reasons. They frequently are—or pretend to be—maimed, crippled, diseased, or otherwise deformed; they can thus be presumed to be weak, helpless, and unable to work or earn a living. Because of this, and because they dress in ragged clothes, one can reasonably assume them to be poor. Finally, when asking for food or money, beggars usually assume a very deferential and servile manner, placing themselves in an inferior position to that of the potential giver. For all these reasons, a beggar can be seen as unable to take care of himself or to hold his own. He has no *mien-tzu*, the prestige component of "face" (see Hu 1944), and thus he is unworthy of respect or even of notice. Moreover, I have argued elsewhere that the poverty of beggars—their inability to support themselves—can be seen as a source of envy and therefore a threat to those who have, that is, the potential givers (Schak 1979; see also Foster 1965, 1972). One informant, in fact, stated that one of the reasons her family gave to beggars was to correct the imbalance between the haves and the have-nots: "When you are so much better off than another, you should give."

A third reason for people to see beggars in a negative light is that they are heterodox. Many informants stated this directly or indirectly. Several, in reference to the beggars' misshapen bodies, to their being *wu-kuan pu tuan-cheng* (the five [body] parts not in their proper place), said, "They aren't the same as we are." Although the phrase generally refers to deformities of the face and head, informants said they referred also to a cripple, a blind person, or to one with a disease. Another informant, who operated a cafeteria (*tzu-chu ts'an*), said that a beggar was of a lower status than a prostitute because, when the latter was not working, she lived a life not very different from a housewife. "You wouldn't be able to tell the difference," he said. "*She cooks at home.* A beggar doesn't. He gets his food from others who have cooked it already."[8] That such a man, who cooked for and served some one thousand people a day, would single out beggars from the students and workers who make up the bulk of his clientele adds to the significance of his statement.

Other informants referred to the relative status of prostitutes and beggars. One considered the beggar lower because she had had many encounters with beggars but none, to her knowledge, with prostitutes. "Beggars are dirty and easy to spot, but one can't tell a prostitute when she isn't working." Yet another informant said of prostitutes, "At least they are more presentable in public. They don't dress in such a ragged, dirty, offensive manner."

Another difference between beggars and ordinary people is their hair. That hair has great symbolic significance has been well demonstrated (Strong 1967; Leach 1958). It is the most readily manipulated part of the body, and thus it can be used to convey a great variety of messages. Moreover, the Chinese, anxious over all sorts of disorder or *luan* (see, e.g., Solomon 1971), have demonstrated great anxiety over hair and what it symbolizes. In both Taiwan and the People's Republic during the 1960s, long hair on males was forbidden, purportedly because it makes it difficult to distinguish them from females. Chinese in America earlier this century were often badgered and bullied by having their queues cut off; what had been a hated imposition of the Manchus to distinguish the Han Chinese from themselves became a symbol of identity to the Chinese away from home. Smith relates how the village bully arranged both this clothes and his hair to effect a more fearsome appearance (1900:213). Macgowan (1912) makes repeated reference to the disheveled, matted, filthy, disorderly hair of Chinese beggars:

His hair, instead of being plaited, is matted and disheveled. No comb could ever find its way through such a tangled wilderness. (P. 292)

His hair hangs disorderly about his face and escapes in loose tufts from his queue. (P. 294)

Her hair was a perfect wilderness of disorder. (P. 296)

His face has a scowl on it, which is rendered all the more forbidding by his hair falling in ragged tufts over his forehead and eyes and giving him a bold and savage appearance. (P. 296)

Their hair was not done up in the ordinary pigtail, but was allowed to hang disordered and uncombed at its own free will. Stray tufts fall down over their foreheads. (Pp. 298–99)

Liong-hiat beggars, too, believing it enhanced their effectiveness, disarranged their hair before going out to beg.

Beggars used a similar ploy in dress, not only by wearing dirty, smelly, ragged, and sometimes strange-looking garments, but also by wearing them in an unconventional manner, as if they were simply thrown onto the body. By defying convention in their appearance, they showed themselves to be unpredictable, outside the conventions of normal society, and therefore a threat, something to be gotten rid of as quickly as possible. Best just to give them a few coins and be done with them.

Finally, beggars are different in that they are frequently perceived as being homeless and not having a normal family structure. Although these perceptions were not correct with regard to the Liong-hiat beggars (see chap. 6), they might have been true of some beggars in the past. In any case, it is easy to understand why such ideas exist. Male beggars, frequently seen begging alone, are often thought of as "bare sticks" (*kuang-kun*), that is, single. Female beggars, even though they often beg accompanied by children, are perceived as having no husband-breadwinner—precisely the impression they are trying to create. Because beggars usually avoid begging in areas adjacent to their own neighborhoods, they often appear as wandering strangers, people without home or roots. The very fact that they are begging points to their having no patrimony and therefore no connection with parents or ancestors. Informants frequently referred to beggars as *bou chin bou chiek*, "without kith or kin," and as *bou ka kho kui*, "without family or home to return to." Since the most basic level of existence for a Chinese is as a member of a kinship group, beggars are heterodox indeed.

Their being perceived as wanderers with at best a loose connection with home and parents is evidence for a fourth reason for viewing beggars negatively—that they are unfilial. It is the moral duty of an adult male to be in a position, both a physical location and a financial condition, to support his parents. Since beggars are not at home and since they are "poor," they fail to live up to these obligations. Mencius said, and Chinese generally accept, that the most unfilial act of all is the failure to produce an heir. A single male is not in the proper marital status to beget one, and a poor man, especially with the lowly status of a beggar, is thought to find it difficult if not impossible to attract a wife. Furthermore, beggars are seen as unfilial in yet another way. The very fact that they beg, that they engage in such a lowly activity, is a great loss of face, a blow to the reputation of the entire kin group. Being poor is bad enough, but begging is much lower and shows a complete lack of self-respect. No one who disgraced his family in such a way could be called filial (see Yang 1945:45; for two rare exceptions, see Schak 1979:119–20).

Finally, but significantly, beggars are considered lowly because they are parasites. Informants often described them as lazy, unwilling to work, unproductive, preferring to take life easy and eke out a living, and worst of all, as being "the most worthless beings in existence."

Besides all this evidence referring to general values in the Chinese cultural tradition, there is evidence of the real-world low status of beggars. One graphic manifestation of this is their association with death. Death is *sang* and is represented by white, in opposition to *hsi*, happiness, represented by red. Death is extremely polluting in Chinese culture to all those associated with it. In villages and urban neighborhoods, a family in which a death has occurred will place a white, diamond-shaped paper above the door with a warning that the house is to be avoided. Neighbors will put up a red diamond-shaped paper on which is written the character for happiness, both to demonstrate that they are not under taboo and as a prophylactic to ward off the polluting effects of the nearby death. Persons associated with the death, particularly the agnatic kin, are polluted for some time afterward and are unable to participate in happy events such as weddings, New Year visits, or temple worship. Those not under obligation to assist the family of the deceased avoid participation in the funerary preparations and activities, although they may still attend the funeral itself. However, beggars voluntarily associate with death in a number of ways. In Peking and Chekiang they acted as pallbearers. In Taiwan a beggar led the funeral procession dressed as a deity but exposing himself to the malevolent forces of the underworld. In Taiwan and elsewhere beggars sought alms at funeral processions, and leper-beggars in Kwangtung went so far as to leap into graves to prevent interment and even to exhume bodies and hold them for ransom (Gray 1878ii:52). Fortune observed them camping in a mortuary area in which there were a number of coffins awaiting burial and using the coffin tops as supports for mosquito nets. "These people seemed to have no supernatural fears of any kind, and were on . . . friendly terms with their dead companions" (1857:56–57).

A second association is related to their connection with death. Because of certain similarities between them, beggars are associated popularly with the fearsome hungry ghosts: both are pictured as deformed beings, as dirty and dressed in rags, and as lacking the proper connections with their ancestors or lacking descendants to care for them; both want something, both must be paid off to get rid of them, and the demands of each carry with them an implied threat; and both are polluting beings (Ahern 1975:208; A. Wolf 1974a:171). Third, as I have already mentioned, people speak of beggars as worthless, and when their status is compared with those of prostitutes or gangsters, beggars come out on the bottom. The only individuals considered beneath them are thieves and strong-arm bandits. Fourth, the idea or concept of a beggar is also used in a pejorative sense by parents scolding or admonishing their children: "You are so dirty! Are you trying to look like a beggar?" "If you don't study hard, you will end up a beggar." One informant said her mother objected to her learning to play the *hu-ch'in*, a two-stringed Chinese violin, because she associated it with beggars.

Wang states that people will sometimes name a child "beggar" in order to fool the malevolent ghosts, beggars being so low that even the fierce and evil ghosts want nothing to do with them (1974:155). Finally, the status of a beggar does not stop with the individual but extends to other relatives, especially children. Many of the children of the Liong-hiat Beggars quit school early rather than suffer the taunts of *"khit-ciaq-kia:"* ("beggar's kid") from their schoolmates, and one man claimed that he would have great difficulties procuring a loan to buy a taxicab in part at least because his parents had been beggars.

On the other hand, there is evidence that points to the worthiness of beggars. There are many folktales linking beggars in various ways with positive supernatural beings, most often with immortals (*hsien*), less frequently with gods (*shen*). In a number of tales, the deity manifests himself in the form of a beggar (Eberhard 1965:131–35; Chiang 1955b:32–36; 1954a:42–44). Two of the celebrated Chinese Eight Immortals, Lü Tung-pin and Li T'ieh-kuai, are reported to have begged, and Li is known as the patron saint of the beggars (Hung 1954:22; Wu Tao-ying 1969:74). There is a statue representing Li on the altar of the Beggar chief of the Liong-hiat group, and this group holds an annual worship festival (*pai-pai*) to fete him on his birthday.

In a number of other tales, miracles are associated with beggars, most often as a result of a giver's compliance with a request for succor (see, e.g., Chiang 1955a:60–64; 1954b:59–63). Such requests must be fulfilled out of compassion or charity, however, and not with a grasping heart or greed for a reward. Otherwise the "miracle" will turn out to be a curse, and the giver will find himself in a much worse condition than he was in originally (see, e.g., Wu Tao-ying 1969:400–401). There are also a number of tales in which beggars themselves are the recipients of miracles (ibid.:397–400).

Aside from folktales, there are a number of legends influenced by Buddhism and Taoism and preserved in official accounts in which beggars are depicted as paragons of such important virtues as filiality, honesty, sexual purity, hard work, kindheartedness and compassion (Wang 1974:226; Ch'en 1726:19–20; Hsü Fang 1954:77–78). There are also stories about men such as Wu Shun, a philanthropist-beggar who begged but used his earnings to buy books for libraries, send poor children to school, or for other charitable, public-spirited purposes.

There is also a very large corpus of folk and now popular literature known as *wu-hsia hsiao-shuo*, "knight-errant stories," the Chinese equivalent of American westerns or Japanese samurai tales. These stories sometimes depict knights-errant as beggars. They are men who have a strong sense of social justice and who go about righting wrongs, particularly those perpetrated by the strong and wealthy on the weak and poor. These knights-errant, although they often appear ragged and somewhat unkempt, and although they often beg for their sustenance, are actually very strong, skilled fighters who are difficult to best. They beg, it seems, because they are unconcerned with the mundane affairs of living, and they desire only enough goods to satisfy their immediate needs (see, e.g., Wu Chia-ch'ing 1971:23–29).

Thus, in three different types of literature, beggars are depicted in a positive light. Moreover, these depictions are supported by cultural values: the Buddhist ideals of charity and compassion in the folktales, the official or Confucian virtues of filiality, honesty, and sexual purity in the legends, and the popular values of the strong, almost Robin Hood–like champions of the people in the knight-errant stories. The nonchalance displayed by these knights-errant toward subsistence activities must also have considerably enhanced their heroic image to a folk who struggled constantly against hunger. Moreover, in both popular Buddhism and popular Taoism, the path to "salvation"—bodhisattvahood in the former, sagehood or immortality in the latter—required that a seeker divorce himself from the desires and cares of the world. Candidates for salvation must become as beggars if they are to have any hope of success, and they must be detached sufficiently from earthly ideas of prestige and self-preservation to beg or to fulfill a task such as sucking pus from a festering wound.

A further evidence of the potential worth of beggars is the fact that officially their status was not inherited. In traditional China there were several categories of people regarded as *chien-min*, "mean people." People in categories so designated—prostitutes, actors, and criminals, to name a few—were not given full civil rights; they were not allowed to compete in the civil service examinations, and their status was passed on to their descendants (see Ch'ü 1961:128–35). Beggars, however, were not "mean people" and were not so stigmatized.[9] There are a number of tales and legends that point to figures, sometimes the same individual, who experienced downward mobility into and upward mobility out of beggary (Eberhard 1965:26–29). In some of these stories, the individuals mentioned were historical figures (Wu Tao-ying 1969:401–2; F. Liu 1936:99), without doubt the most famous of whom was Chu Yüan-chang, who rose from beggar and bandit leader to overthrow the Mongols and establish the Ming Dynasty. Moreover, the most frequently encountered explanation in the folk literature of why people become beggars is that it is their fate (see Wu Tao-ying 1969:395–400), and neither informants nor the folk literature intimated that beggars were beggars because they were morally inferior. Thus, whether a person becomes a beggar is beyond his control; it is not the result of a moral failing on his part.

In fact, people of high morals are reported to have begged. Hsü Fang praised those who were poor but chose to beg rather than become bandits or hangers-on about the rich (1954:78). And some beggars are reported to have been highly moral individuals; so impressed with them was Su Tung-p'o, the eleventh-century poet and philosopher, that he put them on a par with the Jade Emperor himself (ibid.).

There is considerable evidence that because they are unable to support themselves, beggars are considered worthy of support. Many informants and many characters in the folk literature described disabled beggars as *kho-lian*, "deserving of pity," and expressed a willingness to help them. Informants felt the same way about refugees and those who had suffered losses from natural calamities, even though they were able-bodied, because they had lost their means of livelihood. Moreover, one tactic formerly used by beggars in Taiwan illustrates that there were a number of people whose feelings were translated into action; beggars would go through the streets at night announcing their coming by beating a bamboo clapper. Those who wanted to avoid them could easily do so. But there were sufficient people who wanted to give and who were willing to drop what they were doing and take some money out to give to the passing mendicant that beggars continued to use this tactic.

I have established that the authorities and the general public in traditional China recognized the existence of the beggars and their right to exist. Although their primary intent was to control the activities of the beggars rather than to help them, the authorities recognized beggar chiefs and beggars, and at one point in the nineteenth century at least, the government even stipulated the amounts that beggars were to get from each home (Wang 1974:151). Various levels of government also established charity homes and asylums for beggars as well as other poor and unfortunate souls, and although the amount of charity bestowed on them was rarely sufficient, it does demonstrate official recognition of their existence and even a degree of responsibility in relieving their distress. That the general public recognized and, albeit somewhat grudgingly in some cases, accepted them is demonstrated by the fact that alms were freely given on holidays, festival days, and other special occasions (see, e.g., Matignon 1900:241; Gee 1925:16–17; Wang 1974:150), and that lineages, clans, religious groups, guilds, and private individuals also established organized charity for beggars. Kulp even claims that beggars were seen as necessary by people in Phenix Village. "The developed Buddhist hopes to gain 'West Heaven,' but charity and alms are the fundamental means, enjoined by the priests, of gaining that happiness. The beggar provides the object upon which the faithful may bestow alms and pity and thus add to his credit in heaven. This is the basis of the kindly feeling that people take in beggars, loathsome as they may be" (1925:100–101).

The Whys and Whos of Giving

I have shown that within the Chinese cultural tradition one can have a positive or a negative view of beggars. However, this view, while important in deciding whether to give, proved not to be the most crucial factor. As Kulp points out in the passage quoted, one can feel compassion toward beggars even though one views them negatively. What proved to be the most important factor in deciding whether to give, assuming that the giver did not feel coerced, was whether one regarded beggars in general or a particular beggar to be worthy of charity. One had to decide whether they were lazy good-for-nothings who deserved both their low status and their low economic position, or whether they were pitiful beings worthy of charity. One also had to face the uncertainty of not knowing in specific cases. But before exploring this area, let us first look into the more straightforward reasons why people feel charitably or uncharitably toward beggars in general.

There are a number of reasons why a Chinese might choose to give to beggars and several why he or she might not. One group of reasons might be termed religious. Several informants said they gave to make up for bad things they had done or to gain Buddhist merit. Others believed that charity was an important component in "self-rectification" (*hsiu-shen*), a more philosophical concept found in several schools of thought and belief in China. One man, a follower though not a baptized member of a Christian church, spoke of giving because it pleases God. "We all rely on Heaven for sustenance," he said, using the phrase *k'ao-t'ien ch'ih-fan*, an expression used by non-Christians as well. He explained that, since Heaven was the source of all things, it was incumbent upon people to share what they had with others. This is closely related to the idea expressed in

Chinese folktales, though not mentioned directly by any informant, that giving to beggars is as giving to deities.

The idea of sharing was mentioned by several informants. Many expressed the feeling that mendicants had no other way to make a living but by begging, and they voiced sympathy for the ill, the elderly, the disabled, and widows with small children. Some referred to beggars as the "poorest of the poor," thus deserving of charity. One young woman said, "We have so much and they have so little. We should share what we have with them."

Others expressed empathy in a different way. One couple, quite poor themselves, gave to beggars because they pitied them and because they felt beggars were not to blame for their predicament. "Had I been born in those circumstances, I would probably have been a beggar too." Their sentiments were echoed by a bicycle repairman who took pity in particular on people who were too old to work and whose sons (he assumed) had failed to fulfill their filial responsibility to support them; they were thus reduced to begging to stay alive. "Who knows?" he said, pointing to his wife. "We might be in that position ourselves someday, and we would certainly appreciate any help people might give us." In so speaking he was not anticipating his and his wife's future but expressing a moral sentiment.

Other reasons for giving willingly were at least partially remunerative. One informant said her father liked the kind of music beggars used to sing as they wandered through the streets; when he heard them he would go outside to listen and give them money so they would sing more. Many others said they gave to beggars "mourning at the roadside" (*tiau lo-ce*) during a funeral procession. Regarded by some as a service, it was seen by others as simply giving the beggars their due on certain occasions, much as people are more generous on festival days and holidays.

Finally, there are a number of informants who give out of fear or simply to get rid of what they consider to be a nuisance. A proprietor of a small, open-door shop expressed the feeling of many of his counterparts when he said, "I do business. Five or ten [New Taiwan] dollars[10] isn't that much to me, so when a beggar comes by I just give him some money to get rid of him. Otherwise I'm afraid he'll frighten away my customers or make them think I'm stingy for not giving." Others regarded beggars not so much as a nuisance but as a physical or psychological threat. One young man said that beggars were dirty, ragged, and smelly, and that they were strangers. She was uncomfortable at the thought that a "dirty beggar" might touch her. She was also discomforted by the sight of a blind, crippled, or otherwise "unwhole" beggar. She mentioned in particular a young man who used to come around to beg when she was a child and who was mentally abnormal. When confronted by these kinds of beggar, she gave just to get rid of them. "I'm not afaid of these people," she said. "I'd just rather they went away." Another kind of beggar caused her to feel genuine fear, however—the young adult males she would sometimes encounter in the city. They were not beggars in the conventional sense of the word but were somewhat scruffy, tough-looking fellows who might better be described as *t'ai-pao,* "young hoodlums," and who would ask for money "for bus fare home" or some other such reason. As a young, single woman, she did fear this type, and although she knew they were not really seeking "bus fare," she gave them money so they would not follow or bother her.

There were also a number of reasons not to give. Some informants refused because they regarded beggars as undeserving. They saw them as lazy and capable of earning a living by working, or they regarded them as fakes. Some said they did not need to give alms because beggars did well enough. "They get more money than workers (*kung-jen*)," exclaimed one. "Laborers can earn NT$300–400 per day, but a beggar can get NT$500–600 per day. I've even heard of beggars going to bars and restaurants."

That beggars do quite well is true, as is the charge that they sometimes spend money wastefully. One woman who married into a nonbeggar household on the edge of the Liong-hiat community said she had always taken pity on beggars and had given to them before she and her husband began courting. But afterward he would laugh at her when she gave, telling her that if she saw how well off beggars actually were and how they used their money, she would no longer have pity on them. She still gave on occasion, although not to her neighbors, of course, even though she knew that a beggar might not be as badly off as he made himself out to be. The former subdistrict head, who knew the Liong-hiat beggars well and knew that they sometimes gambled, drank, or otherwise "wasted" the alms they collected, also still gave because he knew that despite their bad habits, many beggars had no other way to get a living.

Another reason some did not give was that beggars were not grateful for what they got. "They have no feelings of gratitude (*kam-chieng*). Even if they thank you, they don't mean it. They may even curse you if you don't give."

Although the various reasons for giving or not giving can be isolated and viewed separately, in the minds of most informants, things were more complex. They usually gave not for one reason but for a variety of them. One woman, for example, always gave to beggars who came to her door, and she genuinely felt sorry for them. Coming from and marrying into families with plenty of money and servants to do the housework, she had never had to work in her life. But she also gave because she feared what the neighbors would say if she did not. She feared that a spurned beggar might stand around outside her door, perhaps creating a ruckus, and attract the attention of those in neighboring households. Knowing that she had the means to share with those less well off, regardless of whether they were worthy of charity, they would see her as stingy if she failed to give.

Another group of informants also consistently gave, but they were quite undecided about the worthiness of the beggars. They responded not just to one of the various interpretations of beggars in their cultural tradition but to several conflicting ones; moreover they had not worked out these conflicts and inconsistencies in their own minds. They viewed beggars with pity and charity on the one hand but with scorn and disgust on the other. They recognized that some beggars were worthy—generally those they perceived as unable to support themselves—and they claimed they were quite willing to give to those in that category. But there were also unworthy beggars, especially males who appeared young and able-bodied and otherwise able to work, and they did not feel so charitably disposed toward these. But because beggars were often skilled in presenting themselves to the public in the most effective way, informants said they had problems in distinguishing the truly worthy from those they suspected were not so worthy. They had to make ad hoc decisions in ambiguous cases, and because they were unsure of their judgments, this made them uneasy. Moreover, they would speak of how worthy of support, how pitiful beggars were at one point in a conversation, and at another they would refer to them as useless and worthless. They would say that those who could not work should be supported, but a few moments later that no beggar had the right to beg at any time, that all beggars should have to work for a living "as everyone else does." When pinned down, some said that beggars who could not work should be sent to the Vagrant Reception Center. This way "unsightly" beggars would be kept off the streets.

Because of these conflicts and ambiguities, and despite their altruistic feelings toward worthy beggars, these informants often gave with conflicting emotions and for negative or instrumental reasons. They felt they should give, but because of their doubts about the worthiness of a particular beggar, they also feared they were being cheated or bamboozled but could do nothing about it. Sometimes they gave because they felt a beggar was unsightly or a nuisance, and they just wanted to get rid of him. If there were other people around, they gave because they did not want to be regarded as tightwads. The beggars did not ask for much money, and it was easier to give than not to.

Yet another category of response came from people who gave according to the occasion. For example, some who might not give under other circumstances did so when they encountered beggars mourning at the roadside during a funeral procession. But there were at least four different motivations for giving. One might give because he regarded what the beggars were doing as the performance of a valid service for which they should be paid. He might give because he regarded them as an unsightly nuisance and just wanted to get rid of them. He might give because he did not want others to think of him as stingy, as not giving the beggars their due, even though the services they performed were not requested. And he might give because he felt charitably disposed toward beggars in general.

From the whys of giving or not giving, we can now turn to the whos: Are there some categories of individual more or less inclined to give than others? Many informants, beggar and nonbeggar alike, had ideas on this question. The writer of the Ai-ai Report regarded giving as a feminine characteristic, referring frequently to those who give as "women or those with hearts like women." This view was contradicted by the son of a beggar, however, who said that although some women give large amounts, men are the most frequent givers. Another particularly generous group he mentioned was prostitutes. Because they had similar experiences dealing with the world at large, he reasoned, they felt an empathy toward beggars, and this made them give more. His viewpoint was supported by the former subdistrict head, although he gave a different reason: prostitutes were generous because they had an "easy-come easy-go" attitude toward money and also because they wanted to accumulate merit to absolve them from the karma of their occupation.

Another group that some regarded as generous was twelve- to fifteen-year-old girls. One informant said they gave because they were very good-hearted (*sian-liong*) at that age, but another was more cynical. He said they gave mainly when they were with friends, and their motive was to impress those whom they were with rather than a genuine feeling of charity toward beggars. Chan Lean-heng, who did participant observation research among beggars in Penang, disagrees completely, singling out teenagers of either sex as being particularly uncharitable (1973:35–36).

The one group whose generosity was unquestioned by informants was the poor. Chan reports that they were more willing to give, less condescending, and always acknowledged her thanks (1973:33–34). Beggar informants in Taipei generally concurred with this observation, adding, however, that even among the poor there were decidedly ungenerous, uncharitable individuals. Moreover, some rich people also gave, as was evidenced by infrequent though memorable contributions of NT$50, NT$100, and in a few cases, NT$1,000 from a single donor.

Older women were regarded as generous by some because they were soft-hearted and were worried about having enough merit to negotiate smoothly the courts of hell. Adult males were supposedly sympathetic because they constantly experienced the hardships of the outside world. Former beggars gave because they had experienced mendicancy.

The plethora of expressed opinion on this subject indicates that no identifiable group of persons had an edge on charity, that all categories of people had reason to give, and that in no case was there a universal or majority positive response to the entreaties of beggars. Moreover, because of the wide range of choice and the internal conflicts in the norms that govern such things as charity and worthiness, an individual can justify as morally proper any response he chooses.

CHAPTER THREE

Appeals and Tactics

BEGGARS IN PREMODERN CHINA used a wide variety of tactics in their appeals for alms. There were appeals based on need and worthiness of assistance, in response to which the giver should give for moral reasons. There were requests—or demands—for alms in a coercive manner, with a threat, direct or implied, to do something ranging from creating a nuisance to inflicting severe property damage or bodily harm, the donor giving because he felt compelled to. And there were appeals based on performing some sort of service or furnishing some good, in which case the beggar got alms to recompense him. For the purpose of discussion, these appeals and the tactics appropriate to them will be labeled positive, negative, and remunerative, and each will be discussed in this chapter.

It may be helpful to remind the reader at this point that many of the activities described here and said to be engaged in by "beggars" are not what one might commonly associate with begging. They are included because those who have written about Chinese mendicants, Chinese as well as Western authors, have attributed such behavior to beggars. This problem of defining begging will be taken up again in chapter 9.

Positive Appeals and Tactics

Although initially introduced by Buddhist missionaries, charity became an important virtue in Chinese society at both the folk-value and the religious-scriptural levels. Many folktales, legends, and myths stress the rewards to the generous and the punishments to the miserly, the grasping, and the greedy (see Schak 1979). In the folk concept of

45

judgment, the good acts one did in life were weighed against the bad, and the amount of torment one endured in the hells depended on the balance between the two. Giving alms was one way to gain merit (*chi-te*), which would expiate one's sins. Moreover, in both Buddhism and Taoism, charity and generosity to the point of neglecting one's own needs and comforts were the sine qua non for those who wished to perfect themselves in order to attain Nirvana or sainthood.

The most basic image of a beggar in China was that of one who lacked the very essentials of life, who had no means to get them on his own, and whose survival was dependent on the charity of others. The easiest and most straightforward appeal a beggar could make, then, was based on evoking sympathy and pity for his perceived helplessness and need. The Liong-hiat beggars referred to the characteristics which enabled a beggar to appeal on this basis as his *kho-lian-iu:*, "image of pitifulness." If this *kho-lian-iu:* was based on a real disability, all the beggar needed to do was to make sure it was easily perceived by and made a strong impact on the public. For example, Gee writes of beggars who thrust diseased limbs into the faces of passersby while asking for alms (1925:6). If the disabilities were not real, the beggar would have to fake them. As I have explained, the distinction between beggars whose *kho-lian-iu:* was real and those for whom it was based on deceit was of great concern to the potential giver, but it need not concern us here. The important things at this point are the image presented of one who lacked the physical ability to gain a livelihood, and the appeals on which the request for alms was based, pity and sympathy.

A beggar's *kho-lian-iu:* was based on his perceived inability to get the necessities of life. One such type of person was a refugee, someone who had been self-supporting but who, because of a natural or man-made disaster, had lost his livelihood. Another type consisted of those who station in life made them dependent on others—that is, the elderly, the young, and women—but who had, respectively, no sons, parents, or husband to depend on. The third type was the handicapped, anyone physically or mentally unable to work and care for himself. These factors could be cumulative, the most effective combinations being a group of children or a woman with children, at least one of whom in each case was handicapped. Old Lady Ning, describing her own begging tactics, said, "when [my daughter and I] came to an open gate, I would send her in, for people's hearts are moved by a child" (Pruitt 1945:62–63).[1] Children were so effective that a woman would sometimes "borrow" them from another beggar when she went out to beg. And Peking mendicants who were too weak or ineffective to get alms on their own would kidnap children, cripple them by severing the muscles and tendons of the limbs, and set them out to beg (Bennett 1931:217). Some also used a tactic called "selling coldness" (*mai-tung*), in which an adult "used helpless, recourseless children as living sacrifices from which he profitted. When the weather was cold, he had the child squat near the stoves of a market stall in order to get the sympathy of passersby" (Liu Hsü 1936:178).

Those who had the greatest difficulty begging by means of positive appeals were a strong, healthy-looking teenager or an adult male, although the latter sometimes begged with children, claiming that their mother was dead and he was the only one to look after them. Otherwise such a beggar would have to fake a handicap or use remunerative or negative tactics. Alternatively he could beg either by shouting and screaming as if he were crazy (Liu Hsü 1936:172), or kneel, perhaps banging his head on the street in a most abject, self-depreciating manner (Doolittle 1965ii:377). In the latter case he would receive alms as an object not of pity but of scorn and derision.

Begging by means of positive tactics was usually quite straightforward. Most handicapped beggars simply went to a place where they encountered a good number of passersby and begged, either squatting in one place or walking along the streets. Those who were so handicapped that they could not beg without assistance often went out with another beggar who could transport the handicapped one in a cart, carry him piggyback, or, in the case of a blind beggar, lead him by the hand through the streets. The healthy member of the team could assist his partner in begging or let him beg alone, but the alms were shared. In some cases this was done on a casual basis, but in others a formal relationship existed between the healthy and the handicapped partner. The former made sure that the latter could beg, and he also saw to all his needs—food, clothing, shelter, and so on—in return for which he took all the proceeds from begging. If the handicapped partner was a child, he was probably sold to the healthy partner by his relatives, but in other cases adult beggars willingly entered into such agreements. In Taiwan the handicapped person was referred to as a *khit-ciaq e ke-si*, literally a "begging implement," a term that unfortunately connotes a mercenery and exploitive relationship. But as I will point out, it was not necessarily that way, nor was it so regarded by the Liong-hiat beggars or others in the community.

The first step in begging by positive tactics was to make the public aware of one's plight, something at which, according to observers, Chinese beggars were quite skilled. Macgowan writes, perhaps somewhat tongue-in-cheek: "It is a remarkable fact that with the Chinese beggar these diseases, which constitute their stock-in-trade, are always in the right place. They are never seen on the back of the legs, nor on other parts of the body that could not easily be exhibited to the public" (1912:292–93). He also describes a beggar who had "a huge sore" on his leg which "has eaten away nearly all the flesh from the front part of it. It is raw and bleeding, and the man points to it as you come near . . . [trying] to excite your sympathies" (ibid.:292). To enhance further his effectiveness, a beggar could appear dirty, disheveled, and strangely dressed, mixing an appeal to sympathy with the creation of an aversion to getting too near him.

Another way to attract the public was to use a prop of some sort. These ranged from the very simple—the placard used by a refugee to explain why he is begging—to the more complex. Gee tells of a Soochow beggar who had a pair of false feet made from canvas with hideous sores painted on them "so skilfully done as to deceive even the closest observer as he hurriedly passed by" (1925:7). Matignon describes a man in Peking who had a pair of wax legs, "a pair of stumps, bloody and gangrenous," which he put into a sack when it was time to return home at night. Another, whose plight was all too real, walked along on knee pads, displaying the mummified legs he had lost (1900:228–29). Quite similar to this tactic is the contortionist's ability to twist a limb out of place in order to appear crippled.

Beggars who had no handicap sometimes gave themselves one. Matignon writes of a beggar who amputated his own leg by tying a string around it then progressively tightening the string until the limb was cut off. He then used the leg to "excite charity" (1900:229). Pitcher recounts seeing beggars who cut themselves and severed their tendons, losing the use of their limbs. "We once saw one of these professionals on all fours, being unable to stand erect" (1912:18). A beggar might go to some lengths to keep a handicap. Gee reports, for example, that beggars sometimes kept their wounds open so that they "never seem to get better or worse." Despite the passage of time, "the sore that brings him in the cash is as hideous as ever" (1925:7). Bennett cites the case of a foreign doctor who offered to remove the cataracts from the eyes of a blind beggar. The beggar refused on the grounds that he would lose his source of livelihood (1931:217). Gee recounts a similar case in which, after the operation was successfully performed, the beggar surprised the doctor by saying: "Where am I to go? I have nowhere to go and can do nothing, and now that you have taken away the only means I had of making a living, you will have to take care of me. Formerly I could touch the hearts of people by my appeals as I was a blind man, but now that I have my sight, they will not [sic] longer take pity on me" (1925:19; see also Smith 1890:319).

Another tactic employed mainly by beggars using positive strategies was to choose terms of address that declared the worthiness of the beggar and enhanced the superior status of the giver or suggested a relationship between the two that placed the latter in a nurturing, succoring position. Beggars frequently used kinship terms when calling to a potential donor, but those they used were highly selective, having great symbolic impact. In both Peking and Taiwan, they called passersby "father's younger brother" or "father's younger brother's wife" (Liu Hsü 1936:178–79). In addition, Taiwanese beggars used the terms for father's elder brother and father's elder brother's wife. All of these place the beggar one generation lower and in an inferior but dependent status. Thomson reports the use of *Taipan*, also a status-conferring term, meaning "Boss" and connoting "May you be the general manager of your firm" (1909:176–77). Moule writes that mendicants begging from pilgrims en route to the Hangchou temples "preface every appeal for alms with a pious repetition of Buddha's name" (1902:124), reminding worshippers that charity earns merit for the giver.

Finally, beggars maximized their take by choosing the best places to beg and by begging on the most lucrative occasions. Observers write of them begging in markets, on busy streets, and near temples, places where they would encounter the most passersby. No reference is made to their begging in villages unless they were bandit beggars (see next section) or unless there was a festival of some sort, not only an occasion that would attract a host of people but one on which, for a combination of religious and festive reasons, people would be inclined to be generous. Some beggars even had special songs and dances they performed on festivals and holidays.

Remunerative Appeals and Tactics

Whereas some beggars, or beggars sometimes, solicited alms on the basis of need and relied on gaining the sympathy of the public, others got their living by performing tasks and services and by selling goods. There were beggars who worked, entertained, performed certain functions at life-cycle ceremonies, or manufactured and sold goods. Some of these tasks had no association with begging; non-beggars also did such things, and when beggars performed them, they did so as workers, not as beggars. A number of the services they performed, even those associated with begging, were quite tangible, tasks considered necessary. For some others, however, the benefit supposed to accrue to those for whom the task was performed was much less perceptible, and its performance was probably simply an excuse to ask for money. The activities described in this section are included because those who performed them are called beggars (*ch'i-kai* or *khit-ciaq*) in the literature. The ambiguity and imprecision in the semantic range of these terms will be considered in chapter 9.

Beginning with ordinary work, beggar chiefs in Taiwan used to raise stud pigs (a lucrative but lowly undertaking) and then hire individual beggars to take them to the farmers who required their services and bring them home. Beggars in the south of Taiwan sometimes earned money hiring themselves out as farm laborers; the stronger ones plowed, and the weaker ones weeded (Wang 1974:151). In the Peking area, beggars advertised themselves as dentists at local temple fairs, promising the painless extraction of aching molars. "When a victim is found, they will shout loudly—to drown his howls of anguish" (Bennett 1931:219, 268). In Peking, the government hired beggars to wet down the streets,[2] and beggars there, both male and female, also acted as prostitutes (Matignon 1900:217, 233; see also Coltman 1891: 113–14).

Beggars also made and/or sold products or services. Soochow beggars made small feather ear brushes, which they peddled in teashops to wealthy customers (Gee 1925:14–15). Assistant beggar chiefs, and probably the beggars under them, made grass sandals and chicken-feather dusters (Wang 1974:149). In Canton, beggars provided long, copper tobacco pipes and charged three cash for a few whiffs (Gray 1878ii:63). In Peking, they caught snakes, which they took to festivals to sell to Buddhist women. The women would let the snakes go, saving their lives and earning merit for themselves.[3] The beggars would then catch the snakes again and resell them (Liu Hsü 1936:178–79). Foochow beggars were less devious. They also caught snakes, but they sold them to doctors, who boiled them down to make medicines (Gray 1878ii:61).

There is some question as to whether beggars manufactured their products with the intent of earning money on their sale or whether the articles were simply implements to assist them in begging. Gee suspects the latter (1925:15), and older Taipei informants said that although in the past feather dusters were available only from beggars, there was still an element of charity in buying them, that buyers were often generous in the amount they paid. The beggars themselves did not rely on them as a necessary element in begging but manufactured them only on days when it was too cold or rainy to go out begging. Moreover they were often more interested in using them as shields against arrest than in actually selling them; if a policeman came along and questioned the beggar, he could show the dusters and claim he was peddling, not begging.

In some areas beggars had specific roles at funerals and weddings. Dressed in special costumes—red robes in Chekiang, green in Peking—beggars acted as musicians, bore the trousseau and gifts, carried the banners, and shouldered the sedan chair carrying the bride in the wedding procession. Moreover, they had a right to do these tasks. Bennett reports that a family that attempted to do without the beggars and all the traditional ritual and paraphernalia in favor of a more modern wedding found a host of beggars blocking the gateway to the groom's home when the automobile bearing the bride arrived. It was only after the groom paid the beggars the sum of money they would have earned had the wedding been in the traditional fashion that they left him in peace (1931:216). Stott writes that beggars in Peking, angered at the jailing of one of their leaders, actually went on strike right in the middle of the principal wedding season. One family went ahead, however, choosing under the circumstances a modern wedding, but when the bridegroom suddenly and mysteriously died, the beggars used this as propaganda against the adoption of "evil" foreign ways. This increased the effectiveness of their lobbying effort and resulted in the release of their leader (1927:833).

In Peking beggars performed similar functions at funerals. They acted as pallbearers, musicians, and bearers of the paper models of "spirit" objects to be burned and thus sent to the spirit of the deceased for his use in the nether world (Bennett 1931:216–17).

Beggars in Taiwan had no formal role to play at weddings, although they often attended to receive their due, and according to some informants their presence was believed to bring good luck. But they did play both formal and informal roles at funerals. Informally beggars availed themselves the opportunity to sacrifice at the roadside, tiau-lo-ce, thereby "serving" the family of the deceased by worshipping their ancestors. This act was not originally a tactic used by beggars to exact money from the bereaved family but was done by friends and associates who wanted to pay their respects to the deceased. Beggars merely took advantage of it as a way to get alms, although their performing it is variously seen as a service rendered or an act of extortion.

More formally, in the past, funeral processions were led by a *khui-lo-sin*, a "god who clears the road," who was represented by a large paper model of a person with a man inside to carry it. According to legend, this god was actually an Indian; when demons met up with him, they would run away and hide, and the soul of the deceased was thus kept safe from harm. But because of his encounter with demons, the person carrying the model might be bothered by them in the future. Therefore families would hire a beggar (or less commonly, a gangster) to perform this task. In order to protect himself, the beggar painted his face with many colors. When the procession reached the burial site, the model was burned, and while the coffin was being interred, the beggar lay down on the grave and rolled over once to get rid of the demons. He then had to walk quickly on his return home, taking care not to turn his head or look back. Otherwise he could be killed by the *khui-lo-sin*. For his trouble he was rewarded with all the delicacies, which included a pig liver,[4] hung inside the model during the procession (Wang 1974:150–51).

Another type of service rendered by beggars to secure contributions was to entertain (*be-gi*), and the literature is rich with descriptions of their various performances and skills and the colorful names of them. In Peking beggars told stories at temple fairs. After telling most of the tale, they would stop just short of the climax and pass a plate around. "If the bottom of the dish is not well covered, the act is left unfinished. If the applause is cordial, the dish makes a second round" (Bennett 1931:268).

Other beggars, trained in the martial arts, performed routines, with projectiles, knives, lances, double-edged swords, and battle forks. Some also performed tricks such as swallowing iron balls and then taking them out from various points on the body, balancing objects on the nose or on a chopstick balanced on the forehead, swallowing swords, juggling a variety of objects, and "magically" joining a set of iron rings. Some trained animals—mice, monkeys, goats, and dogs—to jump through hoops, pull carts, put on clothes, and even beg. Others performed the lion, dragon, and other traditional dances (Liu Hsü 1936:171–73; Gee 1925:13–15; Wang 1974:146–47; Doolittle 1865ii:260; Ai-ai Report).

Probably the best-known beggar acts, however, were singing and playing musical instruments. Beggars played violins, flutes, drums, and two guitarlike instruments, the *p'i-p'a* and the *san-hsien*. They also used clappers and strings of cash to keep rhythm. Some used the musical instruments as accompaniment for their signing, whereas others simply played them. Still others made "music" in quite bizarre ways. Wang writes of a "talent" called "striking the seven sounds" (*ta-ch'i-hsiang*) in which a beggar, his face painted with soot and wearing a wreath on his head, went from door to door making "music" by striking seven parts of his body—his knees, hands, shoulders, and so on—in a musical fashion (1974:146). Another strange "talent" was to strike oneself with a brick and then to appeal to the crowd for alms. Liu Hsï reports: "As he strikes himself, he makes a '*hng*' sound, alternatively calling out to the onlookers. The sound is both loud and sad, and it is made with both tune and brogue. As he strikes himself with the brick, he makes a *pha-phak* sound, as if he were keeping rhythm" (1936:75). Beggars sang a number of types of song, the type seeming to vary from place to place. In Taiwan, they sang the *khuan-se-kua*, "songs that exhort to righteousness." Usually sung by blind females and accompanied on the *san-hsien*, these songs told the listener that worldly accumulation of goods would come to naught, that it was far more important to be charitable and generous with one's wealth. Although these songs had a message based on pity and religious duty, many informants found them quite entertaining and paid the beggar to continue singing.[5] In northern China,[6] beggars sang two types of songs, the *lien-hua-lo* and the *shu-lai-pao*. In both, the singer beat out the rhythm on bamboo clappers or with an ox bone to which bronze bells were tied. In the *lien-hua-lo* he sang traditional rhymes with the phrase *lien-hua-lo lo-lien-hua* or similar syllables as a sort of chorus interjected between the lines or at the end. In the *shu-lai-pao* the verse was chanted rather than sung and was spontaneous. The singer would choose whatever phrases suited the occasion, wishes of *fa-ts'ai* ("become wealthy") at Chinese New Year, for example, or flattering lyrics at the beginning of an encounter with a shopkeeper and more scolding, abusive, or embarrassing ones if the mark was slow to make a contribution.

Lu-k'o yü tao-k'o, a Taiwan-made film set in nineteenth-century Shantung, depicted such a situation. A beggar asked the proprietor of a small eatery for some food. When he refused, the beggar, good-naturedly and with a smile on his face, began to sing about the indiscretions (no doubt fabricated) of the proprietor's wife and daughter, much to the amusement of his patrons. Embarrassed, the proprietor quickly gave in.

Although there were a number of stock phrases the singers could use, they were also very talented at ad-libbing. Liu Hsü felt that singing the *shu-lai-pao* was a very creative activity and that it was entertaining enough to be a future path for the beggars in Peking.

Inundated with many new competitors who had been pushed out of the rural area because of hunger and social disruption, the beggars there had seen their ability to make a living greatly diminished (1936:176–77, 180).

Beggars performed special songs and dances in areas other than Peking as well, particularly around Chinese New Year. The Ai-ai Report speaks of "talent beggars" (*gi-khit*), who at festival times "greeted" people, often in song, with messages of good fortune (*kiong-hi*). These beggars also performed the lion and dragon dances, a dance celebrating a promotion, and one called "rowing the wealth boat" (*yao-ts'ai-ch'uan*), which is supposed to signal the coming of wealth to the hearer. All of these dances and songs are of a celebratory nature and are supposed to bring good luck and prosperity to the individuals who pay for them as well as to the community as a whole.

Wang mentions two similar forms of entertainment, the "jumping treasure" (*t'iao-pao*), and "shaking the money tree" (*yao-ch'ien-shu*), both done in the first lunar month. In the former the beggar juggled, balanced, and rolled a ball of mercury in two split pieces of bamboo in front of a shop or at the front door of a house and said "Ah! Head of household. The jumping treasure has arrived at your doorstep. You will have sons and become wealthy." In the latter the beggar tied several coins onto a bamboo stick with a red thread, then begged from door to door, shaking the bamboo and chanting such lines as, "You will have opportunities to prosper. You will have descendants generation after generation who will be scholars and officials" (Wang 1974:146–47).

In these special occasion tactics the beggars took advantage of the season and the custom of wishing others good luck. This was something normally done by friends or relatives rather than strangers, but such a wish was welcome from any quarter, and since it was imperative that no inauspicious act such as displaying anger or offending someone be committed at that time, the good wishes of the beggars were rewarded. If they were not, their good wishes turned to curses (a negative tactic), something to be avoided at any time but particularly on happy occasions such as holidays, birthdays, and weddings.

Another way in which beggars used singing to perform a service for which they were remunerated was to tell fortunes, something at which beggars and other marginal people such as the blind were supposed to be especially talented (Stott 1927:833). Beggars did not always sing as they told fortunes. They sometimes acted as phrenologists at local festivals (Bennett 1931:219), but in Penang, Chinese beggars played a Chinese guitar and sang a song indicating one's luck (Chan 1973:12). Wang described an even more elaborate method in Taiwan. The beggar walked along the streets at night with a lantern, a two-stringed violin (*hu-ch'in*), and a set of sixteen bamboo tallies each with a different verse written on it. The customer drew a tally, and the beggar then sang one of a set of traditional songs to explain the message on it and tell the customer's fortune. The beggar usually sang only a verse or two of the whole song, which ran to "hundreds or even thousands of lines," but some customers liked the songs and the singing so well that they paid more to hear them in their entirety (1974:146).

Finally, beggars rendered a "service" by providing an opportunity for people to give in a conspicuous manner; that is, they gave them an opportunity to gain face. Whereas for some the presence of beggars at a celebration was a nuisance, others welcomed it because it gave them a chance to show all present that they were men with good hearts as well as men of means. One informant claimed that some people wait until there are many others present at a festival before they give to beggars. "They use the opportunity to buy face," he said. Others said that politicians were especially prone to using charitable acts as a means to gain face and votes. They mentioned especially one Taipei City councilman who promoted himself as a champion of the downtrodden, and for a time he skillfully employed the tactic of helping beggars and prostitutes as a means of retaining office.

In traditional times, at least, even retired officeholders felt that their reputations required them to continue to give alms. Stott was told by a beggar chief of a town inhabited solely by ex-Mandarins and retired government officials, all of whom "had to be of an assured financial status." This town was under a fixed tribute to the beggars' guild, and the residents always paid up because "those who deign to live there would lose face if the requisite amount of rice and money were not duly furnished. Ex-Mandarins are still desirous of maintaining their reputations above the common people" (1927:832).

Negative Appeals and Tactics

Negative tactics and appeals are those based on some form of coercion, and they range from making a potential giver feel uncomfortable or creating a nuisance in a shop to outright robbery and banditry. The more forceful means are used mainly by adult males, but the others could be used by a beggar of any age or sex.

Beginning with the more forceful tactics, there are a number of reports in the literature of people the authors refer to as beggars but who might equally be termed bandits or local bullies. Matignon writes of beggars who joined the military in times of war but who were "the first to desert and loot the neighborhood village" (1900:234). Hsiao[7] cites reports of the *kua-tzu* of Shensi, the *chien-tzu-hang* of Kiangsu, the *hua-tzu-hui* of the southeast coastal provinces, and others, all strong, young, able-bodied "beggars" whose activities were a combination of begging, extorting, robbing, and pilfering (1960:457–59). Huc tells of villagers being held to ransom by beggars. Once paid off, they "decamp to go and pour down like an avalanche upon some other place" (1856ii:313–14). Ti substantiates the existence of beggar-bandits at a much later date. In his travels as a Red Guard, he visited the Hangchou area not long after a gang of beggars had been driven away from the Six Pagodas, a popular tourist spot, by units from the People's Liberation Army and other local bodies. The beggars had learned martial arts from their leader and had used their skills and strength to rob tourists and occasionally to rape young women. Ti writes, "No wonder the Hangchou beggars are more barbaric, more heterodox, stronger, and fiercer than those from elsewhere. They have occupied the mountains and forests and have been strong-arm bandits" (1974:382). Bodde and Morris cite two law cases involving individual beggars who attempted to extort money and who, when refused, committed arson against their victims (1971:439, 443).

A little less fearsome were the beggars who merely menaced or threatened intended donors. Gee writes of a number of coercive tactics of this sort. Some beggars went around in pairs and were "often insolent and overbearing in their attitude to one who refuses to listen or respond to their demands for money"; people gave in to them rather than risk their anger (1925:8). Others were entertainers who gave displays of sword swallowing, but who sometimes became angry, perhaps at the miserliness of the crowd, and used the same weapons to menace onlookers and prompt them to make a contribution (ibid.13). Still others were also expert in the use of weapons. They were specialists in throwing the *fang-p'iao*, an iron rod about six inches long, blunt at one end and sharp at the other, and at one time had made their living accompanying shipments of goods and protecting them from bandits. With less demand for their services, they took to demanding money from pawnbrokers. If one was refused, he would throw the projectile "with wonderful accuracy" at a designated object or spot on the wall, displaying his ability to hit what he wanted to. Wishing to avoid further damage or injury, the pawnbroker would quickly come to a settlement (ibid.:15).

In Taiwan there were groups of "tyrant beggars" (*pa-to khit-ciaq*), coarse and wild in their appearance, who extorted money from shopkeepers and wealthy individuals. Often they would first display their skills in martial arts, or they would make the excuse of being victims of a natural disaster, and then they would ask for money. Intimidated by their manner and appearance, people "bore the pain and gave" (Ai-ai Report).

Finally, Macgowan (1912:297–99; see also D. J. MacGowan 1859:297–98) writes of what he calls "wandering criminals," men who had been banished for offenses they had committed. Although the state sentenced them, it took no part in their support. Local government, however, gave them an allowance almost sufficient to buy their rice. To supplement this, it allowed them to beg, seeking alms from local shops. The shopkeepers had a "choice" of either paying their leader on an annual or quarterly basis or of having the criminals call every day for a cash. In this way these men were similar to the local mendicants, but their methods were very different. Each criminal was bound hand to ankle by a chain,

> which he clanked ominously as if to hint that any resistance to his demand for money would end in a fierce and fatal onslaught. [Moreover, while] . . . the ordinary beggar . . . whines out his request in the humblest tones and . . . receives the insults that are hurled at him in the very meekest and the most submissive manner, . . . the "wandering criminals" spoke in loud and domineering tones and in a rough northern dialect that the people of the south did not understand. It was an unknown language, but the clanking chains, fiercely flashing eyes, and savage looks put a menace into the stormy language of the north that prevented the people from resenting this unusual onslaught on their pockets. (Macgowan 1912:299)

Another intimidatory tactic of Chinese beggars involved the use of snakes. A beggar chief in Chekiang told Amelia Stott, "Some of our members find these snakes useful in collecting their flowery dues from greedy-hearted ones. To dwell upon the fierce love of money in men, and especially in women, weighs down the spirit. Often the *tao-fan* [beggar] has to throw a snake round a woman's neck before she will drop her grudging gift. The act invariably arouses in those who behold it so great a degree of terror that they quickly avoid similar inconvenience" (1927:831).

Gee reports a similar tactic, employed against shopkeepers. Beggars in Soochow used a snake called the *tsing-siao zoo*, which typified the green dragon, the bearer of good luck. The beggar would bring his snake into the shop, showing it around and telling the proprietor that it would bring good fortune to his establishment. Although the snakes were harmless, "the darting back and forth of the tongue may frighten the timid, and the shopkeepers gave to get rid of the beggar and his companion" (1925:8). Apparently snakes have been used by beggars for many centuries. In the novel *Walter Margin*, which dates back at least to the sixteenth century, the writer notes that beggars who wanted food often carried snakes. "They need not say a word but just show the snake and that meaning is understood" (Shih Nai-an 1963:562n).

Although reports such as these of beggars using force, intimidation, or fear to extract alms are fairly numerous, it seems that a far more common tactic was simply to create a nuisance, making it worth one's while to pay them off and get rid of them. The main targets of such measures were shopkeepers and well-to-do families holding celebrations or funerals.

Begging at celebrations and funerals has already been discussed, and it was demonstrated that there were some positive aspects to these activities: the performance of services—some essential, some less so—and the bringing of good luck. The presence of beggars at such gatherings, where a lot of people were in attendance, also gave the host an opportunity to bestow charity in a public and ostentatious manner, demonstrating that he was a man of face. But beggars were not altogether welcome at these events. In present-day Taiwan, the services they might once have provided are performed by professional musicians who specialize in playing at funerals and weddings, and by motorized vehicles that transport the coffin and mourners to the grave, or the bride, her party, and her trousseau and dowry to the groom's home. However, there are indications that even in the past some people, at least, considered beggars a disruptive nuisance on these occasions; in these cases the beggars' main strategy seems to have been not to attend but to have their chief collect a sum of money in advance to keep them away (Wang 1974:150; Liu Hsü 1936:172).

The cost to the host differed according to time and place. In Canton the host could invite some beggars, the number depending on his level of wealth, to attend the feast, although they ate at their own separate table (Gray 1878ii:59); in other areas there was a mutually acknowledged figure to be paid (Liu Hsü 1936:172; Gee 1925:25–27).

If the proper amount was paid, all would be well: the only beggars to attend would be those sent by the beggar chief to keep others away. If it was not, the beggars would take "appropriate" measures. Gee describes in great detail how they disrupted a wedding because the host offered the chief a sum too small in proportion to his wealth. Beggars of all descriptions—dirty, ragged, disabled, bizarre in dress, outrageous and grotesque in manner and actions—descended upon the residence and left only when they received what they considered their due (1925:25–27; see also Liu Hsü 1936:172; Macgowan 1912:295–97). In Foochow beggars would meet those mourners who did not pay them off at the cemetery and actually jump into the grave to prevent the coffin from being lowered. Since, according to the principles of geomancy, the timing of the interment as well as the site of the grave were important if one was to secure supernatural benefits, such a disruption represented a serious threat to the family of the deceased (Doolittle 1865ii:262–63: see also Gray 1878ii:52).

A similar system operated in begging from shopkeepers. As I have explained, the main objective was to have the shopkeepers pay off the beggar chief, and there were also mutually understood fees to be paid over a specific period (Shih Ch'ien 1925:14; Gamble and Burgess 1921:274), in exchange for which the chief gave his word to keep the beggars away. If the shopkeeper refused to pay, however, he faced a number of different tactics. Beggars might go individually, in twos and threes, or in larger groups to beg from him. They might stay outside, near the door, perhaps blocking the doorway, or they might go inside, near the counter. They might just ask for money or simply hold out their hand or other receptacle and say nothing, or they might be boisterous, disruptive, or even insulting. They might curse the shopkeeper—curses were feared as well as being offensive (Liu Hsü 1936:175). Some even report beggars pounding the shop floor, beating gongs, and making loud entreaties, which drowned out conversation between shopkeeper and customer, for alms (Doolittle 1865ii:260). One informant, a shopkeeper, said that what he could not endure was the way the beggars would *liam-kieng,* literally "chant scriptures," but in this case referring to the whining manner in which they spoke to him: *"Thau-ke* [boss]. I am ill. Please give me a few dollars." Another said his weak point was the fear of being called *tang-sng,* "a skinflint." Others merely disliked the unpleasant presence of beggars.

In order to reduce the disruptiveness of the beggars, at least, if not the total alms given, shopkeepers resorted to a few tactics of their own. Some played a waiting game. Since only one group of beggars was allowed into a shop at one time, the shopkeeper tried to stall as long as he could before giving. This not only reduced the numbers of beggars he faced in a day, but if he proved a tougher mark, the beggars would frequent his shop less often (Matignon 1900:226). Another tactic was to establish times when beggars could expect to receive alms from shops. In Taiwan the assistant chief would lead the beggars out on the first and fifteenth or the second and sixteenth days of the lunar month (worship days for the general public and the business community respectively), and each beggar would be given one or two cash, depending on the size of the shop (Wang 1974:150). In Penang an arrangement was made that beggars came around only on Thursday mornings (Chan 1973:n.p.). In Foochow beggars went to the rice shops twice a year, after each harvest, and received alms from both shopkeepers and farmers (Doolittle 1865ii:263). And in Peking, although beggars could make daily rounds, receiving two cash each from each shop, one day each autumn was set aside on which they could go to the stores and take what they wanted. "The store-keepers could get absolutely no protection from the police, and could not even protect themselves by refusing to put out their goods. The beggars, if angered by the stinginess of a merchant, were not slow to loot, wreck, or even fire his shop" (Gamble and Burgess 1921:275).

Specifying occasions on which beggars could expect to receive charity not only reduced the disturbance they could create and perhaps the money that was spent on alms, but it also highlighted to the public the "generosity" of the shopkeeper by directing attention to his philanthropy. Moreover, in several of the examples mentioned, there was a sacred significance to the days on which beggars were allowed to seek their alms.

Finally, two other closely related negative tactics are used by some beggars, one based on the association of beggars and contagion, the other on beggars horrifying their marks to make them give. There are many reports of beggars mutilating themselves in front of others while asking for alms: striking themselves with sticks or bricks; cutting themselves to draw blood with sickles, knives, or razors, perhaps sprinkling the blood on a shop floor; driving nails into the head; pounding the head on a wall, a cobblestone in the street, or the head of another beggar; or lighting combustible materials on the top of the head (Gray 1878ii:62–63; Gee 1925:3, 15; Matignon 1900:229; Liu Hsü 1936:175–76; Wang 1974:147). Liu Hsü describes one colorfully named tactic, "boring holes with two eels" (*shuang-shan tsuan-tung*), in which the beggar pushed one hook through his nasal septum and another through the loose skin of his throat (1936:178). There was undoubtedly a fair degree of showmanship in these tactics. Taiwanese spirit mediums (*tang-ki*), for example, sometimes slash their backs with knives, drawing blood, while in a trance, but the cuts they make are very small indeed, much like a minor scratch from a kitten or a thorn. Still, most found it preferable when faced with a beggar mutilating himself just to give a few coins to get rid of him.

Beggars also take advantage of their physical state or appearance to arouse feelings in their marks ranging from mere discomfort to actual fear of contamination. Some point to the very real threat of disease they present, such as the smallpox-stricken beggar, his body covered with running sores, who waved his arm in the face of passersby (Bennett 1931:218), or the leprous beggar, so infected that his ears, hands, and feet appeared to be sloughing off, carried on the back of another and threatening to enter a shop unless the proprietor demonstrated generosity (Gray 1878ii:62). Others emphasize that beggars are dirty and smelly and note the desire to avoid physical contact with them or to prevent them from touching one's person or clothing. Some beggars take advantage of this in a very dramatic way. Waiting until a customer sits down to eat something in a restaurant or at a noodle stand, they then spit or thrust their fingers into his food. The customer, robbed of his appetite, leaves, and the beggar eats his unfinished meal (Matignon 1900:227; Ti 1974:81). Other marks find the physical state of disabled beggars or the ragged, tattered, perhaps emaciated appearance of poor ones very discomfiting. In all these cases it is a simple and relatively inexpensive matter—and one he is very much aware of—just to give a small amount to the beggar to be rid of him.

There are three observations we can make about the strategies beggars choose in soliciting alms. First, although for heuristic purposes we can divide beggar tactics into three types depending on the sort of appeal being made, in actual practice these boundaries were much less distinct. To be sure, there were pure types to be found, disabled worthy beggars who restricted themselves to supplication, entertainers whose art earned them alms, and those who relied on naked force and intimidation. But in the approaches of many, there was a melding of different appeals. A disabled beggar, however worthy he might appear to the potential giver, could also instill a feeling of discomfort or a fear of being touched. One might feel pity for a beggar with a communicable disease but also fear of being contaminated by him. An entertainer might sing well but so loudly as to drown out the conversation between a shopkeeper and his customers. Despite numerous reports that attest to the talent of some beggars, Macgowan reports that some so-called entertainers relied on a lack of talent, a grating sound on the ears, to get alms (1912:229–300). Positive and remunerative appeals, it seems, were frequently enhanced by the addition of a coercive or nuisance element.

Second, it should be noted that beggars frequently took as their primary marks those who were most vulnerable. Shopkeepers were always vulnerable because each transaction was important and because they did not want to lose business. Therefore they were loath to have any customers frightened off because of the action of beggars. Moreover, despite the countertactics available to them, observers note that shopkeepers were really no match for beggars. The latter had too many resources—time and manpower—and too little to lose (Smith 1890:71–72; Moule 1902:124; Macgowan 1912:293–94).

People holding celebrations or funerals were vulnerable only on those occasions, but because these were infrequent, it was even more important that they not be disrupted. Many celebrations—weddings, the birth of a child, and New Year's Day—represented new beginnings. Others—birthdays and days on which supernatural beings were worshipped—were occasions to honor an elder, a deity, or an ancestor. In all of these it was important that nothing untoward happen to interrupt the proceedings or to negate the positive, lucky atmosphere, for that would portend a bad future. Burials, too, had to be properly executed, and the interment had to take place at the proper time in order that the geomantic potential of the graveside flow to the family and descendants of the deceased.

Third, we can ask the question, Why did people permit beggars to solicit alms successfully from them. With the exceptions of those who encountered gangs of beggars who were more like bandits or bullies or those skilled in weaponry and martial arts, most were stronger than those who sought alms from them. Why did they not simply threaten or actually use force on the beggars to keep them away? Moule observed that aside from "shouts and oaths, or shavings thrown in their faces . . . greater violence than this few would dare to offer" (1902:124). How can this be explained?

In addition to the fact that some, even though they might be annoyed, were still motivated by charity, there was also the feeling that one who threatened or used force on a beggar risked some sort of nebulous retribution. In Taiwan I was told that "he who takes advantage of a beggar will suffer a loss for it" (*khi-hu khit-ciaq e sue le*). This extended beyond beating or bullying a beggar but even to arguing with him. The reasons were explained as follows. First, beggars were the "weakest of the weak"; for a normal adult male to use his strength against an old, poor, or disabled beggar was unthinkable. Should a hoodlum, presumably in the hire of someone else, beat up a beggar, he would lose his reputation irretrievably. Not only would he become the object of ridicule among his peers, but such an act would constitute a serious breach of *gi-khi*, the code of egalitarianism among gangsters and other underclass elements. Second, any effort to prevent beggars from begging was seen as interference with their livelihood. While not a desired way to make a living, begging was nonetheless seen as necessary for some people—the destitute, the displaced, and the disabled. What a beggar could get from begging was his due. The secretary of the Ai-ai Chiu-chi yüan, a private charitable organization, said that his institution used to take it upon themselves to pick up all beggars. However, they stopped doing this in 1951 because some beggars, unwilling to go, made a fuss, and public reaction sided with them. Onlookers berated the institution's employees, saying, "What are you doing? If they want to beg let them. They have the right to beg if they want to." So the institution began taking only beggars who were willing to go.

Third, according to Matignon, the use of violence by a shopkeeper may be effective for the moment, but within a few days the beggar "will surely return to burn down the storehouse. Even worse, the beggar might come back and hang himself on the door" (1900:238–39). Such an act would have a far more serious consequence than simply the death of the beggar. Not only would it damage the reputation of the shopkeeper, but it would have drastic cosmological implications. First, the shop would be considered haunted, which would keep customers away. To remedy the situation, Taoist practitioners (*to-su*) would have to be brought in to exorcise the ghost. Moreover, the shopkeeper would probably have to remodel the shop in order to change the flow of geomantic currents the death attracted and to fool the haunting ghost so that he would not recognize the place. Second, since the beggar died an unnatural and unjust death (*ong-si*) his ghost would certainly be a *wan-hun*, one that had suffered an unrighted wrong and would certainly attempt revenge. Only when a beggar breached an agreement between his chief and the proprietor could he be beaten with impunity (Doolittle 1865ii:262).

The beggars' strategy of demanding or expecting only a small amount of money renders unnecessary the use of force against them

or the consequences it is believed to bring. It is simply not worth-
while not to give. Several informants said that the few dollars asked
for by beggars were not worth the harrassment, the effort, or the
time to attempt to outwait them. Better to give them some money
and send them on their way.

CHAPTER FOUR

The Structure and Character of the Liong-hiat Community

THE LIONG-HIAT COMMUNITY began in the late 1960s. It is the continuation of a group of displaced squatters, the Beggars and a number of others, who moved there when their old neighborhood was razed. This chapter will begin by briefly tracing the history and development of Liong-hiat and the Beggar group that preceded it. But because of his central role in its formation and continuation, we must start with a personal sketch of Tiek-kou and his role in the history and development of the community.

The History of the Liong-hiat Community

Tiek-kou was born in 1915 in a poor wood gatherer's family in rural Lotung. The youngest of five sons, he was adopted out— sold—to a childless family for ¥120.[1] His adoptive parents were also poor, his adoptive father being an agricultural laborer, and when they died, Tiek-kou, then about twelve years old, returned to his natal family. He said that since his adoptive parents left him no land or anything else of economic value, he had no obligation to stay at their home, but he did retain their surname, and he has maintained his ritual obligations to them.

He began working at age fifteen as a long-term agricultural laborer (*tng-kang*), but he soon left this for a better-paying job in a factory. From there he drifted from job to job, working on highways, in a logging camp, and on a cane press. In 1937, with the outbreak of war between China and Japan, he began selling pictures and maps of mainland China to people who were interested in following the

65

course of the war there. From there he went into black marketeering, selling fish outside the controls the Japanese had established on the Taiwan market. He was caught once, and though threatened with a prison term, his gift of gab got him off with a fine and confiscation of his goods. With the end of the war in 1945 and the repatriation of the Japanese, the bottom dropped out of the black market, and he had to look for some other way to earn a living. But the times were very bad, and it was difficult for a poor man to find enough work to make ends meet. He and his mate—he began his *tong-ku* (cohabitation) relationship in 1942—wandered about, and it was at that time that he began to beg, attending the ritual feasts of farm families in the countryside in eastern Taiwan. In 1948 he contracted *o-cu-a*, a kind of black-colored pox that swell to the size of peanuts, a disease that is not infrequently fatal,[2] and he and his mate wandered north. After a while, they reached the Taipei area, where they settled, begging for a living as Tiek-kou gradually recovered.

After he regained his strength, Tiek-kou worked for a time as a street sweeper, but he and his mate continued to beg to supplement their income. Gradually he gathered a group of beggars around him, all of them living in a squatter area. It was at this time that he began to acquire his beggar implements, and after he had several working for him, he stopped begging himself. His mate continued to beg for several more years, and his three older daughters were all sent out to beg when they were children. But Tiek-kou devoted himself to other economic pursuits, some connected with begging and some with gambling. He also began to build up a network of acquaintances, sworn brothers, and allies, and through this network he gathered information useful to the other beggars, both as individuals and as a group.

The beggars were not the only ones living in the squatter area. Among the others were some Hokciulang and some former commandos in the Kuomintang army from Swatow. These people, as well as the beggars themselves, were attracted there by the availability of cheap housing or of land on which one could build his own house. The former commandos were also attracted by the gambling that went on in the homes of the beggars. Gambling is illegal in Taiwan, but at that time, because the beggars were thought of as desperately poor, they were a perfect cover; if discovered by the police, they simply claimed they were playing cards or dice as a pastime and that the stakes were penny-ante, hardly enough to justify a charge of illegal gambling. The commandos not only liked to gamble but also acted as bouncers (*pou-piou*) keeping order at the gambling dens.

These people lived as neighbors in the squatter area for many years until the authorities decided to clear it and build a road, and those living there were forced to move. Some public housing was being built to accommodate them, but there were advantages to the beggars and to some of the others not to move there. From the beggars' point of view, whereas the squatter area had been close to Taipei and to the business district of the town in which they lived, the public housing project was relatively far away. Although a bus service was to be provided to and from the new area, it was not as convenient as simply living near to where one wanted to beg, especially for the more disabled beggars who had to be led or helped to their spots. Moreover, one had to take two or three buses from the new area to reach the parts of Taipei where other beggars then sought alms. Finally, the beggars, as well as anyone else, could sell their rights to public housing to people who felt the government was offering a good bargain and who wanted to upgrade their level of accommodation. With the money they received, the beggars could then build other squatter structures and still have a generous amount of money left over for other purposes.

So Tiek-kou began to look for a new place for the Beggars to squat. At that time one of his sworn brothers, who had once been mayor of the town, proved to be very useful. He owned some land on which the city had plans to erect a public building, but that project was some years off, and the government had not yet purchased the land, which was still in agricultural use. From the point of view of the beggars, although it was not quite as centrally located as the original squatter area had been, it was only a few bus stops further down the road, and it was certainly preferable to the public housing area. Tiek-kou negotiated a rent for the land and then consulted with the beggars and with those Hokciulang and commandos interested in coming with them. They approved the deal and soon moved to the new area, which was called Liong-hiat. Those who moved included the beggars, several Hokciu families, and three former commandos who by then had become integrated into the Beggar group.

Having a new place to squat did not solve their problems, however. When the group moved, there was nothing on the land they rented except some old, broken-down chicken coops on what is now one side of the central pathway. They began to build new houses or improve on already existing structures, but as soon as they made any progress, the police came in and tore down what they had built. Since the land on which they lived was earmarked for public use, the government did not want any residences built on it, for this would create problems when it came time to clear the land and erect the proposed public building. Repeated appeals to the police and to city hall brought no results, so Tiek-kou and Iek-a, the subdistrict head, finally called on the city government and issued them with an ultimatum: either let the residents build suitable living quarters on the land or they would erect tents, and a tent city of poor people would be very embarrassing to the city council.[3] De facto permission to build was then granted, and Liong-hiat soon became habitable.

But the problems of the community were still not over. The Liong-hiat area, like much of the low-lying land in the Taipei Basin, is subject to flooding.[4] To escape the worst effects, many of the residents wanted to add onto their homes a low-ceilinged loft (*phia-cui-lau*) where they could go and take their valuables to escape the floodwaters. For a long time, because they were squatters, their requests were ignored by the bureaucracy of city hall. Then Tiek-kou and Iek-a went to see someone higher up in the city government. The result of their visit was positive, and the Liong-hiat residents were given permission to improve their houses, adding to their height. Tiek-kou had succeeded again.

He got yet another concession from city hall when he lobbied successfully to get the road that runs in front of Liong-hiat paved. This road, formerly a dirt path, was muddy in rainy weather and dusty in dry. It was an inconvenience to those in Liong-hiat and the surrounding area. When some funds for road works became available, Tiek-kou succeeded in getting a portion of them spent on the road in front of Liong-hiat rather than on some other road.

The neighborhood became more livable with the paving of the pathways in the area and the erection of the public toilet by the TCS late in 1973 (improvements in which Tiek-kou played no role). Since that time the only changes have been the building of several new houses and the rebuilding of some of the old ones. Tiek-kou's role as leader will be discussed further in chapter 7. For now we will turn our attention to how Liong-hiat functions as neighborhood and a community.

Community Relationships in Liong-hiat

As explained in chapter 1 and as is apparent from the preceding section, besides the Beggars, Liong-hiat also includes a group of

Hokciulang and several Hokkien-speaking households that I have lumped into a residual category called Neighbors. In some ways it is a misnomer to refer to Liong-hiat as a whole as a community. A community certainly exists among the Beggars. One also exists, although the bonds are weaker, between the Beggars and some of the other families. But there are several households, both Hokciu and Neighbor, who have relationships with the Beggars in only two ways: they live nearby; and they share a water supply and bill. I will now examine the various segments of Liong-hiat and analyze the relationships within and between them, the fights, quarrels, disputes, and ignoring of neighbors on the one hand, and the friendships, neighborliness, and mutual care and assistance on the other. I will also document the degree of communal feeling that exists between various families in Liong-hiat and describe the attitudes residents have toward their neighborhood.

Relationships between the Beggars are basically friendly and are characterized by a good deal of cooperation and mutual assistance. As the map shows (p. xii), homes in Liong-hiat open onto an L-shaped path with another smaller path off to one side, giving a public courtyard effect. Doors are usually open, and people spend a lot of time either outside chatting across the path, or inside each other's houses, visiting in a neighbor's front room (*kheq-thia:*). Tiek-kou's front room is an especially popular place where anyone, resident of Liong-hiat or visitor to the area, can gather, even if no one from his household is present, to chat, smoke, munch snacks, drink tea, and play cards. Others' front rooms also serve as gathering places, though in a more limited manner, the guests usually being friends of the household head.

Besides visiting each other, the Beggars frequently borrow items from neighbors and even borrow or use rooms in their houses. The most frequently borrowed item is water. Since they do not have running water, people get it from outside and store it in large cisterns in their homes. Boiled water for drinking is stored in thermos flasks. It is not uncommon for someone to run out of either boiled or unboiled water in the middle of a task and go next door and take what they need, often without saying a word. Later, when it is more convenient, they will replenish their water supply. But no one expects that "borrowed" water will be returned amount for amount. They assume that it will work out more or less evenly in the long run.

Another item that is "borrowed" is the television. Not all families have sets, and when people who do not have a set want to watch television, they just go to the home of someone who has one and sit down and watch, even if no one in the host household is watching. Children frequently gather in one home to watch television even when they have sets in their own homes. They do this because it is more fun to watch with friends or because they want to watch a different program from the one being viewed at home.

A facility that is frequently borrowed is a bathroom. Some of the Beggars, particularly the single ones, live in very small, even one-room houses, and these and many other homes do not have bathing facilities. In fact the bathing facilities in those homes that have them are quite rudimentary, consisting of a room with a wood or concrete floor, a metal tub, a supply of water, and a small hole at the base of the wall to allow the used bathwater to flow into the sewage ditch outside. But these rooms are available to those whose houses have no bathing facilities, and it is not uncommon to see someone, towel in hand, walking away from the homes of Tiek-kou or a couple of the others, having just had a bath.

Another facility sometimes borrowed is a front room, the reason being to give a banquet. Usually this is done because the would-be host has no suitable place to entertain guests himself. For example, when Kua:-chui gave a banquet to thank those who had contributed labor to help him build his house, he used his father-in-law's front room because his home was not yet finished. O-niau hosted a ca-tered meal at A-ieng's place to thank him and Tiek-kou for their help to that point in getting her and her family their identity cards. Pai-kha-e, a single beggar, gave a banquet during the annual city festival in the home of A-tan.

Another reason people loan their front rooms to another for a ban-quet is religious taboo. After a funeral ceremony, the relatives and some close friends of the deceased accompany the coffin to the grave-yard, where it is interred. The relatives must maintain a solemn deport-ment for a considerable period thereafter, but other mourners, once they have offered incense to the deceased and the corpse is removed for burial, are supposed to return to a normal state of happiness. To facilitate this, the head of the family of the deceased gives a banquet for them, and although he personally abstains, he urges the guests to eat, drink, and enjoy themselves. But his own house is still under taboo and cannot be used for such purposes, so he uses the homes of his neigh-bors. When A-sek-a's father-in-law died, several families, including Lau Lim, one of the Hokciulang, loaned their front rooms as places for the guests to eat and drink. Others did the same at the funeral of A-pui-a, Kua:-chui's mate.

Minding others' children is also quite frequent in Liong-hiat, and it demonstrates the extended family, villagelike atmosphere found among the Beggars. Often this is done quite informally. As there are many children around, one can simply go off on an errand, leaving the children to play with others, more or less in the care of older siblings, neighbors, or anyone else who is about. If a mother plans to be gone for several hours, she might make a more formal arrangement and ask that a neighbor keep an eye on her children and perhaps feed them if they become hungry before she returns. Neighboring mothers and teenage females are especially willing to watch others' children, but men will help out too.

This sort of assistance is often given spontaneously. A-ieng once happened along as A-tho's daughter-in-law was trying to hang out clothes and watch her rambunctious eighteen-month-old son at the same time. He picked up the child and played with him for the several minutes it took the boy's mother to finish her work then handed him back and went on his way. A-sek-a's oldest daughter was washing her clothes one Sunday afternoon when her sister, who had been minding Niau-bu's young son, brought him in. He had been playing outside and had gotten quite dirty. Seeing this, she told her sister to bring him over. Then she bathed him and washed his clothes before sending him home with her sister.

In another incident involving care for children, and one displaying a quite different sort of concern, a group of people were chatting and playing cards in Tiek-kou's front room when Kua:-chui's five-year-old daughter did something that displeased him. He picked up a thin stick and hit her with it, but after two or three blows, the stick broke, so he began to use his hand. A-tan apparently felt the girl had been punished enough, however, so he rushed over and picked her up then held her in his arms until her father's anger subsided.

Incidents such as these are quite common, as are such acts as picking up and comforting a child who has fallen down or giving a treat to a neighbor's child while giving one to one's own. They illustrate both the degree of familiarity and the closeness of the bonds between the Beggars.

The Beggars also frequently shop for each other. Quite often I would be talking with someone in the morning when a neighbor would pass by, shopping bag in hand, and ask if there was anything the person needed. Alternatively, someone might see a neighbor on her way to the market and simply give her money, asking her to pick up some specific item or whatever might be a good buy that day.

During the initial fieldwork period, several Liong-hiat families either repaired their houses or tore them down completely and built solid, brick and concrete, two-story structures in their place. Those doing so often recruited labor from their neighbors or neighbor's relatives. Several in Liong-hiat are skilled masons or carpenters, and others were willing to work as laborers on such jobs. This recruiting was mutually advantageous. The laborers and tradesmen got opportunities to work and could do the jobs when they did not have outside employment. The builders, as neighbors and longtime friends, were able to pay less than the going rate for the labor, thus reducing the cost of the house. In addition to the wages paid, each builder gave a banquet for the workers when the job was near completion, providing good food and plenty of wine. Only one builder did not pay cash wages to all those who worked on his house, but as a contractor, he had provided work in the past for those he did not pay, and he promised to continue to do so in the future.

Loaning money to each other is another form of mutual assistance in the community. Sometimes the money is given as a loan; no interest is charged, but the loan has to be repaid as soon as possible. A beggar receiving such a loan is obliged to go out to beg each day until it is fully repaid. Persons wanting to borrow money to gamble, on the other hand, have to pay a high rate of interest, and some in the community, particularly Tiek-kou's wife and his oldest daughter, earn money making loans to gamblers. The most common form of credit, however, is the rotating credit association (*he-a*).[5] This is often used to raise larger amounts of money, from a thousand to several tens of thousands New Taiwan dollars, over a longer period of time. It is also a way to save money and to earn interest on one's capital. Participation in rotating credit associations was widespread during the initial period of fieldwork, partly because so many people needed large amounts of money to make the desired improvements on their houses. Many persons were in several rotating credit associations at the same time, in some as organizers (*he-thau*) and in others as ordinary members (*he-kha*).

The most important form of mutual aid in the community is an outright gift or donation in time of crisis or emergency. During the initial field study, four individuals or families needed and received such help, one of them twice. Two had serious illnesses, one was hit by a motorcycle while crossing a street, and two persons died. Niau-chi-hi:, who was hit by a motorcycle, and A-tan, who suddenly developed a bleeding ulcer, were both in hospital for considerable periods. Many community members gave money to their families to help with the expenses, and A-tan, also thanks to his neighbors, had a constant supply of milk powder. A-pui-a developed uterine cancer and, for a time before she died, was under the care of a doctor in Kaohsiung, a city in the south of Taiwan. Most of the Beggar families contributed several hundred New Taiwan dollars each to her mate, Kua:-chui, to assist him, and they contributed again at her funeral. A-sek-a's father-in-law's funeral cost over NT$30,000, a sum far in excess of what he could afford. Relatives paid half the expenses, but the neighbors also gave NT$200–400 each for a total of NT$7,000. They also assisted in the funeral, making funeral clothes, taking donations, and preparing food. A-sek-a himself still paid about one month's earnings, but he nonetheless had a more manageable burden.

Another instance of mutual assistance occurred when Lau-liong got into a fight and severely injured another man in the arm with a knife. Details of the incident and the settlement will be given in chapter 7, but a good portion of the NT$70,000–80,000 it cost to settle the dispute came from the community in the form of contributions to Lau-liong himself and as a levy imposed on the winnings in Tiek-kou's gambling dens.

Besides the extension of assistance and the feelings of neighborliness among the Beggars in general, there are also groups of close friends among them. Three men in particular, A-sek-a, A-ieng, and Be-bin, frequently invite friends to eat with them. It is also common for friends to drop by their houses in the evening, and, after accepting the obligatory bit of food, send out for some wine to help them pass the evening hours as they chat. It is also not uncommon for someone, male or female, who has just had a big win at a gambling den to invite a group of friends out to a small local restaurant (*mi-tiam-a*) to eat and drink.

Groups of women also spend a lot of time talking and visiting together, either in front of their doors or in the home of someone involved in a drawn-out, menial chore. Such groups usually consist of women of approximately the same age, but one woman, A-tho, is sought out by many women in Liong-hiat, including some from non-Beggar households, for advice or just as an interesting, kind, and understanding person to talk to. A-tho is blind, and she spends most of her time at home sitting on a tatami-covered sleeping platform just inside her house. But she is rarely alone; there are almost always neighbors or members of her family sitting on the platform chatting with her.

With the exception of those who seek out A-tho, adult networks of friends are almost always made up of the Beggars and some outside acquaintances; they never include the Hokciulang or the Neighbors. But groups of friends involving the Beggars' children, especially the males, cut across such boundaries. There are several recognizable age cohorts in Liong-hiat that include all the children of the same sex and age in the area. Most of the Hokciulang have been neighbors of the Beggars for many years, so their children grew up together, and none of the adult Neighbors, even those who them- selves almost totally ignore the Beggars, make any attempt to restrict their children or tell them not to play with the others.

There are two negative aspects to community interactions: disputes and quarrels and, much less frequent, taking advantage of someone in a vulnerable position or taking delight in someone else's misfortune. As one might expect, young children quarrel more than anyone else, but adults shrug this off as an unavoidable aspect of childhood. They generally try to remain aloof from children's quarrels, for they feel that involvement will lead to disputes between parents, something they want to avoid if possible. Instead, if a mother sees her child quarreling, she goes over to break up the squabble and send her child home. She shows little sympathy if her child is hurt in a scuffle and is likely to say, "That's what happens when you run around outside all the time. If you stayed in more, you wouldn't get into so much difficulty." Nor does she show much sympathy if her child is the victim of a bully but says, "You see? I told you not to play with that bully. Next time maybe you will heed what I say."

But quarrels and fights are not restricted to children. They also occur among adults, and for a number of reasons. One person might be using a hose to fill water containers in his house when another comes by, disconnects the hose, and fills his own water container. Words might be exchanged, but nothing else comes of the incident. The failure to repay loans or to repay them on time is another cause of contention, and it often prompts the creditor to curse or even strike the debtor a few times. Again, such matters rarely go further. More serious disputes arise when someone takes or tries to seduce another's mate. These cases end with a more formal settlement in- volving Tiek-kou as arbitrator and requiring the payment of damages (see chap. 6).

Insults or other unacceptable behavior by one who has been drinking or arguments between people who are gambling can also lead to serious disputes, even fights. Tua-kho-e frequently gets into such situations when he is drunk. He boasts in a very aggressive and annoying manner, insults people, or attempts to force his affections on a woman. Such behavior often invites a beating, if not at the time, later on when he is asleep.

O-baq-e also got into a fight as a result of his drinking. One evening he went to A-sek-a's house to see friends. He had been drinking, but he wanted to drink more, so he sent A-sek-a's daughter out for more wine. He was not content to drink alone, however, and he asked others to share the wine with him. A-sek-a refused because he had been having stomach trouble. Hiong-a was there too, but he was not interested in drinking any more either. So O-baq-e became angry and began to argue with Hiong-a. A-ieng heard the noise from outside and went in to calm the situation. He told O-baq-e to settle down, that there was no reason to argue about such a trivial matter. All seemed well, so A-ieng left, but before long, O-baq-e began to argue again. A-ieng returned and tried to quiet him for a second time. But O-baq-e picked up a small footstool and hit A-ieng in the face with it. A-ieng left but soon returned with a sword, and he struck O-baq-e with the side of the blade. A-ieng ended up with bandages on his head and cheek, and O-baq-e spent a couple of days in hospital. The incident was soon forgotten, however. One informant later remarked that both disputants were like hoodlums. "They see such exploits as adventures. The scars that result are badges of courage, evidence of their bravado and manliness" (ta-po khi-khai).

Not long afterward, A-ieng was involved in another incident. One evening he invited Kua:-chui to go out gambling with him. At first Kua:-chui declined because he had no money, but A-ieng flashed a big roll of bills and said he had plenty for both. They started gambling, but after a while, Kua:-chui began losing heavily. He looked to A-ieng, but A-ieng ignored him. He then asked A-ieng for money, but instead of giving it to him as he had promised, A-ieng retorted, "What do you mean, coming to gamble when you don't have any money?" A-ieng continued to berate him and then, with a conspicuous gesture of noblesse oblige, gave him some money in a way that caused Kua:-chui a serious loss of face. Kua:-chui left and returned with a knife. He confronted A-ieng, the two argued, and he stabbed A-ieng in the arm.

Lau-liong was also involved in a dispute in a gambling den. One night a number of people were gambling in Tiek-kou's dice room when Lau-liong made a pass at O-niau. She turned him down, and, his pride hurt, he began to revile her. A-hong, a young man from outside, told him to go outdoors, where he would not disturb the gambling, if he wanted to argue. Lau-liong pulled out a knife and hacked A-hong's arm, severing some of the tendons. It took Tiek-kou, A-ieng, and the subdistrict head several weeks to settle that dispute, and the cost to Lau-liong and to the community as a whole was considerable (see chap. 7).

Not all such disputes ended in violence. A-sek-a once accused Touq-pi:-a of cheating while they were playing dice. The two argued for quite some time, cursing and shouting very loudly at each other, but others separated them, and the two cooled off before any fighting broke out.

A number of other incidents occurred between the Beggars during the period of fieldwork in Liong-hiat, but soon after each, despite the amount of anger and even violence displayed, the disputants forgot about their quarrel. Giok-khim, one of the Neighbors, commented, "They are like children. They quarrel frequently, but then they quickly forget why. So they make up and become friends again." And even with the amount of violence arising out of the disputes, particularly involving knives, Giok-khim never felt any fear for her personal safety, despite the fact that her husband, a seaman on a merchant ship, was frequently away. She said that violence was always directed at the offending individual in a quarrel. It was never random. "I feel as safe here as anywhere else I have lived," she commented.

Giok-khim also felt secure against theft. She remarked that once in a while a child, perhaps tempted by the thought of buying a snack, might take a few coins left lying about in plain sight, but she had never had anything taken from her house, nor had she heard of such incidents happening to others. A number of informants confirmed this observation, and the subdistrict head explained, "Beggars do not steal. That is not their way. They ask (*kiu*) for money, but they do not steal (*thau*)."

The other negative aspect to relationships in Liong-hiat is that people are sometimes taken advantage of, especially when they are down on their luck. O-niau and Hana are two cases in point. O-niau was reared in the community. As a child, she took her mother out to beg. When she became so old that passersby, rather than giving a few coins, would scold her for not going out to work so that her mother would not have to beg, she went off to work as a teahouse hostess, and from there she became a call girl. She earned good money, about NT$2,000 per night when she worked, and she was quite generous, especially to Tiek-kou and A-ieng, to whom she gave money, and to the young males in Liong-hiat, whom she frequently treated to food and wine. But when she became pregnant and could not work, no one except Tiek-kou helped her at all. He gave her a bit of money now and then and arranged for some of his relatives to take care of her baby after she gave birth so she could return to work. But others seemed almost to take some kind of delight in her predicament, and they treated her in a condescending manner. She had been high and mighty, but she had fallen.

Hana, but contrast, was a newcomer to the area. When she came, she had a lot of money, supposedly from a divorce settlement. She wore nice clothing and gold jewelry, but she loved to gamble, and before long, her money, then her jewelry, were gone, lost in the dice and card games she frequently played. When she came, she started two rotating credit associations to build a home, but she had to default on her payments, something taken very seriously by the Beggars. As a result, her house was leased to give her a chance to pay her debts, but when she could not raise the money she needed, it was sold. Hana was quite bitter when I talked to her about her losses. She complained that when she came to Liong-hiat, she had plenty of money and had been very generous, lending to whomever asked. Now that she was penniless, when she asked for a loan— usually to gamble—She was refused.

Some households keep to themselves almost entirely. The man who bought Kua:-chui's old house after his mate died is the most extreme example of this attitude. Previously the house had opened onto the smaller of the two pathways in the area, as had those facing and on either side of it. The new owner, however, bricked in the doorway and put a new one in the rear. He said he did so to make his front door a bit closer to the main road, but any difference was marginal. Others maintained that his actions were meant to demonstrate that he was not part of the Beggar community and he wanted nothing to do with it.

There were a few other households in the area that maintained an almost separate existence. Lau Kho, a Hokciulang, formerly a carpenter and later a pig farmer, associated only with some of the other Hokciulang. When the TCS was planning its projects in the area, cementing in the pathways and building a public toilet and bathhouse, it wanted to use a bit of the land his pigpen occupied, but he refused to cooperate. As they needed that piece of land, TCS representatives tried to negotiate with him, but he would not budge. Getting nowhere, the social workers finally reported this to the municipal government. Since the government was a joint sponsor of the project, and since the pigpen itself was an illegal structure on land not owned or rented by Lau Kho, the police were called in to dismantle it. Any positive feeling Lau Kho might once have had toward the Beggars was erased by this incident, and he never interacted with them in any way afterward.

The Ngs, Hokkien speakers and migrants from the south a few years before, were another family that had little to do with the Beggars. They spoke no ill of them, and the preschool-age children in the family played with Beggar children their age, but that was the extent of their interaction. In fact, adults in this family had no social dealings with anyone else in Liong-hiat but associated with some of their relatives living in the Taipei area instead.

Another household that led an isolated existence was made up of three Hokciu cobblers, all bachelors in their forties and fifties. They simply lived in the area. They had no dealings with anyone, not even their Hokciu landlord, who lived next door. One night, while the other two were away, one of the cobblers, despondent over his recent discovery that he had cancer, hanged himself from one of the beams. The other two moved away the next day from what had become an unlucky house.

There was one other Hokciu household that had little to do with the Beggars; it consisted of an old man in his fifties, his adopted son and daughter-in-law, and his natural son. Relative newcomers to the area, they had lived there only a few years. The old man spent his days with his old circle of friends, all fellow Hokciulang from outside Liong-hiat. He would leave after breakfast in the morning and not return until evening, when he would have a meal, then go to bed. His adopted son, very busy with his work as a sales representative for a plastics manufacturing company, was home even less. Only the natural son spent a fair amount of time in the area. He attended high school in the evenings and worked at home during the day pounding gold leaf for inlaying in stone (*ta-chin*). He associated with others in the area enough to know who people were, what they did, what their relationships were, and what sorts of interesting things had been happening, but he was not part of any social network in the area. This family moved away quite suddenly one day. The natural son, having a trade skill and a high school education, felt himself to be a cut above the other young men in Liong-hiat, and one evening he got into an argument with Touq-pi:-a, Tiek-kou's son, calling him a "beggar's kid." Touq-pi:-a ran home and came back with a samurai sword. Seeing this, the Hokciu man ran inside his house, so Touq-pi:-a hacked the locked door several times with the sword. The family left the following morning.

Other families had closer or at least more cordial relationships with the Beggars, however. For example, Lau Ong, from whom they got their water, while not a frequent visitor to Beggar households, did occasionally go over to chat or play a few games of cards. His wife, busy with her housework and with running a small prepared-food stall at one of the local markets, had little time to socialize, but she frequently exchanged large notes for the coins and small bills the beggars collected to make change for her customers. His daughters, all in secondary school, had little to do with the Beggars' daughters in their age groups, all of whom were working in factories and had different circles of friends. But one son had been quite friendly with other Liong-hiat males his age until he became more involved in the social circle revolving around his apprentice training. He still came around occasionally to see his old friends, however.

Giok-khim, one of the Neighbors, had very friendly relationships with other women in her age group, especially Tiek-kou's daughters and Chieng-cui's wife. She was more educated than they were and had much more experience in the outside world, but she never acted as if she felt herself superior in any way. She and others often did their work together, or one of them would come chat with her while she was washing clothes, preparing food, or watching her children. She also participated in rotating credit associations organized by various Beggars, and she donated money to those families that had experienced a crisis.

Many of the non-Beggar household members avoided the virtually incessant gambling games in the Beggars' houses; indeed they despised gambling as much as they did begging. But a few would join the card games on occasion, or in some cases on a more frequent basis. It was quite common for non-Beggars to participate in rotating credit associations organized by Beggars, although Neighbors and Hokciulang were generally more wary and would investigate more carefully who the organizer and other members were and what sorts of outstanding obligations they had. Considerably fewer non-Beggars made donations to Beggar families undergoing a crisis, but there were some who did. Lau Lim even allowed A-sek-a to use his front room for a banquet following the funeral of the latter's father-in-law, and his wife offered incense to the deceased's spirit.

Close friendships of members of non-Beggar households were not with the Beggars, however. The Hokciulang spoke a first language quite different from Hokkien and perceived themselves as a group apart. Their networks of friends included each other and people outside Liong-hiat, mostly fellow Hokciulang. The Neighbors, a more disparate cohort, had no common bond that brought them together as the Hokciulang did, and their friendship relations were with outsiders. Close personal relations existed between the younger generations of all groups, but these tended to weaken as people grew older and became involved with schoolmates and workmates.

Perhaps the most significant link between a Beggar and any of the non-Beggars was that between Tiek-kou and the main body of Hokciulang. They had been neighbors before the move to Liong-hiat and had known one another quite well. Moreover, it was a joint decision to make the move to that area. Tiek-kou found the vacant land, then discussed the possibility of a move there with A-liong, the spokesman for the Hokciu families. Each then consulted his own group to get its approval.

The Hokciulang also accepted Tiek-kou as community leader and prevailed upon his skills and abilities when they needed them. For example, A-liong needed Tiek-kou's help when he became involved in a dispute with a man from Ch'üan-chou. A-liong had received some money from this man but was unable to return it when the man came to him with an urgent request for repayment. The man from Ch'üan-chou, depressed over a number of things, committed suicide, and his fellow Ch'üan-chou-men came to A-liong to avenge his death. Frightened for his safety if not his life, A-liong went to Tiek-kou, who agreed to mediate with the Ch'üan-chou group. He managed to convince them that A-liong and the man to whom he allegedly owned money were actually business partners, and that the money in question was the other man's portion of the invest-ment. The money was not a loan at all, and it need not be repaid. The Ch'üan-chou group accepted the story and renounced any inten-tion to take revenge on A-liong. He has been grateful ever since to Tiek-kou, and he and the other Hokciu families of long-standing association recognize Tiek-kou as community leader.

In their feelings toward the area, most of the Neighbors and the Hokciulang saw it simply as a place to live—and a place to leave when their finances made it possible for them to do so. Several Neighbor families did, in fact, leave the area between mid-1974 and late 1977. Giok-khim was one of the first to do so. Although she had generally good relations with others in the area, she had wanted to move for quite some time. Her reasons ranged from wanting to live in a better house to a fear that her children would begin to pick up bad habits from the Beggars' children. She and her husband had been planning to move after he finished the voyage he was on as a merchant seaman and found some other kind of work. But she sud-denly moved one day while her husband was still away at sea. She later said that two recent happenings had prompted her action: a dwelling owned by one of her relatives had become vacant; and her three-year-old daughter began to imitate the playtime gambling of the Beggars' children. The latter incident had upset her greatly, so she took advantage of her opportunity to move and left. The main group of Hokciu families, although they manifested an overall negative attitude toward the area, felt stuck there. They could foresee no possibility of a move because none had the money to afford it. Moreover, they had been neighbors with the Beggars for as long as twenty-five years and had made the necessary accommodations.

The feelings of individual Beggars toward others in their group and in the neighborhood are more mixed. At one level they see much that is positive about the community, the cooperation, mutual aid, and friendships, and the fact that as beggars, they are accepted by others. Indeed, this is their neighborhood. Moreover, with the completion of the projects carried out by the TCS, many have also begun to feel a bit of pride in the physical area as well. One morning A-sek-a and A-ieng were clearing a small patch of bare ground alongside the newly laid concrete pathway and planting flowers. They said they wanted to beautify the area. Several others stopped to watch and to make comments, and Siong-a, Sia-pue's nineteen-year-old son said proudly, "We are going to become a community (*she-ch'ü*), the Liong-hiat Community."

At another level, just as the non-Beggar families do, the Beggars also recognize the negative aspects of the area, especially the gambling. Even those who are heavy gamblers themselves see gambling as an evil and something their children should avoid if possible. They also feel very strongly the stigma of living in a beggars' den, and many want to spare their children this. Some, particularly in the younger generation, hope to be able to move away. Chieng-cui, with two small children, frequently expressed this desire, but he is trapped both by his financial situation and the responsibility of taking care of his blind, mentally unbalanced mother. A-sek-a has no plans or hopes of moving his whole family, but when his son left school, he arranged through a relative to get him an apprenticeship in Taipei, away from Liong-hiat. He said that his son had begun to *ouq-phai*, "pick up bad habits," from some of the other young males in the neighborhood, and he wanted to get him into better surroundings.

The attitudes of the young people toward the Beggar community and their strategies for mobility will be discussed at length in chapter 8. At this point it is sufficient to say that they are very cognizant of the negative aspects of the Beggars' social life. Suffering as they have for, so to speak, the sins of their parents, they are sometimes bitter in their condemnation of the begging, gambling, and loose sexual behavior of some in the adult generation. But, undoubtedly stung by the stigma they have sufferered as "beggar's children," they are also defensive toward the one group of people among whom they have found acceptance. To condemn the community as a whole would be to condemn themselves. Moreover, they would be condemning their parents, who are, for all their faults, still their parents and people whose good points outweigh their bad. Thus the younger generation defend the community against outside insults and condemnation. They object very strongly when others refer to it as a "beggar's den." None try to deny that there had been people there who begged or that there are still active beggars there. But they point out that there are fewer beggars than before, and that none of them, the second generation, beg. In their defensiveness they also interpret some actions by outsiders as slights when it is doubtful they are intended as such. As an example, a hawker came by one evening offering bruised fruit, which he probably had not been able to sell during the day, at a reduced price. Cieng-a interpreted this as an act of condescension, however, and she cursed him, "Who do you think you are, that you can come and sell us second-rate merchandise. Just because we are poor doesn't mean you can treat us this way!"

Despite the quarrels, fights, and failings of character of some in the community, the Beggars are a tightly knit group. Two of the TCS social workers, who also worked in other communities of squatters and poor people, frequently commented on how cohesive (*thuankiat*) the Beggars are, and how much they see themselves and act as a community rather than simply as neighbors whose relationships are based only on proximity of residence. The Beggars, too, are conscious of their being a group, and they demarcate the social boundaries of their community in comments they make. When I saw a person I did not know and asked who he or she was, an informant would either identify the person by name and relationship to someone else in the community or say simply, "He is an outsider." Membership in the community means the sharing of a special affective bond. One informant, speaking of the failure of the Ng family, one of the Neighbors, to contribute to the funeral expenses of A-sek-a's father-in-law, said, "We have *kam-chieng* (affective bonds) among one another, but we have no *kam-chieng* with them." And Chieng-cui summed up the community bonds as he explained why there were such close relationships between members of the Beggar group. He quoted a Chinese saying, "Distant relatives are not as good as close neighbors" (*oan-chin pu lu kin-lin*), and he added, "We have been together for a long time, and we have established good relationships with one another. If I am in trouble, these people will help me, so if they are in difficulty, I must help them."

To conclude this chapter, we may note the paradoxical nature of social relations in the Beggar community. On the one hand, there are strong feelings of solidarity, supported by acts of cooperation and mutual assistance. On the other, there is a surprising amount of quarreling and fighting. This is a combination one would not expect to find in a Chinese community,[6] where people tend to keep the lid on dissension if possible because, once ruptured by an open conflict, bonds of friendship, kinship, even cooperation are extremely difficult to restore. Harrell states that although hostile relationships may be ameliorated, "it is almost impossible for an overt conflict to be resolved" (1982:138), especially when people of any consequence, such as adult males, are involved. He goes on to give an example of a dispute between two political rivals that finally reached the level of physical violence resulting in one man beating the other. Afterward, even though compensation was paid and a banquet was given to show that all was forgiven, the dispute was not forgotten. Outwardly the men were civil to each other, but further cooperation between them was virtually precluded (ibid.:144–49). Crissman reinforces this view. He says that people will suppress a dispute for years, allowing it to break into the open only when it is possible for one to leave the village. Disputes that do become public, often resulting in the disputants siding with rival factions, ramify beyond those directly involved; the wives of all the parties will afterward avoid washing clothes with each other and their children refuse to play together (personal communication).

Why is it, then, that people in Liong-hiat readily erupt into conflict, yet just as readily forgive and forget? Enquiries into this matter produced nothing other than a general unwillingness to discuss it and Giok-khim's remark that the Beggars fought and forgot as children did. A number of characteristics of the Beggar community appear relevant, however. Foremost is the effect of the stigma imposed on the community because some engaged in begging. While it has not prevented them, it has limited individuals' efforts at extending their networks of close relations outside the community, and it has produced strong emotive feelings toward those inside and toward membership in the community itself. As will be shown later, some persons who were expelled for violating community norms returned to Liong-hiat after spending some time outside. A further factor is

Tiek-kou's leadership and his ability to resolve conflicts. This will be discussed at length in chapter 7. At this point it will suffice to say that he is highly respected and well liked, and this has made it possible for him to exercise some influence over the Beggars' behavior and to impose sanctions on those who misbehaved. Finally there is the fact that most households in the Beggar group were linked not only as neighbors but also through a network of kin and fictive kin ties (see chaps. 6 and 7). Taken together, these factors explain how conflict and harmony coexisted in Liong-hiat.

CHAPTER FIVE

Economic Activities

BEGGING IS THE MOST noticeable and outstanding economic activity carried out by the Liong-hiat residents who are the subject of this book, and it is the activity responsible for their sociological categorization. As table 1 indicates,[1] at the time of the research, the majority of households relied on begging for at least part of their income, and it was the primary source of income for many. Moreover, from what I was told, begging was at least as important an economic activity in the past.

Important as begging is and has been, however, it is not the Beggars' sole means of making money, and it is becoming less and less important. This chapter will first outline the begging activities and strategies of the Liong-hiat Beggars and then examine the other income-producing activities found in the Beggar community. Following that will be an analysis of the rewards of each in terms of income and risk involved and a look at the Beggars' level of living. Finally, some comparisons will be made between the socioeconomic life of the Beggars and of others in Taipei.

The range of tactics available to the Liong-hiat beggars is a good deal narrower than that of beggars in traditional China. This is due mainly to four fundamental differences in the social conditions of present-day Taiwan as compared to those of China in the past. First, begging is against the law in Taiwan, and although a policeman must catch a beggar unquestionably in the act of begging, if caught, the beggar can be sent to the Vagrant Reception Center (Yu-min Shou-jung So), where he will be kept until someone acts as a guarantor and takes responsibility for him or until he is considered rehabilitated. Although it is not a

TABLE 1
Household Reliance on Begging

	Past (N = 21)[a]	1974 (N = 24)	1978 (N = 17)
Number reliant	16	16	12
Degree of reliance			
Completely	NA[b]	8	5
Mostly	NA	3	1
Some	NA	3	2
Tiau-lo-ce only	NA	2	4

a. Difference in N, the number of households in the Beggar community, reflects its size and make-up. "Past" refers to a period several years prior to the initial study.
b. NA = not applicable.

prison and those kept there are not considered criminals, the inmates are not allowed to leave, and this restriction on their freedom is anathema to the beggars. The Liong-hiat beggars fear nothing more than incarceration there.

Second, social attitudes are changing, especially in Taipei, the seat of the national government, where a large proportion of the residents are less traditional in their outlook. In a smaller city or town, where a far greater percentage of the population is native Taiwanese, more attention is paid to traditional festivals, and beggars, whose presence at a festival gives people an opportunity to display charity, are an accepted part of the atmosphere. But in Taipei, although there are some very important and well-attended temples and some widely celebrated festivals, there is also a large proportion of people, especially the educated middle and upper classes of mainland Chinese origin, who at best have no interest in such events and may even be opposed to them on the grounds that they are wasteful of resources and superstitious in origin. These people are also less tolerant of related customs and practices. While they may be sympathetic toward the plight of beggars, on humanitarian rather than on religious grounds, they are also concerned with the "face of the nation" (*kuo-t'i*), and they consider the presence of beggars unsightly and a national shame.[2] The police respond to the feelings of the local population and are much more diligent in apprehending beggars in Taipei than they are elsewhere.

Third, the economic conditions in the Taiwan of the 1970s were far better than those of the China of the declining years of the Ch'ing and the early years of the Republic. Taiwan has enjoyed spectacular and virtually continuous economic growth, especially since the 1960s, and there has been little problem in finding employment or supporting oneself. By contrast, in the Peking of the early decades of this century, the police winked at begging; Gamble and Burgess report that according to one high-ranking police officer, "there were so many poor people in the city that the police could not take care of them all in the poorhouses, and so had to let them beg for a living" (1921:276). It is not surprising, therefore, that beggars in present-day Taiwan tend to rely mainly, though not exclusively, on positive tactics, playing on the sympathies of the public.

As in the past, sympathy is based on age, sex, physical presentation, and the public's perception of one's ability to support oneself and one's dependents. Thus those with handicaps, the aged and the very young, and single females and males with small children have little trouble begging. Teenagers and young or middle-aged adults, especially males, are generally unable to use a positive appeal unless they use some sort of ploy. These principles are manifest in the tactics and appeals used by the Liong-hiat beggars.

The reason a number of them beg is quite genuine, as many are handicapped or otherwise physically or mentally unable to work. Several adult females are blind, a number are elderly, one is thoroughly crippled with muscular dystrophy, and another is mentally deficient, although that is not the appeal she uses when begging. There are also several handicapped adult males. One lost one arm and partial use of the other in an industrial accident. A second lost half his leg because of bone cancer. A third has tuberculosis, a fourth has a mild though chronic dermatitis that makes his skin look red and scaly, and a fifth has a horribly scarred face, half a nose, and a patch over the socket where one eye used to be, the result, he said, of an untreated case of syphilis. There are also a number who are old and sickly. Most are unable to work, but a few take advantage of their handicaps, enhancing their *kho-lian-iu:* (pitiful image) in various ways.

Aside from the physically disabled, there are three women who have no spouse to support them. Two are widows, and the other is an "adopted daughter-in-law" (*sim-pu-a*) whose husband divorced her. All three are elderly, and none is in good health. Another woman, although she has a spouse, cannot rely on him because he is a morphine addict. Between using the drug and spending time either running from the police or in jail, he is not much help to her.

Others in Liong-hiat who beg, as well as some of those just described, use some sort of ploy. The most common is for a woman to beg with children. Although it is not always the case, passersby assume that the children are all her own and that she is their sole source of support. According to informants, whether the potential giver assumes that the "missing" adult male has died or deserted them or that there never was a permanent male and the children are illegitimate makes no difference; the children are objects of pity in and of themselves, and a woman on her own with children to support is also an object of pity because in the normal course of events she should be able to be dependent on the support of a male.

The *kho-lian-iu:* of a woman begging with children is enhanced if one or more of the children are handicapped. And because of the lack of awareness of fundamental hygiene and preventive medicine, including immunization, in Liong-hiat, where a majority of adults is illiterate, a number of children have had polio. One, for example, is Be-bin's younger son, whose legs are so misshapen that he cannot walk at all without crutches. His mother, Ti-bu-a, takes her son, about five years old in 1974, out in the mornings to a spot near the entrance of a primary school. There, some of the children going to school are so moved that they give away their spending money. Ti-bu-a gets about one-third of her daily take in an hour or so each morning. Several informants also spoke of a young boy from southern Taiwan who was born without arms. His *kho-lian-iu:* was so good that, according to one, he had already earned enough for an apartment building by the time he was five.[3]

Reversing the roles, children sometimes take out handicapped parents. This is not so much a ploy as a necessity, but nonetheless it is quite effective. Children of blind women have to lead them out to beg, and Hiong-a's daughter has to carry her mother, crippled with muscular dystrophy, piggyback.

Begging with children had declined by 1974 as compared with the past, however, because most of the children were older by that time. Children are a great asset to a beggar as long as they still look too young to work, but once they near their teens, they become a liability. Several of the beggars' children related how, by the time they were ten or eleven, instead of drawing sympathy from the public, they were chided. "You are so old. Why do you let your mother beg like this? Why don't you go out to work and support her!"

Adult beggars sometimes beg with a handicapped adult, using the latter in much the same way as mothers use children, to get the sympathy of the public. Several of the women in their forties or fifties, who look too old to have young children of their own, occasionally take out A-m. In her seventies, A-m has a wizened face, looks old and frail, and to top it off, is blind. Her *kho-lian-iu:* is very good. The accompanying woman claims to be her daughter or a neighbor and says that A-m is dependent on her for support. Liong-hiat males have also taken out other males when the occasion presented itself. Pai-kha-e, an amputee, now gets along on crutches. But before his cancerous leg was operated on, it was so painful that he could not walk, so either A-kim or Gong-a would put him into a cart and take him to the marketplace. There, with Pai-kha-e displaying his diseased limb, his partner would call out to shoppers to be charitable to his unfortunate neighbor. Although the partner was an able-bodied adult male, he was not chided for failing to support Pai-kha-e as older children are when accompanying a parent. The children are perceived to be kinsmen and are regarded as obligated to support their parents if the latter cannot support themselves. But one has no such obligations toward a neighbor. In fact, the assistance rendered by Gong-a and A-kim to Pai-kha-e was seen as a charitable act.

There were no "beggar implement" relationships in force in Liong-hiat in 1974, but several living members of the community, A-m, A-kou, A-chun, and Cap-sa:-hou, had once been Tiek-kou's implements, as had three deceased ones. As Tiek-kou moved into other economic activities, the beggar implement relationships lapsed, and he no longer collected their earnings or guaranteed their needs. Despite the fact that he had at one time taken all their income, his relationship with them was never viewed as exploitive, either by the implements themselves or by others, including non-Beggars, in the community. Instead people saw Tiek-kou as taking his just compensation in exchange for necessary care and services rendered.

Children rarely went out on their own to beg. In fact, by the time most of them were old enough to venture out without an adult, they felt so ashamed that they went to beg even with a parent only quite unwillingly. Only one, A-suat, the daughter of A-pui-a, would go out to beg of her own volition. By the time other children reached their teens, most absolutely refused to accompany anyone to beg, regardless of the occasion. A-hui was the only teenager to beg, and she did so only infrequently as a means to supplement her income as a factory worker. Moreover, she did not beg in the customary manner, crying for alms in the street, but would approach an adult and, claiming she had lost her purse, ask for a few dollars for bus fare home. This ploy enabled her to gain sympathy without exposing herself to the shame of begging. Moreover she was by no means unique in getting money this way. While not common, it is by no means rare to be approached by a teenager and asked for bus fare or the like in the downtown areas of Taipei.

Two adult males also have to use ploys in order to beg. One, Kua:-chui, is in his thirties and is strong and able-bodied. When he goes out to beg, he takes his four children, the oldest of whom is only five, with him and tells passersby that they have lost their mother and that he has to stay home and take care of them. Whether or not people find this story convincing, he is quite successful. The other, Be-bin, is somewhat older. Not in the best of health, he none-theless appears able to work, so he simply leaves the begging to his wife. She takes her younger son out in the morning and goes out with three of her children in the evening. Be-bin accompanies but he does not beg with them. Instead he stands several meters away, mixing with the crowd, and watches for the authorities. Should the police come near, he gives a signal, and his mate and children get up and wander about until they leave. Then they resume begging.

As in the past, some of the Liong-hiat beggars make themselves up (*hua-cong*) in order to appear more pitiful or strange. Before they go out to beg, they put on dirty, ragged clothes, disarrange their hair, and smudge their hands and faces with dust. Some have what could be called uniforms. Ti-bu-a dresses in baggy, black pants and a black jacket. Tua-kho-e wears a tattered military fatigue jacket and a woolen stocking cap pulled down as far over his forehead as possi-ble, so that he "won't be recognized." He also carries a student book bag and a *pian-tong*, a small metal box usually used to carry food, as a receptacle for money.

The only prop anyone in Liong-hiat uses is a photo of several of the older women, A-m prominently in front. When one of these women begs, she shows the picture to people and claims that she is the sole support of the group of women. However, it is not uncom-mon to see beggars, particularly young children, using props. On the day of an annual regional festival (*pai-pai*), there were numerous beggars on the bridge linking Taipei to the celebrating suburb. Sev-eral were young children who looked thin and sickly and appeared to be sleeping. Many had a note beside them explaining why the child was begging, and a few even had letters supposedly written by doctors. Another example of this tactic was found in a Taipei news-paper story about a young boy, blind, mute, and crippled, who was regularly seen begging at a pedestrian bridge in Hsinchuang, a small town outside Taipei. Beside him were a bundle of things wrapped in a cloth, a receptacle for collecting money, and a note reading, "Please good people, warmly bestow alms to save this poor, unfortu-nate, ill orphan." According to the newspaper, the local people were very generous to the boy, and he received quite a lot of money (*Chung-kuo Shih-pao,* 3 Dec. 1977:7).[4]

Tiek-kou strongly denied that any Liong-hiat beggar used any of the more radical make-up tactics or props that were used in the past such as false limbs or drugs to make one appear blind. Those, he claimed, were tactics used by "spies"; they would attract the attention of the police and greatly increase the risks of arrest. He added that under the martial law conditions that existed in Taiwan, the authorities took a dim view of those who attempted to disguise themselves to the extent that they hid their identity. He was very wary of anything that might attract too much notice.

For similar reasons the Liong-hiat beggars also used tactics based on remunerative and coercive appeals very sparingly. In 1974, A-tong's mate was the only one who was still entertained, playing the *hien-a* (three-stringed guitar) and singing in one of the large markets. A-tho used to do this, but she has stopped begging. Nor does anyone manufacture the chicken-feather dusters anymore. The one remunerative tactic in common use is to *tiau-lo-ce* (mourn at the roadside). It is employed mainly against wealthy families, those who can afford the extra expense, and it is more accurately called a coercive tactic. Most of the older beggars, even those who engage in no other begging activities, participate in this when the occasion arises. But not many outsiders prefer the presence of beggars at the funeral of their family members to the guarantee of Tiek-kou that none will attend. Not only is the cost greater—each of the eight to one dozen beggars who *tiau-lo-ce* receives about NT$100, whereas one can pay Tiek-kou off for NT$500–600, — but most regard the presence of beggars as an annoyance and more often with disgust. Only a small number of people welcome the presence of beggars at funerals, and they either see this as an opportunity for charity or, in the case of some described as hoodlums, as an opportunity to display noblesse oblige and to gain face.

Thus it is Tiek-kou who profits most from funerals. His ability to make money in this way is, of course, dependent on his being able to call in the beggars should a family refuse to pay him, but since it is he who finds out about the funeral in the first place, it is also he who creates the opportunity to profit from it. When he does learn of a funeral, he may contact the family directly, or, since he is so well known, the family may contact the subdistrict head and pay off Tiek-kou through him. When the beggars *tiau-lo-ce,* they keep the money they receive; when a family pays Tiek-kou off, the money is his, although he sometimes treats the beggars to snacks and wine.

In recent years, Tiek-kou has changed his role at funerals. Instead of simply going to the family and receiving payment to keep the beggars away, he now participates in the funeral procession. In fact, he leads it, carrying the flag and guiding it along the road, choosing the route, and signaling the vehicles that carry the casket, the offerings, and the mourners, when and where to stop. This has not traditionally been a part of the role of beggars at funerals in Taiwan. In the past it was done by a man of some status such as a subdistrict head. But few such men are interested in doing it anymore, so Tiek-kou has appropriated the role for himself. No one invites him. He simply appears and takes up the flag. Nor is he particularly welcome. Many would prefer not to have any beggars, even beggars who do not look or act like beggars, attend a family funeral. But in this role he does no one any harm, and he is out of the way. For his part, he gets the same amount of money as he would simply by keeping the beggars away, but he also gets to hobnob with politicians and other people of means and influence in attendance, something very important in conducting his affairs (see chap. 7). Furthermore, by playing a positive role in the proceedings of the funeral, he achieves a modicum of respectability. He can say that he is working for a living.

The only other tactic that could be considered coercive by those in Liong-hiat is that used by Tua-kho-e and others who beg from shops, but this is mildly coercive indeed. They do not make any trouble, as beggars did in the past, but just ask quietly for money from the shopkeeper. They make no threat of force but are simply an unsightly annoyance. This was confirmed in one case by an informant who owned a shop in a part of Taipei where Tua-kho-e occasionally begged. The shopkeeper said he gave him money because of his appearance, his scarred and gruesome face, and because he disliked having him around. When I asked if Tua-kho-e ever threatened or made trouble, he replied, "He wouldn't dare. All I would have to do is threaten to call the police and he would leave immediately." No one in Liong-hiat used any of the more drastic coercive tactics described in chapter 3.

The other strategies used by the Liong-hiat beggars are to find a good place to beg, and to take advantage of holidays and festivals. In terms of place, Ti-bu-a begs near a school in the morning and in front of a theater in the evenings. A-tong's mate goes to a large marketplace near a well-frequented temple, and Pai-kha-e goes to a bus stop, usually in the mornings. Cap-sa:-hou sometimes begs at the entrance to the pedestrian ramp of a bridge. When the occasion warrants, some of the beggars may go to a temple, a festival, or a performance of a puppet show.

Most of the Liong-hiat beggars avoid Taipei and beg in the surrounding suburbs, where they are less likely to attract the attention of the authorities. The exceptions are A-tong's mate and Tua-kho-e. The market where A-tong's mate begs is in a very old and heavily Taiwanese section of town, and because of the almost carnival atmosphere there at night, few object to a singing beggar. Tua-kho-e begs from shop to shop in parts of Taipei, but he never sits in one place on the street, and he keeps alert so that he can avoid any police in the area.

There are also certain times of the year that are better for begging than others, and among these, festive occasions are especially good. Of the holidays, Chinese New Year is reported to be the best. People have money then and are generally more free with it. It is also imperative not to do anything at that time—such as being stingy—that might offend the supernatural powers or the spirit of the occasion. Even the police, who are supposed to arrest beggars, turn a blind eye at these times.

But all festivals are good times for begging: *Ch'ing Ming, Tuan-wu, Chung-ch'iu, Chung-yüan* or Ghost Festival, the *chiao* or cosmic renewal festivals, festivals for local patron gods, family-centered festivals, and even purely secular holidays; all these are lucrative occasions for beggars. At all such times and at local festivals, one will see many more beggars than usual sitting in the streets or going from door to door. So profitable are the local festivals, in fact, that some beggars beg their way around the island, nomadically following the local festival calendar.

One of the most noticeable alternative ways some of the Beggars earn money is through gambling. They do this in two ways, by gambling successfully or by operating gambling dens. Many of the Beggars are frequent gamblers, and a few are either skillful or lucky enough to be consistent winners. Some also gamble less frequently but come up with big wins often enough to be termed professionals; that is, they earn a significant and relatively constant portion of their income from gambling. In one of the more remarkable episodes, Kua:-chui won NT$30,000 in three days playing mahjong. This happened shortly after his mate died and while his new house was being completed, these events leaving him heavily in debt. "He felt himself in a must-win situation," A-ieng said. "He is a good gambler, but he was very lucky then." Kua:-chui is one of the successful gamblers in Liong-hiat, as are A-ieng and A-chun.

However, most of those who gamble in Liong-hiat lose more than they win. The effects this has on their lives and on those of their family members will be discussed in chapter 8, but as long as they continue to live in Liong-hiat, these people continue to gamble. Many do so as a way to pass the time. As beggars they are stigmatized, and this limits their outside associations. Most of the senior generation are illiterate, and this further limits the things they can do with the large amounts of free time they have. But many also gamble because of the hope that luck will ride with them and bring them a big win, and because they lack the willpower to stop, even though they frequently suffer losses.

There is almost always a game of something going on somewhere in Liong-hiat. The four games played most often are mahjong, casino, *su-siek-phai* (four-color cards), a Chinese game played with small, thin cards of red, green, blue, and yellow, and *sit-bat-a*, a game played by throwing four dice into a bowl. Some also play twenty-one and poker, and many know the Japanized versions of English poker terms such as *sutureeto* and *furashu*. The hard-core gamblers like dice best because it is a faster game. Their excitement shows as they play, displaying their individual styles of talking to the dice or clicking them against the side of the bowl before a throw.

Aside from gambling itself, four people in Liong-hiat operate gambling dens (*kiau-tiu:*). Tiek-kou has three, one downstairs for recreational and low-stakes games, and two upstairs for more serious gambling. A-ieng has one, A-tan has one for mahjong only, and Kua:-chui has one outside Liong-hiat. Only two of the dens are single-purpose rooms. A-tan's mahjong room is a small one just off his front room, large enough only for a table, some chairs, and some space for a few onlookers to stand, and Tiek-kou's dice room had once been a kitchen, from which everything has been removed except for a single, naked forty-watt bulb suspended from the ceiling. The dice bowl is placed in the center of the room on the floor, the participants squatting or kneeling around it, their bets in front of them. The other gambling dens are in front rooms or bedrooms of people's houses.

Those who operate gambling dens earn money both by "taxing" (*khau-se*) the hands, that is, charging an entry fee, and by taking 3 percent of the winnings. Amounts they make vary, depending on the frequency of customers, the size of the stakes, and the type of game played. Dice, for example, is more rapid than card games; more games can be played in a given time, so the den operator makes more money.

Hard figures on what people earned through gambling were difficult to come by. Gambling is illegal, and except for mahjong, it is frowned upon by the outside community. Both those factors made it difficult to talk freely with people about it. People were reluctant to let me see the gambling dens, the opportunities I had coming mostly by chance. Moreover, in one sense, the less I knew about gambling, the better: should there have been a police raid or should it have been discovered that some information had leaked out, I could have been held responsible, and that would have jeopardized the relationships I had established. Further, a number of informants were ashamed of their own or others' participation in gambling and were somewhat embarrassed when I asked questions about it. When I did inquire, I got vague answers or no answers at all. Informants would often say simply that gambling was just a bit of fun between close friends and neighbors and that the stakes were low. Every once in a while, however, someone would give up a bit of information, usually about Tiek-kou.

Tiek-kou, it was said, takes in as much as NT$2,000–3,000 per day. This may sound like a lot, but one informant explained that if a succession of people play cards for about twelve hours, and if each player brings NT$1,500 into the game (by no means an extraordinary figure, given the amounts wagered in "friendly" games), the take for the den operator is about NT$1,000. If the gamblers play dice, the take is even higher because of the more rapid turnover. Two to three thousand New Taiwan dollars, then, does not appear to be too high a return for someone operating three dens, as Tiek-kou did.

Tiek-kou, however, does not keep all the money he gets from his dens. Whereas the other den operators keep all profits from their dens, Tiek-kou keeps only four of the ten shares in his. He gives two each to A-tan, his son-in-law, and to Kua:-chui, his godson. The remaining two are for running expenses: occasional gifts to the police and handouts to some of the young men who help keep order in the dens.

In addition, Tiek-kou shares some of his profits with three others, two directly and one indirectly. After he and A-iu: established their sworn brother and co-husband relationship, he gave A-iu: money when he needed it. He also gave money to A-m after she became too old and frail to beg as actively as she once had. She had been one of his beggar implements, but a special relationship existed between her and his children, they referring to her as their *lieng-bu* (nursemaid). Thus he continued for some time to give her money after he had allowed his economic relationships with his beggar implements to lapse, and he still gives her a room in his house to live in. A number of years ago, he attempted to ensure her support by arranging a fictive adoption of a son for her. This man, Chai-thau, was in his late teens at the time, and Tiek-kou's hope was that he would work to support her in her old age. But Chai-thau has not worked regularly enough to support even himself, and some of the money Tiek-kou occasionally gives to A-m finds its way indirectly to him—not something Tiek-kou had intended.

Another source of income for some in Liong-hiat is prostitution. In Taiwan prostitution has often been a secondary occupation for women in beggar communities,[5] and a den in a municipality to the south of Taipei is well-known as a brothel. In Liong-hiat, two women have voluntarily become prostitutes. O-niau did so because her family was quite badly off and she was too old to help her mother beg any longer. Moreover, prostitution was the best of the options open to a pretty but unskilled and uneducated young woman such as herself. At first she worked in a teahouse in Tamsui, but she left to become a call girl in Taipei, where she specializes in Japanese customers. With her income, she is in the best position of anyone in Liong-hiat to help her family (mother, younger sister, and younger brother), but she does little for them. She does give her mother money occasionally, but she spends most of what she earns gambling or taking her friends out to eat and drink.

Niau-bu is the other voluntary prostitute in Liong-hiat, but her reasons for taking up this work were somewhat different. According to her older sister, Niau-bu became a prostitute because she is vain and lazy. She wanted to have money and pretty clothes. Given her lack of education and job skills, she undoubtedly chose the correct profession. She could earn as much in two days in a teahouse as she would in a month on a factory assembly line, the only other line of work open for her. Niau-bu worked in the same teahouse as O-niau did for a few years, but then she left to marry Niau-chi-hi: and has since stopped.

Several other Liong-hiat women became prostitutes involuntarily, after their parents "pawned" (*tng*) them to teahouses or brothels for a three-year term.[6] The first parent to do this was A-sek-a. He had borrowed a large sum of money by organizing a rotating credit association (*he-a*), but one of the members defaulted, leaving him with the responsibility of repaying the others—"I had no other way," he said. "At the time I owed over one hundred thousand [New Taiwan] dollars, but I had no money to repay it. I sent her to a teahouse in T'aoyüan."

The next parent to act was A-tho, who needed money to finance the wedding of her second son. She also sent her daughter to a

T'aoyüan teahouse, but later on, she "redeemed" her, buying out what was left of her contract, and put her in a local teahouse, where she makes more money and is closer to home. She also has a younger daughter working in the same teahouse. That girl is too young to become a prostitute yet, but it was widely believed in 1974 that she eventually would.

A-tho was followed by Hiong-a with one daughter and then by Bebin with three. Neither of them pleaded any special economic grounds other than that they were poor. However, both they and A-tho stopped begging after indenturing their daughters.

These daughters work under two different systems, the "free" (cu-iu) and the "restricted" (bou cu-iu). In the restricted system the father is paid an agreed upon sum in advance. His daughter is given room, board, clothing, medical, and personal expenses. The prostitutes are kept under close watch; hoodlums accompany them if they go out for any reason. Because of the informal networks between hoodlums and brothel keepers throughout Taiwan, it is difficult for the prostitutes to escape. Under the free system, no initial amount is paid to the parents. The women are free to come and go as they would on a regular job, and they earn a commission, a percentage of what the customers spend on tea, liquor, snacks, and sex. They also keep any tips.

A few others in Liong-hiat have engaged in what could also be considered acts of prostitution. These women owed money as a result of gambling losses that they were unable to pay, so they exchanged sexual favors for cancellation of debts. They did this on an ad hoc basis, and no one in the Beggar community categorized them as prostitutes. But the results of their mates' finding out what they had done were sometimes explosive. In one case a man left his mate, and in another, the shocked, enraged man attacked his mate's lover with a knife.

A number of persons in Liong-hiat generate income by working at regular or irregular jobs. Four adult males are skilled construction workers; two are masons (tho-cui-kang), one a carpenter, and one an ironworker. Two others drive three-wheeled carts at the Central Market, one on a permanent basis for a wage, the other on a per haul basis. One male in his late teens has a motorcycle repair shop, another is an apprentice, two others are in the military, and an additional five work off and on at various laboring and factory jobs doing such things as construction work and making shipping crates. One adult male works as an unskilled laborer, and another occasionally goes out on his trishaw cart to buy and sell scrap metal.

Only one female who has children living with her works regularly for income except by begging; she cooks and does odd jobs at construction camps where her husband works. But all nine of the single teenage females work. Eight are laborers (*lu-kang*) in factories. The other, Hiong-a's daughter, also wanted very much to work in a factory. But her parents told her in stark, economic terms that her mother could make more begging than she could in a factory, and that she was needed to take her mother out. As I mentioned already, she was later indentured to a teahouse. Four other females work as street hawkers. One young married woman does so on a casual basis, usually around holiday periods. Another works quite regularly, many hours each day. And two young girls sell *giok-lan-hue* (magnolias) on the streets of Taipei for a few hours each day after school.

On the whole, the females are far more economically active than the males. With the exception of Hana, who is living off money from a divorce settlement, all females who do not have to look after children or are not in school do something to generate income. This includes the old women, such as A-m, A-kou, and A-chun, and some of the younger, pre-school-age girls: the former beg and the latter accompany adults who do. Girls under ten are also more likely to be required to go out begging with parents or other adults than are boys of a similar age, one consequence of which is that they are less likely to receive an education.[7]

Of the males, four are supported by their mates who beg, and they do virtually nothing to generate income themselves. These men are the objects of some derisive comments, especially that they *ciaq-nng-png*, literally "eat soft rice," or live off women, but otherwise they are as accepted as anyone else in the community.

But the most stark contrast in work force participation is between the teenage males and females. All the females, but only two of the eight males in that age group, are active on a regular, full-time basis. Most of the males work once in a while, but they often hold a job for only a few days to a week or two, and then they quit to take it easy, either hanging around the gambling dens or going out with friends. Their parents do not like this behavior, but they do little about it. Nor are most of the young men happy with themselves. They realize that they are not fulfilling their duties toward their parents and siblings and that such a course of action will get them nowhere in the future, but only one, Ho-a (A-tho's son), had the resolve to do anything about it during the initial fieldwork period. He had been one of the most notorious of his age group for drinking and gambling, but one day he came home and announced that he was going to Kaohsiung to work as a construction worker. After a few jokes and bets that he would not last long doing such demanding physical labor in the hotter southern climate and for less pay than he would get in Taipei, he went. He was still there when I left the field six months later, having returned only once, to attend the local festival for a few days.

There are two other activities by which Liong-hiat people generate income. Three men, Sia-pue, Tiek-kou, and A-tan rent parts of their houses to others. The rentals they receive are small, however; A-tan, with four tenants, receives NT$2,000[8] per month, but the others get at most one-fourth of that figure.

The other income-generating activity is participation in rotating credit associations. As these operate in Liong-hiat, the organizer (*he-thau*), in exchange for organizing and guaranteeing the association, receives an interest-free loan. The lenders (*he-kha*), depending on how early or late they bid out the money, either pay or receive interest. According to informants, if one stays in beyond the halfway point, he stands to gain, and if he is the last to withdraw the money, he stands to gain about 30 percent over his invested capital. For most Beggars, participation in rotating credit associations is like gambling; they never know beforehand whether they will come out ahead. Gamblers generally lose, being tempted to withdraw funds or borrow against them when they are without money to gamble. There were several cases of gamblers taking as little as NT$48 on the hundred. But among the Beggars there are some who have sufficient excess capital and willpower to stay to the end and use the rotating credit associations as a way to make money.

Data on income from the various economic activities of the beggars were difficult to come by. Some informants were simply reluctant to discuss it. Others said their income varied considerably from time to time. But many really did not know how much they took in. It was not a fixed amount, and they did not keep track. What was important to them was that their income was sufficient to meet their needs, and these needs were also quite variable.[9] If one had more money, he might buy better food or spend more on wine. Another difficulty was in the tendency either to exaggerate the spectacular or to try to appear much poorer than one really was. Thus, when A-ieng said that Kua:-chui was a good gambler who "can make over NT$2,000 a day," it was more accurate to say that he sometimes made that much, but he certainly did not do so every day or even most days. By the same token, claims by Ti-bu-a that she made only NT$70–80 per day begging were equally incorrect; her husband said she made several hundred, and she told others in the area the same. The figures that follow are based on checks and cross-checks, information given by other community members, and on estimates of expenditures.

Under normal begging conditions, a beggar can make NT$300–500 per day. For Ti-bu-a, this means going out twice in a day, morning and evening, but for Pai-khe-e, three to four hours in the morning in front of a bus stop are sufficient to make NT$300. Beggars with families to support, such as Ti-bu-a, A-tho, and A-tong's mate, go out to beg almost every day, but those who live alone and do not gamble can make enough to support themselves, about NT$10,000 per month, going out less frequently.

The amount a beggar makes depends on how pitiful or worthy he can make himself appear to be and on the spot from which he begs. Income per day can vary with an outstanding donation; according to Ti-bu-a, most donations are of the order of NT$0.50–2.00, but she sometimes gets gifts of NT$10–100, and on one occasion she received NT$1,000 from one giver. On special occasions, beggars make higher than usual amounts. At some of the local religious festivals, they bring in NT$1,000–2,000 in a single day, and at such times beggars from other areas around Taipei and even from other cities also come to beg. Although Tiek-kou makes the most money from funerals by keeping beggars away, given a chance to *tiau-lo-ce*, a beggar can make a quick NT$100, and if he is lucky, he might be able to go to more than one funeral a day. Tiek-kou usually makes money from two to three funerals a day, about NT$500 from each.

The amount of money gamblers make was the most difficult figure to come by. Despite hearing about occasional successes such as Kua:-chui's NT$30,000 in three days, I was unable to collect any systematic data on this topic. First, no one keeps track of how much he or she won or lost over a period of time. Second, no one relies exclusively on gambling for income. Only Kua:-chui derives the greater portion of his income from gambling itself, but he also operates a gambling den and has a 20 percent share in another, and he and his mate sometimes beg. A-chun is also a net winner at gambling, although on a much smaller scale. Her other income comes from begging, government welfare payments, and occasional handouts from one of her six sons. Third, gambling is illegal, and in terms of actual law enforcement, much more illegal than begging. Participants and other community members are quite secretive about it and usually far more reluctant to talk about it than they are about begging or prostitution. Thus, on the subject of gambling, little can be said other than that most of those who gambled lost more than they won.[10] A-sek-a, his wife, Be-bin, Hiong-a, and Tiek-kou all gambled frequently, but according to their children and other informants, although they sometimes won, more often they lost, and they were certainly net losers.

Data on earnings of those operating gambling dens was also difficult to obtain, but at least in the cases of Tiek-kou and A-tan, some information was forthcoming. Tiek-kou's dens gross NT$2,000–3,000 per day, of which he keeps 40 percent. A-tan makes NT$100–200 on his den. Like Tiek-kou, he has other sources of income, including a 20 percent share in Tiek-kou's dens.

The amounts prostitutes make vary with the system they are in. Those in the restricted system receive their room, board, expenses, and a small amount of pocket money. The parents of those from Liong-hiat receive NT$120,000 for each daughter for a three-year term. Be-bin thus made NT$360,000 for his three daughters. In the free system, the parents receive nothing from the teahouse or brothel itself, but filial daughters give much of the money they make to their parents. The prostitutes/hostesses themselves get commissions and tips. Fees for sex are split seventy-thirty between the prostitute and the house. A-tho's daughter, who has worked under the free system since she was redeemed from the teahouse to which she first went, makes about NT$1,000 per day, most of which she gives to her mother. O-niau, as a call girl rather than an employee of a teahouse, is under neither system. She is paid directly by her customers, mostly Japanese tourists, and makes about NT$2,000 per day.

Income from other employment varies with the job. Beginning with the Liong-hiat males, the most lucrative lines of work are in the construction trades. Skilled carpenters and masons earn NT$250–300 per day as workers and NT$300–350 as contractors. Lau-liong and A-sek-a do both. Ang-a, an ironworker in a small factory in the traditional sector, enjoyed a raise in wage over the Chinese New Year in 1974, taking his monthly earnings from NT$3,000 to NT$4,500. Unskilled male laborers, whether in construction or in a factory, earn NT$200 per day. One of the two cart drivers, Sia-pue, earns approximately NT$3,000 per month on a per haul basis, while Ai-khun, who drives a cart on a wage basis, earns NT$4,500. Cui-a, operating a motorcycle repair shop in Liong-hiat, nets NT$4,500–6,000 per month. Apprentices' wages vary with the trade they are learning and how advanced they are. Their period of training generally is about three years, but it is actually determined by their progress in learning. Their wages vary from NT$1,000 to NT$2,000 per month. A-tong, the scrap monger, works very little and earns only a few hundred per month. Most of his income comes from begging, usually by his wife, but occasionally by himself as well. Those in the military receive the lowest pay and are actually a net debit to their families; wives or fathers of servicemen in Liong-hiat send NT$300–400 per month to their husbands or sons to help them meet personal expenses.

Monthly income figures for Liong-hiat workers are subject to variations brought about by a number of factors. For those hired on a daily or per job basis, the availability of work can maintain or reduce their incomes. For construction workers, the weather also plays a role; heavy rain can preclude outside work, but if a job is at a stage where indoor work can be done, the weather may have no effect. If a job is rushed, workers can increase their incomes by working overtime. Construction and factory workers get an extra half day's pay plus dinner for an additional three to four hours work in the evenings.[11]

Remuneration rates for females in Liong-hiat depend on whether they work in factories or as hawkers. Factory workers in 1974 received a basic wage of between NT$1,100 per month in a galoshes factory and NT$1,400 in an electronics assembly plant, both for a six-day week. In addition, workers get regular bonuses for good attendance, for not being late for work, and for eating their meals at home rather than in the factory facility. They also occasionally work overtime, for which they receive the same rates as for normal working hours. These increments took their monthly incomes to NT$2,000 or more. Finally, at various holidays during the year, they receive bonuses on a profit-sharing basis.

Hawkers earn considerably higher incomes. A-tho's two daughters, selling magnolias on the streets in Taipei, make a profit of NT$0.50–1.50 per flower (which they sell for NT$2.00–3.00) and earn about NT$50 for three to four hours' work. This is not much, but it is about 50 percent more per hour than female factory workers earn. Cieng-a, Tiek-kou's daughter, works considerably harder and earns a great deal more. She sells all sorts of items—small toys, socks, plastic flowers, inexpensive decorative items and trinkets—usually in the underpass in front of the Taipei railway station. At night, she peddles chicken wings and feet stewed in soy sauce in one of the entertainment areas of Taipei. She works long hours but, depending on her luck, makes NT$400–600 per day. Her work is not without its risks, however. She is not a licensed hawker, and she has no fixed shop. She either uses a pushcart or, more commonly, spreads her wares out on a cloth on the ground. This form of hawking, known as *ta-a*, is illegal, however. It is considered a public nuisance because the hawkers block the already congested streets, overpasses, and underpasses in the busy parts of Taipei. Being unregistered, they also pay no tax, although that does not appear to bother the authorities since many people who cannot afford a shop are able to earn a living this way. Some say that the government dislikes such hawkers because of the bad impression they make on foreign visitors and tourists, but since they are concentrated in areas frequented far more by Chinese than by foreigners, particularly tourists, this is probably not a serious objection. Whatever the reasons behind the policy, the police are not supposed to allow people to do business in this way, and when policemen are spotted, the alarm is given and the hawkers quickly pick up their wares and scurry off. If one is caught, he is subject to fine and arrest. In the month before Chinese New Year, 1974, Cieng-a was arrested three times. She was able to talk her way out of a fine the first time but had to pay NT$300 on each of the second and third occasions, an amount that ate severely into profits. On the third, she also spent two days in jail and was threatened with a five-day term if caught again. As she had already bought and paid for her goods, a consignment of socks, she could not stop completely but had to be very careful and curtail her activities until the spate of vigilance, brought on by the approaching holidays and local election, subsided. Still, she continues to hawk illegally in Taipei. She began her working life as a clerk in a department store but found the low pay and long hours unacceptable. She dropped out of school in the seventh grade, and although that makes her well educated by Liong-hiat standards, she is not qualified for any better line of work. Hawking from a ta-a is the most lucrative line of work acceptable to her. Problems with the police, fines, and periods in jail are simply business costs.

Nor are other economic activities of the beggars without their risks. Begging is illegal, and although the local police are generally quite tolerant, and beggars virtually have to be caught red-handed to be apprehended, they do risk arrest, and some have been taken in. When they are caught and not simply released sometime later, they can be fined; Ti-bu-a once had to pay several thousand New Taiwan dollars. Much worse, they can be sent to the Vagrant Reception Center.

Gambling is also illegal, and the law is much more vigilant toward it. The police are generally tolerant of friendly, penny-ante games and mahjong games among family and friends, but they are supposed to crack down on professional and high-stakes gambling. However, for a certain consideration they sometimes turn a blind eye. This is why Tiek-kou retains 20 percent of his profits for operating expenses. Part of this sum goes to the police. They, in turn, either leave him alone or tip him off in the event of a raid. Still, running a gambling den is not without its risks. Police from a higher jurisdiction can make raids, and there are also times when pressure from above forces local police at least to be seen to be doing their duty.

Another source of risk and expense is from the *lo-mua:* (gangsters). They do not try to limit gambling but instead take a cut. Each area in Taiwan has its *lo-mua:*, and each gang must control its territory (*te-pua:*) or it will lose it to another group. So they collect money from those in their territory who are vulnerable, and in exchange they protect them from the predations of outside groups. Tiek-kou and the others have befriended the local *lo-mua:* and pay them off.

Prostitution is not illegal if the prostitute is registered; in fact there are government brothels, classes I, II, and III, in Taiwan. But there are risks and costs in that work too. Both venereal disease and pregnancy make a woman stop working for a shorter or longer period of time and consequently lose income. When O-niau became pregnant and had to stop work, she was in dire financial straits. Only Tiek-kou's aid saved her from having nothing at all. She also faces another risk. Having no identity card,[12] she cannot be registered. If she is caught by the police—and hers is a very visible line of work—she can be jailed or sent to the Vagrant Reception Center, where she would have to stay for about six months while she was checked out, her identity established, and an identification card issued to her.

Income figures for households vary considerably. Data on this topic are incomplete, and some information is grossly inaccurate. All who gamble tend to disguise the extent of their losses or gains and degree of participation. Thus income and expenditure figures do not reflect this activity. Moreover, probably because I was initially brought into the community by a social worker from the TCS, some, even after many months of research, never quite dissociated me from that organization, and they gave me very low income figures in order to appear more worthy of welfare.[13] Nonetheless, some families were relatively forthcoming regarding their incomes and expenditures, and three even kept rather exhaustive records at my request for a one-month period.

Families from whom I obtained approximate though reasonably accurate income figures are listed in table 2.

To put these figures into perspective, they can be compared with a Taipei City average (second quarter, 1974) of NT$10,229.6 per family, NT$1,930.1 per capita (Taipei Shih 1974:16). But data on expenditures reveal that the Beggar families are worse off than they appear.

TABLE 2
Family Income

| Family Head | Number in Family | | Number of Income Producers | Family Income[a] | Per capita Income |
	Adults	Children			
Sia-pue	6	1	4	NT$10,000	NT$ 1,429
Tua-kho-e	1	0	1	10,000	10,000
A-sek-a[b]	4	2	3	8,000	1,333
Pai-kha-e	1	0	1	10,000	10,000
E-a-cai	2	1	1	5,000	1,667
Hiong-a[b]	4	1	1	9,600	1,920
Be-bin[b]	4	3	1	13,000	1,857

a. Figures are for a one-month period, June 1974.
b. Kept records.

Except for the two single males, the families listed in table 2 spent NT$3,000–6,000 per month in repayments to rotating credit associations. Thus Sia-pue's income for general household expenditures was only NT$7,000; A-sek-a's was NT$4,850; Be-bin's NT$7,000; and Hiong-a's NT$3,600. For some, these repayments represent a greatly improved level of housing, but for others, Hiong-a for example, they merely reflect gambling losses.

The greatest single expenditure other than on rotating credit association repayments is on food. Families spend NT$70–100 per day on nonstaple items, generally buying whatever vegetables and other foods are cheap and in good supply. Expenditures on protein foods tend to be the least expensive items: belly pork, fish, legumes, and legume products, especially the various forms of bean curd. Several Liong-hiat families are classified as *p'in-min* (literally "poor people," this is the designation officially given to those eligible for government welfare), but as most are grade two poor (*erh-chi p'in-min*) rather than grade one poor (*i-chi p'in-min*), they are not able to get cash welfare payments. They are eligible to receive rice and other items from government agencies and private charities at Chinese New Year and other important holidays, however, and many are able to put away a three- to four-month rice supply at Chinese New Year. When they purchase rice on the market, they usually buy *tan-bi*, rice from government granaries that has been in storage for some time, or *chui-bi*, broken rice, both of which are about half the price of the second-grade rice that those not so poor buy.

Although they cut corners on food, usually eating the cheaper items, their diet is comparable to that of blue-collar squatter families among whom I have done research. But the Beggars are more likely to feast on festival days, be they special ones or merely the bi-monthly offerings to local gods and ancestors on the first and fif-teenth of the lunar month, or in the event of an unexpected windfall from gambling or begging.

The Beggars show a higher than average expenditure on alcohol, however. The three families that recorded their expenditures each spend between two and four times the reported Taipei average on liquor (Taipei Shih 1974:104), and other individuals in the community also appear to drink more heavily than informants in other areas.

The housing standard of those who remodeled or rebuilt is much higher than that of other squatters, and in terms of rooms, even higher than that of many middle-class families in Taipei. Several of the remodeled homes have two stories and several bedrooms in addition to a kitchen, dining area, front room, and bathroom and are fifty to one hundred square meters in area. Many squatter structures in Taipei are under ten square meters and consisted of a single room and a loft for sleeping and storage. They have no toilet or bathing or cooking facilities, and they are often dark and dingy inside. Middle-class flats are usually about fifty square meters in area and consist of a kitchen, bathroom, toilet, three bedrooms, and a front room. The remodeling of the homes in Liong-hiat cost the owners NT$40,000–50,000, a bargain because they were able to do much of the labor themselves or on an exchange basis, and they often used second-hand building materials. They also save on housing because they pay no house rent, although they do pay a small rent on the land at a rate of NT$63 per *p'ing* (3.344 square meters) per year. Tiek-kou's rent of NT$3,000 per year, the equivalent of a month's rent for a house the size of his, is the largest of anyone in the community.

The one disadvantage the Beggars suffer in their housing is that, like squatters elsewhere, they have no running water but must get it from the tap at Lau Ong's house. But one enterprising Beggar, Kua:-chui, built his new house next to the public toilet and bathhouse built by the TCS. Since the TCS built this structure in cooperation with the municipal government, it does have running water, and a pump and reservoir on the roof provide water for the showers and for flushing the toilets. Kua:-chui simply ran a plastic hose from his house to the reservoir and siphoned off water as he needed it.

Although most of the stem and nuclear family households have remodeled their houses and have relatively large living accommoda-tions, not all the Beggars do. Two lone Beggars, Pai-kha-e and Tua-kho-e, each live in one-room accommodations, and four nuclear families live in houses of two to three small rooms, as cramped and dingy as any in Taipei. Three of these families have members who are heavy gamblers; the other has stopped begging, preferring to get by on the income of one adult son.

How do the Beggars compare materially with others in the Taipei area? In per capita income, to the extent that my figures are representative, the Beggars are below average with the exception of the two single beggars who are relatively comfortable. However, these figures must be seen in the light of the large outlays for housing in rotating credit association payments and, in most households, for gambling. This puts them well below average in terms of normal, everyday consumption.

In terms of diet, clothing, and other personal items, the Beggars are comparable with low-income families I know in other parts of Taipei. On the basis of interviews and shared meals[14] with many of them, I found that their diets appear basically adequate with the exceptions of low intakes of animal protein and iron. The former is obvious from interviews and observations, the latter from the fact that many postpubescent females suffer from iron deficiency anemia (*phin-hiet*). A trained nutritionist might find other inadequacies. In terms of clothing, all in Liong-hiat except the older and poorer community members, A-m, A-kou, and A-chun, who get theirs second-hand from various relief agencies, wear inexpensive but newly purchased garments. Warm winter clothing appears in adequate supply except for footwear. However, it is not uncommon in Taiwan to see people, particularly children, wearing only wooden clogs on their feet even on cold winter days. And even wealthier people often wear only slippers inside their (unheated) homes. Thus this is not a significant indicator of poverty.

With regard to housing, those Beggars who have remodeled old or built new homes are on a par with the middle class in terms of space and number of rooms—hence privacy.[15] Their homes are substantially larger than the flats of lower-income families. Some other squatter houses in Taipei are comparable in size, but most are not. As several in Liong-hiat have building skills, Beggar houses are adequately constructed, although most used second-hand brick (less than half the price of new), and their houses are not well finished. In other ways, however, there are significant differences in Beggar housing. Because the Beggars are squatters, they have no running water. Thus they lack such basic amenities as bathing and toilet facilities and kitchen sinks. They also lack legality and thus a feeling of security and permanence, although none of them worry about what they would do if their houses were eventually razed. They have dealt with such problems before and assume they will be able to do so again. Moreover, obtaining legal housing was out of the question. Although some have recently spent up to NT$50,000 on their accommodations, that is only a small fraction of what is required as a down payment on a legal house. And even if one were able to come up with the deposit, it would be difficult to imagine who, given the Beggars' occupations, might lend him the remainder. As for renting, even a small two-room flat costs about NT$1,500 per month. Given their actual disposable incomes, that is an expense they can neither afford nor rationally justify.

Furniture and household items in Beggar houses are similar to those found in poorer homes. One family, in which there are two babies and four older children under twelve, has a washing machine. Two people own small motorbikes. A few have refrigerators or television sets, some have cheap phonographs, and most have radios and electric fans. All homes have enough tables, chairs, beds, wardrobes, and dressers, and the larger ones have sofas and coffee tables. Most of the furniture is in decent repair, but none of it is fancy or of good quality.

Overall the Beggars are materially on a level with low-income families in the Taipei area. However, in one crucial area, education, their expenditures are well below average. There are exceptions. Hiong-a, Be-bin, and A-tho all have sons in middle school and make some sacrifices to this end. But for most, money that could go to some more productive use goes into gambling. Paradoxically, Be-bin and Hiong-a are among the most fervent gamblers. By contrast, many low-income families in Taipei, even those so poor that they receive government welfare, make great sacrifices to get children academic or vocational training beyond grade nine. More will be said on this in future publications.

Compared to poor people in other countries, the Beggars are better off than many. Their diets are not completely adequate, but neither are they grossly deficient. Moreover, no one in Liong-hiat regularly goes hungry. They use inexpensive and sometimes second-hand items, but none of them ever has to scavenge through household garbage or rubbish tips.[16] Their housing is like "permanent" squatter housing anywhere, but it is basically sound. Also, some newly constructed houses are made largely of brick rather than timber, and thus the danger of fire is much reduced. The Beggars are poor, but, reflecting the rising economic level of the society in which they live, they are not destitute. Further comparisons of the Beggars with the world poor will be made in the final chapter.

CHAPTER SIX

Kinship Relations

W ANG SHIH-LANG, writing about nineteenth- and early twentieth-century beggars in Taiwan, described them as "ten or more households living together in a mixed-up manner" (1974:152). At first glance, the Liong-hiat Beggars appear the same. There are a number of couples cohabiting and a number of individuals who have had several sexual partners. Several families rear children not their own, and some individuals act upon the most tenuous, convoluted, and distant kinship ties or create fictive ties where none exist in order to establish or maintain an alliance. Arthur Wolf has described several forms of marriage and adoption found in northern Taiwan that vary according to the ideal forms of procreative and descent relationships and the amount of prestige they confer on the participants. Those forms that are lowest in prestige, those that deviate farthest from the ideal norms, he describes as "compromises made to accommodate social and economic reality" (1974b:129).

That such phenomena occur should not be surprising in light of the many studies of low socioeconomic status groups elsewhere in the world (e.g., Stack 1974; Rodman 1971; Lewis 1959, 1965, 1968; Liebow 1967; Hannerz 1969). On the other hand, and again in light of these studies, it should not be surprising that, on closer examination, the situation in Liong-hiat is more orderly than it first appears. There are people cohabiting, but there are more who are married. There are some who have had several relationships, but there are far more who have had only one relationship and whose relationships have endured for many years. There are examples, and probably more of them, of sexual behavior that would be completely unaccept-

109

able in other communities, but there are also limits to what individuals will accept of others in their community.

This chapter will explore the kinship relations and kinship behavior of the Liong-hiat Beggars. It will discuss relations based on sex, sexual relations and sexual behavior, fictive kinship including adoption, and extended kinship. Finally, it will demonstrate that kinship relations in Liong-hiat conform to an order, albeit not the same order that outsiders profess to conform to themselves, and that many of the deviations from the outside norms are indeed "accommodations to social and economic reality."

In discussing relations based on sex, I will be speaking sometimes about marriages, sometimes about cohabitation relationships, and sometimes about either or both. To avoid ambiguity—or to specify it—the following usages will apply: *marry* and *cohabit* will be used according to their literal meanings; *conjugal relationship* will be used as a neutral term to refer to any established union based on sex; *wife, husband,* or *spouse* will specify a marital relationship; and *mate* or *partner* will refer to a consensual union or to a general or ambiguous situation.

In order to understand the sorts of relations practiced in Liong-hiat in proper perspective, it will be helpful first to outline briefly the system of marriage found traditionally in northern Taiwan. The most authoritative accounts and analyses of it in its various forms are found in Arthur Wolf (1974b) and Wolf and Huang (1980), and the next several paragraphs rely heavily on those works.

Although in Taiwan there was only one jural form of marriage (*kiat-hun*), there were a number of variations on it, the one chosen determined by the financial condition and other considerations of the families involved. The variations differed in procedures and ceremonies, and more importantly in rights transferred to the wife-taking family and in prestige conferred on both wife-taking and wife-giving family groups. In what Wolf and Huang call "major" marriage, the form seen as the norm, the marriage was arranged by the parents of the bride and groom. The groom's family paid a negotiated bride-price, and the bride took a dowry with her when she went to her new home. For the bride, marriage transferred membership in her natal family to membership in her conjugal family and transferred from the former to the latter the rights to her labor, her sexuality, and her reproductive powers. This was done in three steps: she left her natal home, and the door was closed behind her, symbolizing that she was no longer a member of that household; she was led across the threshold of her conjugal home and presented to her senior-generation in-laws, which made her a member of their family and a daughter-in-law; and a short while later, she and the groom bowed to his ancestors, making them husband and wife and completing the transfer of rights. The wedding itself was accompanied by as much ostentation as could be afforded, the dowry being paraded through the streets en route to the groom's home, and the arrival of the bride being met with feasting. The degree to which these procedures were followed and the amount spent on the marriage determined the amount of prestige the two families received. Marriage in which traditional wedding rites were celebrated with a never-married woman marrying into her husband's household were classified by Taiwanese as *tua-chua*, "taking a daughter-in-law in the grand fashion."

Some families either could not afford a major marriage or had special requirements that made it necessary for them to choose one of several forms of minor marriage. There were two basic varieties of this, the marriage to an adopted daughter-in-law (*sim-pu-a*)[1] and the gradation of arrangements that can be called uxorilocal marriage. In the former a girl was adopted into her future husband's family when she was young, sometimes even still suckling at her mother's breast. A bride-price was paid at the time of adoption, but it was only 10–20 percent of that which would be paid for an adult bride. When the girl left her home, the door was closed behind her, and she was presented to her future in-laws upon crossing the threshold to her foster home. This transferred family membership as well as rights to the girl's labor. However, she and her future husband did not worship his ancestors together, signifying the beginning of marriage and the completion of the transfer of conjugal and reproductive rights, until they were older, usually sometime in their teens. Then, when the foster father felt it was time, according to custom there was a private ceremony on the eve of the Chinese New Year, after which "brother" and "sister" became husband and wife. But even this formality was often ignored. In many cases there was no worship of the ancestors or ceremony at all. The father simply announced that it was time for the couple to begin their conjugal relationship. In this sort of marriage there was the same transfer of rights, although over a longer time period, as in the major form. But because there was usually no public ceremony or conspicuous consumption, there was little prestige conferred to either of the participating family groups.

Uxorilocal marriages were even more different from the major form. In these, rather than a daughter being married out, a husband was "called in" (*ciou-sai*). Moreover, instead of the transferral of the reproductive powers of the bride to the groom's family, usually at least one of the sons produced by the marriage—the precise arrangement was negotiable—was filiated by the mother's descent group. Also negotiable was the degree of affiliation of the husband with his wife's kinship group and, correspondingly, the degree to which he estranged himself from his own. He could live with and work for his parents-in-law for a specified period, until they died, or forever; he could even be fully adopted into their descent group and take their surname. The exact arrangements also determined the amount of wealth exchanged between the bride's and groom's families.

If the *sim-pu-a* marriage was low in prestige, uxorilocal marriage was even lower. There was rarely a ceremony, a feast, or a public display; indeed, given the loss of face accorded by this type of union, it was best if it went unnoticed. The real reason for the lack of prestige is not the lack of ceremony but the fact that the groom served his wife's parents and contributed to their descent group. However, for some males the choice was between a uxorilocal marriage and none at all, and in those circumstances the former was preferred.

Farther down the continuum of prestige is not a different form of marriage but one in which one or both parties was previously married—what Arthur Wolf called "second marriages" (1974b:152). Traditionally in such marriages, the woman was brought in without ceremony, often in the middle of the night and through a side or back door. Such a marriage violates Chinese ideals and beliefs for both the bride and groom. Regarding the woman, Ning Lao T'ai-t'ai passed on advice given to her, "A good horse does not carry two saddles, a good woman does not marry two husbands" (Pruitt 1945:116). For the male, since the bride was supposed to be a virgin and an already married woman obviously was not, such a marriage lacked prestige, although it could be said that only a male himself lacking prestige would enter into such a union. It was also believed that in marrying a widow, a man placed himself in supernatural danger, that the soul of the woman's deceased husband would return to haunt his widow's second mate (Hsu 1948:104). The woman's natal and conjugal families could also lose face on account of such a marriage, the former for failing to instill proper morality into their daughter, the latter for being too poor to afford to keep their daughter-in-law at home after her husband died.

Finally there were cohabitation relationships (*tong-ku*) which, while not legal unions, nonetheless were accepted and governed by clearly defined rights. Such unions were expected to be long-term (in fact many marriages in present-day Taiwan begin this way). A male was expected to support his mate, who was expected to work in his household. He also received full sexual rights, but he did not have the right to filiate the children, who took their mother's surname. A man in such a relationship, to make his offspring legally his, had to adopt them formally. Since these were not marriages, no wealth was exchanged between families, and since parental arrangement was the sine qua non of marriage according to Wolf and Huang (1980:119–20), such unions necessarily lacked prestige.

Aside from the form it took, a union was also less prestigious if one of the partners was deformed or unwhole in some manner (*wu-kuan pu tuan-cheng*). Thus someone who was blind, deaf, dumb, crippled, diseased, or mentally retarded was less acceptable as a marriage partner, and usually only one who was also lacking in prestige or wealth would marry such a person. Alternatively, one who was unwhole but wealthy might attract a healthy marriage partner but one low in social status.

Lacking in prestige as some of these forms of union are, the worst fate that can befall one is not to form a union at all. Such a person not only loses out on the *lau-ziat* (excitement) of having children about, but he also fails to provide descendants to his ancestral line and to ensure care for himself in his old age and in death. Examples of all these less prestigious forms can be found in Liong-hiat.

Relationships Based on Sex

Let us turn now to relations based on sex in the Liong-hiat community, beginning with the most common aberration, *tong-ku* relationships. Long-term cohabiting couples I have known both inside and outside the Beggar community appear to be well accepted by their neighbors. Several informants said they saw nothing wrong with cohabiting, particularly if there was no alternative, such as if one member of the couple was already married. In fact, many refugees from the Chinese mainland found themselves in these circumstances; they were on record as having spouses on the mainland but had been unable to bring their conjugal families with them when they came to Taiwan. Being alone, many wanted to marry again, but unless they could prove that the mainland spouse was dead or had remarried, they were unable legally to take a new spouse. Communications between Taiwan and mainland China being very limited, this was next to impossible, so many simply formed new unions by cohabiting.

Only one Liong-hiat Beggar cohabits for this reason, but there are two other reasons for cohabiting rather than marrying, and both apply directly to the Beggars. First, in the folk view, for the male, one of the basic requirements for marriage is to have a sound economic base and a *cit-giap* (occupation). Although beggars can make a decent living, this does not qualify as an occupation. Second, marriage is marked by a feast as luxurious as the family can afford. Beggars are supposed to be poor; they are not supposed to have the kind of money needed to afford a wedding banquet. Actually they often can afford a banquet, but in the past they would forego one in order to maintain their "business image." Thus the older-generation Beggars were inclined to cohabit, at least for the initial period of the union.

That marriage is a more prestigious and desirable state than cohabitation is demonstrated by the fact that a number of Beggar couples who were unable at first to marry changed the legal status of their relationship to *kiat-hun* when they were able to. Moreover, when younger members of the community, the offspring of the Beggars, formed conjugal relationships, they all married; none chose to cohabit. This will be discussed in greater detail later.

Among the forty-six adults in the Beggar community at the time of the initial study, none were married in the *tua-chua* (major) fashion. Only six couples and one widow could be said to have had "conventional" marital histories—that is, they were or had been married, they had not had a cohabitation relationship, and they had not experienced a broken marital relationship except by the death of a spouse. Of those with "unconventional" histories, there were four couples who had cohabited for several years before marrying, five couples and five individuals who had had more than one *tong-ku* relationship, three individuals who had divorced and then formed *tong-ku* relationships, three others who had divorced and remained alone, and three who had never had any type of conjugal relationship at all. Of the forty-six adults, at least sixteen had had more than one conjugal union.

Most of those with unconventional histories were of the older generation in the community. All were over thirty years of age, thirteen were in their late forties, nine in their fifties, and two were sixty or over. Moreover, only six of these individuals had never depended on begging for their livelihood during their adult lives. One of the six was a cart driver; his paramour was a divorcée who brought a substantial sum of money with her when she first came to the community; another was a gangster (*lo-mua:*); his paramour was a divorcée and a former teahouse hostess; yet another was a prostitute; and the last of the six was an idler and inebriate who lived off the begging income of his "adopted" mother. One additional individual usually made his living as a construction worker, but he had also begged from time to time between jobs. The remaining twenty were active, full-time beggars either prior to or at the time of the study. In fact they were first-generation Beggars, and many were among the original members of the community.

Most of those with conventional marital histories were young, in their twenties, at the time of the original study. The exceptions were the carpenter, A-sek-a, and his wife (forty-seven and forty-one years old), A-tan (forty-nine), a retired serviceman from Swatow and the husband of Tiek-kou's eldest daughter, and A-m (seventy-two), a widow. The others were all children of the Beggars. Of this group, only A-m had begged for a living during her adult life. Offspring of Beggars had accompanied their parents when they were young, but none begged at the time of the study, and it does not appear likely that they ever will in the future. They have all found more acceptable and prestigious ways to make a living (see chap. 8). Two of the males are construction workers and one is an ironworker (*thiq-kang*). Another is a taxi driver. The other two husbands, both sons-in-law of Tiek-kou, make their living from gambling and other illicit activities. Both share in the profits of Tiek-kou's dens, and one of these has his own gambling den as well. The other is also a small-time *lo-mua:* and may have had additional income from those activities. Thus all the married children of the Beggars have a *cit-giap*, and, unconventional as some of these may be, they can rely on more or less steady incomes. Moreover the *cit-giap* at which they work, even gambling and petty crime, are more respectable and acceptable to society than is begging.

Within the community, to the older generation at least, cohabitation relationships are quite accepted and indeed are, to all intents and purposes, the equivalent of marriages. There is no discernible difference in the quality of the personal relationship between the partners; cohabitation relationships are often of much longer duration, but the individuals involved are also much older. The same terms of reference—*thau-ke* for the male and *khan-chiu*, *cu-png-e*, and *gua hit-e cha-pe* for the female—are used in either. Finally, both *kiat-hun* and *tong-ku* unions form the basis for establishing households and units of procreation. Although by convention and law it is the descent line of the female that has the right to filiate any children born to her out of wedlock, no one ever mentioned this as a problem. It is a fairly simple matter for the father to arrange an adoption so that children he has begotten become legally his and bear his surname. There was only one case in which a mother claimed a child she bore out of wedlock who was living with the father, but she did so because she wanted money to give up her right to the child, not because her descent line wanted to filiate it (see Adoption and Fostering, p. 130ff.)

There is a possible advantage for a female beggar in choosing to cohabit rather than to marry. One of the hazards of begging is being caught by the police. If she begs as female beggars often do, with small children and can demonstrate (by means of her identity card)[2] that she is unmarried and is the sole support of her children, she can usually play on the sympathies of the authorities and escape punishment. Thus there are good reasons why a female beggar might prefer to cohabit.

The attitude of the younger generation toward cohabitation is quite different, however. None of them gave the impression that they were ashamed of their own parents for failing to marry legally, and some spoke quite openly about it when asked to explain the existence of ancestral tablets representing different lines on their altars.[3] But when they formed conjugal relationships themselves, even though some had premarital sexual relations, they usually married before setting up coresidence. Moreover, to most of this cohort, a formal marriage along with working for a living at a *cit-giap* were highly symbolic of a break with the begging activities and the life-style of their parents. For example, Cieng-a and her husband had a child two years before their wedding, but they waited until he finished his military obligation before formally marrying and moving into a home together. They set up a neolocal residence in an apartment purchased by Cieng-a, a quite deliberate step that removed her both physically and symbolically from the Beggar community. Ang-a, A-tho's eldest son, continues to live in his mother's household. His wife was pregnant when she came to join him after running away from home because her parents would not consent to her marrying a "beggar's child," but they married as soon as she came to live with him. She is a dutiful daughter-in-law, and he is a filial son, helping to support his natal family from his job as an ironworker.

The trend in the community appears definitely to be toward marriage. Six of the last seven unions formed prior to the initial study were marriages, as were five of the seven formed between 1974 and 1977. The cohabitations involved the prostitute O-niau, Kua:-chui, and Tiek-kou, who took up with a former teahouse hostess for a time; the last two were both of the older generation. The marriages all involved children of the Beggars, and all the husbands except Tiek-kou's son, Touq-pi:-a, had fairly well-established jobs or trades. Touq-pi:-a was twenty and had received his draft notice, so he was just living at home and waiting for his induction into the army.

The older generation and those with unconventional conjugal histories and situations can be divided into two categories. In the first are those whose conjugal histories are only marginally unconventional but not so unconventional that they would attract much attention or disapproval in neighborhoods similar in socioeconomic level to Liong-hiat. Three males were unconventional only in that they were well past expected marriage age but had never had a conjugal relationship. One former military man (A-iu:) left a wife and family in Swatow to whom he was unable to return and later shared the wife of Tiek-kou. Two females and one male were divorced, and another male had a broken cohabitation union. The remaining individuals in this cohort had cohabited. Two couples formally married several years later. Both had originally delayed marriage because they were too poor to afford even the minimal celebrations that customarily accompany it. In addition, one of the males had lost his identity card and was unable to get a new one until after the end of the Japanese occupation of Taiwan in 1945. The six remaining couples had all had cohabitation unions, but these had proved to be quite durable. In 1974, five of the eight cohabitation unions had endured over twenty years, one for sixteen, and one for thirteen; the remaining union lasted for only seven years, but it was broken by the death of the female partner, not by a failure of the relationship.

Four individuals in this cohort had had two conjugal relationships. Sia-pue's mate-then-wife had one child by another man before she joined up with him. A-tho's first partner left her for another woman, after which she took up with A-kim, who had previously left the woman with whom he had been cohabiting. By 1974 both A-tho's and Sia-pue's unions had lasted over twenty years. Tiek-kou, widowed after some twenty-five years with his wife, brought in a former teahouse hostess to live with him in 1975. His children objected to this out of loyalty to their mother, and after about a year, Tiek-kou sent the woman away. He did this both to placate his children and because in the meantime, his son, Touq-pi:-a, had married and sired a son. Touq-pi:-a explained, "Now that my father has a grandson, he no longer needs another woman."[4]

The individuals and couples in the other category present quite a

different picture. All had been involved in multiple conjugal relationships. One female had divorced her husband and then worked as a
hostess in a teahouse, where she met her present mate (A-ieng); he had
divorced his wife and broken one cohabitation union before joining up
with her. Another woman (Ti-bu-a) had had three cohabitation relationships, the last of which she formalized into a marriage. Her husband
(Be-bin) had divorced a wife and had three cohabitation unions before
meeting her. A female (Hana) had her first child in a cohabitation
union, her next two in a marriage, and was divorced and living with a
married cart driver in 1974. Two other women (A-su and Cap-sa:-hou)
had each had children by three different males, and another (A-pui-a)
had had children by at least four. Her daughter once remarked, "My
mother doesn't know herself how many men she has had children by."

   These two categories differ in more than degree of conventional-
ity and stability of conjugal relationships. Those in the second are
also less stable and less conventional in other aspects of their lives.
Some have a reputation for being sexually active outside the relationship they are in. Several are very heavy gamblers. A-ieng, a former
hoodlum, had once been a morphine addict; in 1974 he was a heavy
drinker, and he also got into several fights, using weapons in some
of them. Except for Cap-sa:-hou, who is mentally deficient, those in
this category who beg are said by their neighbors to do so because
they are lazy and do not want to work, not because they are unable
to make a living any other way.

   In terms of size, there were twenty-two individuals in the first
category and only eight in the second. Yet the community tended to
be characterized in terms of the actions of those in the second category by outsiders, neighbors, and even by some of the children of
the Beggars, who spoke of the behavior of these adults as *luan*,
"chaotic," a very strong term of condemnation in Chinese. Their
disapproval of the older generation and the manner in which this
motivates them will be discussed later.

   Of the three males in the community who have never had a conjugal relationship, two are beggars. Gong-a, about fifty, has some kind of
chronic disease that causes his skin to peel and gives him a rough
appearance. He lives with A-tho and A-kim, the latter from the same
county (i.e., his *tong-hiong*) and his sworn brother. Why he has remained single I cannot say. When I asked him, he simply said he was
too poor. He appears to have normal sexual desires, however. He
frequently spends his money in teahouses, and it is commonly held
that he had made advances toward A-tho while A-kim was in prison on
drug charges. She turned him down, and apparently this incident

caused no major disruption in the household, because Gong-a still lives there.

Tua-kho-e is the other single beggar. He is the prodigal son of a well-to-do family in Taipei. As a youth he spent his money on wine and women. He contracted syphilis, which he left untreated, and consequently lost one eye and most of his nose and has a horribly scarred face. Both literally and figuratively "having no face," he left home. On his own and having no training or discipline to take up any kind of work, he became a beggar. He still feels a measure of pride based on his family of origin, however; he said he had never married because the only woman he would be able to get as a wife would be a beggar, and he considered that beneath him. On one occasion he invited a prostitute to come live with him, but that arrangement lasted only a few days. "She kept asking for money all the time," he explained, "and she wouldn't keep the place clean."

Chai-thau is the third single male. He is the "adopted" son of A-m. He does not beg, but neither does he work very often. He reportedly once had a clerking job with the city government, but he quit because someone criticized him. Since that time, he has worked only very occasionally. Having failed to establish himself economically, he says he is too poor to look for a mate.

Their poverty obviously has some bearing on why Gong-a and Chai-thau have remained single, but as others in the community poorer than they, E-a-cai for example, have been able to attract mates and form unions, it is not a sufficient reason. E-a-cai's union with A-pui-a broke up in part because he was poor and a brighter prospect turned up for her, but he came out of the union better off than before entering into it, with two adopted children. In the case of Chai-thau, personal rather than economic factors appear to be more important in his remaining single. He is intelligent and perceptive, and he can be quite sociable when he wants to be. But he is frequently withdrawn and alone, and he is drunk more often than he is sober. These factors, coupled with his inability to endure a situation in which he is open to criticism, seem far more significant in his remaining a bachelor.

Another reason why beggars, males in particular, might remain single was offered by some outside informants: that they are essentially wanderers who like being without ties, free to come and go as they please. This hypothesis does not explain the situation of any Liong-hiat beggars, however, most of whom are quite settled, but it is easy to see why outsiders might have this impression. Beggars rarely beg in areas where they live, and thus they appear to be strangers. They do not beg in full family groups and in fact use the excuse of a broken family as a way to gain public sympathy. Moreover, it is difficult in a Chinese cultural context to imagine someone who is a member of a normal family having to or being willing to beg. One with a family should be able to call on the resources of his kinship group and should be unwilling to jeopardize its reputation. Furthermore, there are some beggars who wander, for example those who follow the festival circuit or those who live in one place for a while, several weeks to several months, then move on. Among such people who came through Liong-hiat during fieldwork there, however, some were single, but most were in family groups—couples with children. One family, in fact had four children, the oldest in his mid teens. To generalize from those observed in Liong-hiat, beggars tend to be both sedentary and in family groups. Those who remain single do so for a variety of personal reasons, not because their lives are too unstable to take a spouse.

What is really more remarkable than the number of males who remained single is the fact that so many beggar males, given their relatively poor and unstable circumstances and the stigma attached to their profession, were able to attract mates and form unions. Beggar males desire mates for the same reasons as other males do, for procreation, sexual satisfaction, domestic services, and companionship. In addition, they have another important reason, for help in begging. As I have explained, females are naturally much more able to evoke sympathy than are males, especially if they can claim to be the mother and sole support of several small, famished-looking children. Moreover, they have an easier time avoiding arrest. On the other hand, for a male who looks healthy and able-bodied, it is difficult to beg, so he needs a female to beg for him. This is precisely the pattern found in Liong-hiat. Men with partners do not beg themselves but send their wives or mates out to beg for them. Hiong-a even told his son that the reason he had cohabited with his mate, who had muscular dystrophy, was so she could beg for him; he could then stay home and pursue his favorite activity, gambling, assured that there would always be money coming in.

Although most of the males have been successful in attracting mates, it is revealing to look at the women with whom they have formed unions. I have already noted that one of the factors conferring prestige at a Chinese marriage is the physical state of the marriage partners, and for the bride in particular, this includes her sexual state. Of the seventeen Liong-hiat females in conjugal unions in 1974, only four were without some sort of physical "blemish." Five were either blind or disabled. Eleven, including three of these, had had sexual intercourse with another man prior to forming the unions they were in at that time; eight had had previous unions; one had worked as a teahouse hostess; and two had been raped by their stepfathers. Thus, on the criterion of physical state, only four would have been able to enter first-grade marriages according to orthodox standards. The others would have been considered second- or third-rate brides. Traditionally such a woman might have been fobbed off by a slick go-between on an unsuspecting family, which probably would have accepted the trickery but bemoaned their terrible fate in having such a bride. Otherwise, if they were not been sold into prostitution, these women might have gone as brides to second-rate men, men who themselves were poor, crippled, or diseased.

In forming unions with beggars, the Liong-hiat women did just that, they went to second-rate males. Their mates, in addition to their physical and economic state, are second-rate because they are beggars, according to some informants "the lowest, most useless things on earth." The stigma of having begged extends even to their children. Two of the younger adults related the difficulties they had in marrying. Chieng-cui had to have a nonbeggar member of the community, A-ieng, appeal to his intended bride's parents and convince them that he was a good young man and not a beggar before they would consent. Cieng-a went so far as to buy an apartment for herself and her husband to live in after they were married. Such a contribution from a bride is most unusual, but she hoped, by demonstrating her capabilities and her self-removal from the beggar life, to place herself beyond the condescension and criticism of her parents-in-law.

For the older generation, the beggars themselves, however, it is doubtful that the males obtained their females in the traditional fashion, that is, from the women's parents. Most of the conjugal relationships in this group at least originated as cohabitations rather than as marriages. Moreover, most of the women there appear to have been attracted to the community and to their mates by the life-style. While beggars are not rich, and while they rarely accumulate large sums of money over a long period, they can bring in large amounts on particular days, and when they do, they frequently spend it in an "easy come, easy go" fashion, gambling, feasting, and drinking. There is a sort of partylike quality to life in Liong-hiat, and there is little arduous work or evidence of self-discipline. Furthermore, some of the women were beggars themselves before meeting up with their mates, and some also had left previous unions, obviously dissatisfied with them and what they had to offer. The conjugal relationships of the beggars appear to

have been formed on the basis of mutual attraction, not in the traditional manner of parental arrangement.

Another characteristic of the conjugal relationship in Liong-hiat
that demonstrates the inferior status of the Beggars as partners is
that many of those who grew up or lived there for a long time before
forming a union formed an endogamous one. Of the ten unions, all
marriages, formed by the Beggar children, only half attracted outsiders as mates, and one of these was a marriage to the niece of the
man's stepfather, a relative. All the parties to the other five unions
grew up in the Beggar community, less than a minute's walk from
their partner's doorstep. Furthermore, one first-generation Beggar
woman had a cohabitation union with first one and then another of
the males living in the community. Another, after losing her mate to
a woman in another community, formed a second union with a
fellow resident of Liong-hiat.

I did not question people about the large number of endogamous
unions because most, when they did talk about them, seemed uneasy, and I felt it would be damaging to their feelings of self-respect
and ultimately to our relationship to do so. But I strongly suspect
that the reason for it, propinquity aside, is the deep sense of shame
and inferiority that the Beggar children feel. While a male might feel
somewhat confident talking to a female with whom he has grown
up, the risk of becoming attracted to an outsider only to have her or
her parents reject him because of his background is frightening. A
female might feel the same way. Another factor that would reinforce
this is that all of these endogamous unions took place when the
participants were quite young, most of them under seventeen, and
at that age, their outside social experience and the confidence they
could gain from it would not have been strongly developed. Thus
they entered into unions that complied to the letter with the Chinese
rule of thumb, *men tang hu tui*, that the families of a marrying couple
should be of equal standing and well matched. Not only were these
matches class-endogamous, but they were restricted to within an
even narrower range.

Sexual Relations and Sexual Behavior

In the orthodox Chinese tradition there are three general rules
regarding sexual behavior. First, the descent line (usually in the
person of the father or husband) with control over a woman controls
her sexuality. Second, the purpose of sex is procreation rather than
recreation: thus individuals should not be promiscuous either before

or outside of marriage. (Although on one level a case may be made for this rule to apply to males, in practice it was applied far more stringently to females.)[5] Third, throughout her life a woman should have sexual intercourse with no more than one man, her husband. Thus she should enter into no more than one union.

When one applies these rules to the Beggars, the most obvious observation is that they are frequently breached. From the incidence of premarital relations and pregnancies it is obvious that almost all of the Beggars' children who have married had sexual relations with their partners beforehand, and several were either pregnant or already parents at the time of the wedding. Although this violates rule 2, and its incidence would certainly have been much lower and have attracted a much stronger reaction under the traditional system of "blind marriage," it is also not infrequently breached by young people outside the Beggar community as well. One young woman, a factory worker from a Hokciu family, stated that it was quite common for her co-workers, also females, to have relations or to cohabit with their boyfriends before marriage. Moreover, many university students, who are usually from a higher socioeconomic stratum than the informant just cited, have told me that premarital intercourse is not uncommon among their fellow students and that they saw nothing wrong with it if the couple had already decided to marry. One informant, a Taiwanese shopkeeper and the father of four teenage children, said that although such things were much rarer when he was a young man, they are fairly common now; young people living together before marriage are simply referred to as *tsai lien-ai te kuo-ch'eng chung*, "in the process of love." The acceptance of this behavior is based on the assumption that these cohabiting couples will eventually marry. In the words of one informant, "It's not really promiscuous behavior. It's just 'boarding the train before purchasing the ticket' " (*hsien shang ch'e; hou pu p'iao*). With the exceptions of those who have worked as prostitutes, the other Beggars' children have all married the persons with whom they had premarital relations. Thus their behavior, while outside the ideal, seems well within the operative norms of their outside contemporaries.

No comparable information about the older generation came to light except that the incidence of cohabitation relationships either preceding or in place of marriages was quite high. In 1974, of the eleven older-generation women in conjugal unions, nine had previously had unions with other men. Compared with the standards and norms of the outside community, this is a far more serious matter than is the behavior of the younger generation, especially in light of what seems to be quite rapid change in sexual mores over the past two decades. When discussing these two sets of behavior with informants outside Liong-hiat, it was the women of the older generation whose behavior was more strongly disapproved of. Some pointed out that widows with small children from poor families often remarried because they had to in order to survive, but they felt the situation was quite different for the Liong-hiat women, most of whom had simply left their previous mates. Within Liong-hiat itself, however, no one condemned women for entering a union after the breakup of a prior one.

But some members of the younger generation show strong disapproval toward women whom they regard as *sui-pian*, "loose." These are women who have had either a series of unions or relations with men outside the unions they were in at the time. When younger persons such as Cieng-a and Ang-a condemn members of the older generation for their "chaotic" behavior, it is women such as these to whom they refer. In addition to their dislike of such unstable personal behavior, they also cite cases of women who exchanged their favors to pay off gambling debts, a frequent result of which is the breakup of their families.

Young people did not condemn promiscuous or loose sexual behavior in those who were single, although most of them eschewed such conduct themselves. All the males regarded as loose in Liong-hiat were single. Excusing such behavior in males could simply be the acceptance of a double standard, although the prostitute O-niau was not condemned for her sexual behavior either. She was one of the more attractive females in the community, and all the other females her age had been married for several years. Moreover, no one in the community had ever sought her as a wife. When asked why, no one mentioned her sexual behavior. Instead they pointed out that she was an inveterate gambler; gambling is not only an expensive habit but also the primary cause of domestic conflict. Nor did anyone condemn her for her occupation. She simply took the most lucrative road available to her, one that several others had seriously considered before deciding against it.

Rule 1, male control over female sexuality, appeared to be adhered to more closely than the others, although it was sometimes manifest in a quite paradoxical manner. Whereas this rule usually means that the controlling male restricts the woman's sexuality, there are several cases in Liong-hiat in which the male traded on it. Tiek-kou, for example, shared his wife with his sworn brother, A-iu:, for several years before her death. A-iu: was a retired serviceman from Swatow, and, having a wife and children in mainland China, he did not take another mate in

Taiwan. But Tiek-kou's wife built up a heavy gambling debt to A-iu:, and arrangements were made to pay off the debt by granting him conjugal privileges. Tiek-kou had no objections to this arrangement. In fact he was quite willing to go along with it. Not only was it an inexpensive way out of the debt, but it also demonstrated his magnanimity (*to-liong tua-e*).[6]

Two other cases involved stepfathers who raped their stepdaughters. One, E-a-cai, afterward told Bi-kuan that she must then become a prostitute. When she protested, he gave her an alternative, to marry Lau-liong, one of the less savory young men in the community. She chose the latter. The other, Be-bin, traded extensively on his stepdaughter's sexuality. Once she went out for a walk in the evening with Lau-kheq's son, and they returned rather late. Be-bin berated her and demanded to know if she and the man had had intercourse. She admitted that they had, although some said she did so only to avoid a beating. Be-bin then confronted Lau-kheq, who suggested that his son simply marry the girl and that be the end of it. Be-bin refused and demanded compensation far in excess of what the young man and his father could pay. Tiek-kou was called in and suggested a sum more in keeping with the financial capacity of Lau-kheq's family, and a two-table banquet.

Be-bin tried the same tactic when his stepdaughter was in a hospital. He accused some members of the hospital staff of having sexual relations with her and again demanded compensation. They ignored his demands, however, and he got nothing. Some people in Liong-hiat said he was merely using his stepdaughter to get money, and they compared his tactics with the *hsien-jen-t'iao*, a badger game in which a woman seduces a man, and, in the middle of the act, her "husband" walks in on them and demands money. These feelings were confirmed when, a few years later, he sold his stepdaughter and his natural daughters into prostitution.

In all, five Beggar families sold or had daughters go into prostitution. Tiek-kou—or, more precisely, his wife—was the first. While in her teens, their daughter Niau-bu, willingly but with her mother's encouragement and her father's consent, went to work in a teahouse in Tamsui. She left a few years later to marry; her husband did not want his wife to work as a prostitute.

In the period between the initial and the follow-up research in Liong-hiat, four other families, as their daughters became old enough, indentured them for three-year terms as prostitutes. One did so to finance the wedding of a son, another when the rotating credit association of which he was head folded and he had to pay off his creditors. The other two did so to improve their standard of living and stop begging. One then left the community entirely and set up a *pachinko*[7] parlor for a while before retiring to live off the earnings of his daughters.

Although there is much sexual behavior in Liong-hiat that does not meet with either the ideal or the operative standards of the outside community, there are limits to what the Beggars will accept. It is not permissible to seduce with impunity a female whose sexuality is under the control of another. The ability of Be-bin to sue for damages allegedly done to his stepdaughter by the young man and by the hospital workers, even though he was unsuccessful in the latter case, illustrates this principle, and there are several other cases as well. Pai-kha-e was once punished for seducing A-go's mate. The three of them had been chatting together one evening when they felt hungry. A-go went to buy some snacks, and Pai-kha-e miscalculated the time he would be gone. A-go returned to catch them in the act. He was a jealous man, and not without reason, for he had caught his mate with other men before. This time he angrily demanded compensation, NT$2,000. Tiek-kou, called in to settle the matter, argued that Pai-kha-e be given the choice of hosting a one-table banquet in A-go's honor or publicly kneeling in punishment (*huat-kui*) for an hour before the image of Li Thiq-kuai, one of the Eight Immortals and the patron deity of the beggars. Pai-kha-e chose the former, but A-go demurred on the issue of the money, still wanting to collect. He changed his mind when Tiek-kou brought up his mate's earlier unfaithfulness, saying that if A-go insisted on further compensation, he would run the risk of being accused of playing the *hsien-jen-t'iao* or, worse still, being thought of as one who "wears the green hat," a cuckold.

Other cases of seduction and taking unwarranted liberties with women under the control of others involved Tua-kho-e. On one occasion he seduced Thi-thau-a's mate, and on another he fondled Thi-thau-a's daughter. Tua-kho-e was a large, strong man, while Thi-thau-a was small and sickly. Because of this, Thi-thau-a simply swallowed his pride and did nothing. But his hotheaded teenage son, Niau-chi-hi:, was not willing to overlook these insults. So one night when Tua-kho-e was drunk, he got together some of the neighborhood toughs to beat up Tua-kho-e. On another occasion, Tiek-kou saw Tua-kho-e peeking under his youngest daughter's dress while she was asleep. He did nothing at the time, but he told Niau-chi-hi: (his son-in-law), who, several weeks later, rounded up the same gang of youths and administered another beating to Tua-khoe.

Afterward Tiek-kou, as community leader, advised Tua-kho-e to leave Liong-hiat. He did so and lived elsewhere for a while. But after several months he slipped quietly back into Liong-hiat and resumed residence there.

Another offense that draws a reaction is mate stealing. E-a-cai and A-pui-a had been cohabiting for several years when Kua:-chui returned from prison. Soon afterward, A-pui-a announced that she wanted to move in with him. There was nothing E-a-cai could do to stop her, so he asked for compensation. Tiek-kou was called in to fix the amount. Kua:-chui paid, and the matter was settled. A-tho also received compensation when her first mate left her to live with a woman in another beggar community.

Other acts also brought strong negative responses. Niau-chi-hi:'s mother was known as a loose woman, and this was tolerated. But soon after her mate died, too soon in the opinion of many, she took up with another man. Because she had not waited a "decent interval," people felt she lost face for her children. The negative reaction was so strong that she and her new mate left Liong-hiat to live in another beggar community.

In another incident, Tho-bak-e walked in on Be-bin one afternoon when he and his wife were having sexual intercourse, his stepdaughter, at his insistence, looking on. Some said he had been having her watch them for some time in order to train her to become a prostitute. Tho-bak-e, however, was horrified. She even feared that, having witnessed such an evil thing, some evil would befall her. As word spread of Be-bin's actions, he soon lost favor in the community. Although he was not advised or physically forced to leave, he knew he was no longer welcome there. It was not long afterward that he sold his stepdaughter and natural daughters into prostitution and bought a house elsewhere.

It is thus clear that there is a good deal of aberrant sexual behavior in Liong-hiat. It is equally clear that the behavior of many, probably the majority of individuals, while not meeting the ideals of the outside community, is within its operative standards. Moreover, although there are some actions that are tolerated in Liong-hiat but would invite strong condemnation outside, there are definite limits to what is acceptable to the Beggars.

The key to whether aberrant sexual behavior is accepted by the Liong-hiat Beggars is whether it violates male control over the sexuality of females. This can be demonstrated by dividing such behavior into four categories: (1) premarital coitus and pregnancy, and, especially among the older generation (it was too early to tell what might happen among the younger), entering into more than one union; (2) selling one's daughter into prostitution, sharing one's mate with another, entering into prostitution, and, for a female at least, being regarded as loose; (3) rape of one's stepdaughter and Be-bin's having his stepdaughter witness sexual intercourse between him and his mate; (4) seduction of another's mate, mate stealing, and Tua-kho-e's fondling of Tiek-kou's eight-year-old daughter.

Category 1 behavior is commonplace and drew little reaction. Whereas premarital coitus and pregnancy would certainly have been thought of traditionally as violating the father's control over his daughter's sexuality, such acts are now widely viewed as a de facto part of the courtship process, and the principle of marriage by courtship rather than by arrangement is well accepted. Behavior in category 2 and especially category 3 is less common. That in category 2 is accepted with some reluctance and shame, while that in category 3 is seen as downright bizarre and regarded with shock. Yet the violation of female sexuality—selling daughters, sharing a mate, stepdaughter rape, and Be-bin's actions in front of his stepdaughter—were performed by the male exercising control. While reaction to such behavior was negative, it did not result in immediate or direct sanctions. It was only the acts of category 4 that drew sanctions, fines, and punishments, and it was only in these acts that one male violated the control of another over a female's sexuality.

Fictive Kinship

Frequent use is made of fictive kinship in the Beggar community, and it appears to have three main functions: the adoption and fostering of children; the extension of one's network and set of alliances; and the use of the kinship metaphor to honor someone or to bring greater moral and affective content to a relationship between people not related in some commonly recognized form. This section will examine and analyze the various forms and uses of fictive kinship by the Liong-hiat Beggars.

Adoption and Fostering

Both adoption and fostering are found in Liong-hiat. In adoption there is a change in both line of descent and residence. The purpose of adoption is to continue a line of descent by providing an heir or the potential parent of an heir. Fostering involves a change of residence only. Usually it is the rearing of the child of a deceased friend as a favor to the friend and the child.

With respect to children, the Beggars are in most ways no different from other Chinese. The economic value of children aside, most of the Beggars have a strong desire to form families, to raise descendants, and to enjoy the *lau-ziat* (excitement) associated with the presence of children. Most adults, even the single males, have some sort of special relationship with a child: only two adult males do not. But of the twenty-four Beggar households in 1974, in only ten had there been no real or fictive adoptions as a means to achieve this desire. Not all households had natural children. Moreover, children born to consensual unions legally take the surname and belong to the descent line of their mothers; thus some males had to take extra measures to have children filiated with their line of descent. On the other hand, several households had more offspring than they wanted or could afford to rear, so they adopted some children out.

None of the adoptions in Liong-hiat are of the most orthodox form, the *ke-pang-kia:*, in which a son is adopted from a brother or close agnate. In this form, the child changes residence but not surname; he acquires obligations to an extra set of ancestors and access to an extra inheritance (A. Wolf 1974b:141–42). As this sort of adoption implies a reasonable level of wealth, stability, and both closeness and propinquity to one's agnatic kinship group, it is not surprising that it is not found among the Beggars.

A less ideal but still quite common form of adoption, the *bieng-lieng-kia:*, is found, however. In this form the child changes residence and surname; he has no ritual obligations toward or rights in the estate of his natural parents. Neither the child nor his parents has a biological link with his adoptive parents. He usually comes from far away, the idea being that he will not be able to contact his natural parents again. Very often money is involved in this form of adoption, at least in the case of males, and, as Arthur Wolf found elsewhere (1974b:142), the beggars refer to this form of adoption simply as a "bought" (*khit-e*)[8] rather than a *bieng-lieng* child. In Liong-hiat, A-tan, who is impotent, adopted both a son and a daughter this way. He paid NT$5,000 to the parents of his adopted son and NT$1,000 to the middleman (*kai-siau-lang*). For his daughter he paid only the middleman. E-a-cai paid nothing when he adopted his stepson and stepdaughter after A-pui-a left him to live with Kua:-chui. Although A-pui-a remained in the community, the children were loyal to their adoptive father; in fact they resented very deeply the fact that their natural mother left them (cf. M. Wolf 1972:177–78), and they did not become reconciled with her until much later, when she was dying of uterine cancer.

The other case of *bieng-lieng* adoption was the arrangement made for A-iu: to adopt an unborn child. Having no family in Taiwan and being a coresident in Tiek-kou's house, he was "given" Tiek-kou's third daughter as his child. She did not change her surname or residence (they lived in the same house anyway), but her first son was pledged to A-iu:. After the child was born, his parents went to the District Office (*ch'ü-kung-so*) and told the clerk he had been sold to A-iu:. The child was then registered as A-iu:'s and given his surname.

There were other cases of official change of surname, in two of which males in cohabitation unions legally adopted their natural children. Such children would normally take their mother's surname, but if she (and presumably her kinship group) agrees, the father can *jen-ling*, "recognize and adopt," them. The District Office must be notified, however, since records are kept there, and the children must be formally assigned to their father's line. Bok-cong did this. He was cohabiting with a woman who had had children by other men, but she bore him a son whom he formally adopted. Hiong-a, who also had a cohabitation union, formally adopted his three children as well.

A-tan, who adopted his children from outside the community, also had them registered in his surname, but he went one step further. He paid the District Office clerk NT$1,400 in each case to have them registered as his natural children so there would be no record of their having been adopted.[9] He said he planned to tell the children some day that they were adopted because he knew they would find out from others sooner or later anyway. In fact his daughter, aged seven, had already heard from neighbors that he was impotent. But he wanted to "give them face" by having them listed as natural.

The other form of adoption found in Liong-hiat is the *sim-pu-a* (adopted daughter-in-law). Sia-pue's youngest daughter was adopted and was originally intended to marry his eldest son. Bringing her in also meant that his natural children could be spared the embarrassment of having to accompany their mother when she went out to beg. But Sia-pue's eldest son refused to marry her. In fact, he left home in his teens, not returning until she was married out to Lau Lim's son.

In addition to these various forms of adoption, in which a change of surname and of line of descent is involved, there were also a few cases of *kia-ku*, "fostering." This is a situation in which one rears a child for someone else, usually a deceased close friend. The child changes residence but retains his original surname. As one informant explained, "We have a duty—*gi-bu*—[to the parents] but no authority—*guan-li* [over the child]." Although one can get official recognition that one is rearing a child of another in his stead, no legal formalities are necessary.

In Liong-hiat, two people were rearing the children of deceased Beggars. A-chun cared for the young daughter of Khe-o, a former hoodlum and later a beggar who died of tuberculosis, and A-iu: looked after A-cui-a's son and daughter until he himself died. Since that time, the daughter has married and moved out of the community, and Tiek-kou's family has reared the boy.

In both cases it was Tiek-kou who arranged for the guardians to care for the orphans. He also arranged for A-m to be the "adopted mother" (*iu:-bu*) of Chai-thau. Chai-thau was orphaned at age fifteen, and his family had at one time been neighbors of A-m. Tiek-kou's motive was to provide A-m with a son who would soon be able to go to work and support her. The plan failed, however, as Chai-thau, though not a beggar, has worked only intermittently in his adult life, and he mostly relies on A-m's income from begging and handouts from neighbors in the community for support.

Another case, similar to *kia-ku,* is that of Iok-lan. In 1974 she was seven years old and living in the home of A-tho and A-kim. A-kim is her natural father, but her natural mother is a woman from T'aoyüan, the daughter of the chief of the beggar community where A-kim took refuge for a time when the police were seeking to arrest him for using morphine. Although Iok-lan's natural mother did not want the responsibility of rearing her, neither would she consent to A-kim and A-tho legally adopting her without the payment of NT$10,000 (more than twice the monthly wage of A-tho's son, Ang-a). A-tho was quite willing to care for Iok-lan but was unable to pay the demanded sum to adopt her formally and to make her a legal member of her household. Iok-lan's surname is legally that of her mother, but within Liong-hiat she is known by A-tho's surname, as are all of A-tho's own children.

Aside from those who adopt or gain access to children, there are also those who adopt out or sell them. A-pui-a sold her second child, a daughter, for reasons that she never made clear. She also allowed her one-time mate, E-a-cai, to adopt two others. A-tong sold his fifth child, a son, soon after the birth. A-tong's family was poor. He had tuberculosis and was unable to do much that required physical effort. He both begged and worked as a scrap monger, but most of the time he just stayed at home or gambled, leaving his blind wife with the responsibility of begging enough to support the family. When his fifth child came along, they already had two sons and two daughters. They decided they did not need another, so they sold him for NT$5,000.

There was almost a third case of child selling. After his mate died, Kua:-chui considered selling his stepdaughter, A-suat. He had four children of his own, and A-suat, at age nine already an accomplished beggar, could have fetched around ten thousand New Taiwan dollars from a beggar family in southern Taiwan. Medical treatment for his mate before she died and her subsequent funeral expenses had been quite costly. Moreover, he had just built a new house. He was persuaded not to sell her by her maternal grandparents, however. Not only did they not want to see her sold outside the community, but they pointed out that without a mate, Kua:-chui needed her all the more to look after her younger siblings.

Other Fictive Kin Ties

Aside from adoptions and foster parenting, there are three other forms of fictive kinship found in Liong-hiat. Two are between generational seniors and juniors and use the idiom of parent-child. One of these uses the prefix *gi-*, which denotes "loyalty," "righteousness," and "faithfulness," attached to the appropriate kinship term, for example, *gi-pe* (father), *gi-kia:* (son), and *gi-ca-bo-kia:* (daughter). The other uses the prefix *khe-* in the same manner. Some informants took the *khe* to be *kheq*, the word for "guest," but others insisted it was the word for "contract." Although there is a certain logic to the first rendering, the second is correct, and both Mandarin and Cantonese have that term as well. The third type of fictive kinship is based on the sibling model, and it is used especially by males. Although the "sibling order" of a set of fictive brothers, based on age, is well known, the term usually used does not differentiate between older and younger but simply was the collective term for "brother." The term itself, *kiat-pai e hia:-ti*, refers to "worship," the men involved usually becoming "brothers" through collective worship of a particular god or/and of each other's ancestors. The term is frequently rendered "sworn brothers." All three of these forms of fictive kinship can be illustrated by relationships involving Tiek-kou, usually as the central figure.

Informants from outside Liong-hiat made no distinction in contemporary usage between *gi-* relationships and *khe-* relationships (see also Wang 1974:155), using the two terms interchangeably. But an examination of their application shows that the two are used differently in Liong-hiat, and this usage accords with what some informants said about *gi-* relationships in premodern China. According to them, *gi-* relationships usually occurred between two men, one the senior and quite frequently the patron or teacher of the other. The latter regarded the former as a "father," not in the literal sense, but socially, indicating both respect and a debt of gratitude. No extensive ceremony marked the establishment of the relationship, and rights, duties, and obligations varied with the individual bond. But the *gi-pe* (*gi-*father) often gave his *gi-kia:* (*gi-*son) a bowl of rice, symbolic of the provider role of the father, and at the senior's funeral the *gi-kia:* wore the mourning clothes of a son, perhaps with a touch of red to symbolize a fictive relationship. Afterward he was obligated to make occasional sacrifices to his *gi-pe*'s spirit.[10] *Khe-*relationships, on the other hand, were simply close relationships between two unrelated persons, and the kinship idiom was used to attract into, encourage the development of, or recognize the existence of the affect ideally associated with the kinship dyad in question. Although not literally correct, I will render *gi-* as god- (e.g., godson) and *khe-* as fictive (e.g., fictive son).

Tiek-kou's godsons are neither his clients nor his pupils. He formed these relationships as a result of his anxiety over lack of an heir, his wife's first four children (one stillborn) having been females. He first took Kua:-chui as a godson. Kua:-chui has relatives elsewhere in Taiwan, but he had wandered away from home and had very little regular contact with them. When he drifted into Liong-hiat, then in his teens, he was practically kinless. But soon after settling in the community, he got into a fight while gambling and killed a man. While he was in prison, Tiek-kou, unable to rely on Kua:-chui to provide him with an heir, took another godson, Siong-a, the newborn third son of his sworn brother, Sia-pue. According to the arrangement made, if Tiek-kou had no son or failed to have a son survive to adulthood, Siong-a would formally adopt one of his sons out to Tiek-kou, and that son's ritual obligations would then be toward Tiek-kou's ancestral line. Not long afterward, Tiek-kou made similar arrangement with A-tho, taking her second son, Ho-a, as his third godson. Thus, although different in many respects from the godsons of premodern times, Tiek-kou's would look after his spirit after death.

About a year after his taking Ho-a as a godson, Tiek-kou's wife gave birth to Touq-pi:-a, making it unnecessary for him to adopt an heir from outside, but the established relationships and bonds between Tiek-kou and the three godsons were not abrogated. The rights, obligations, and exchanges between Tiek-kou and the three have varied over time and from individual to individual. As children, Siong-a and Ho-a came every New Year to *pai-ni* (give a New Year greeting) and to receive *ang-pau* (lucky money).[11] Siong-a is also among the young males who get occasional amounts of money for helping to ensure order at the gambling dens. But Kua:-chui is a full partner of Tiek-kou's dens and receives 20 percent of the proceeds. Moreover, Tiek-kou has afforded him preferential treatment on a number of occasions. Kua:-chui is one of the more disliked persons in Liong-hiat. He is a bully and has not stopped short of threatening and abusing others when he wanted to get his way. He has sometimes reneged on his obligations to pay his share of the water bill, for example, and he has also gotten into fights. Others have been advised to leave the community for less, but Tiek-kou has never moved against Kua:-chui. Inquiries as to the reason produced the reply, "He is kin, and Tiek-kou will not move against his kin."

Tiek-kou also has a goddaughter, the prostitute O-niau. His relationship with her is different from those with his godsons in that he was not attempting to continue his line of descent. Because her mother, Cap-sa:-hou, never stayed with the same man very long, O-niau never had a person whom she regarded as a father, so Tiek-kou took her as a "daughter" and has acted toward her as both a protector and a father figure. When O-niau got into trouble with the law over begging or prostitution, Tiek-kou used his influence to help her. When she was pregnant and could not work, he did not laugh at her, as others did, but instead helped her out. When she had her baby, he arranged for it to be taken care of by his kinsmen in northeastern Taiwan. Finally, working with a contact he had in the District Office, he was instrumental in finally getting her family members their identity cards. She, in turn, "treats him like a relative," in the words of one informant. She calls him "A-peq" (father's older brother), as do Siong-a and Ho-a. Moreover, although she has no obligations to do so, she sometimes gives him money as a gift or for safekeeping.

O-niau's relationship with Tiek-kou did not come about simply because he took a liking to or pitied her, however. Its origin was in his relationship with her mother, who was one of his beggar implements. Tiek-kou formalized his relationship with all his beggar implements by making them *khe-* kinsmen; the older ones, all female, became *khe-ma* (fictive mothers), and the younger ones, *khe-kia:* or *khe-ca-bo-kia:* (fictive sons and daughters). He found his three fictive mothers, A-m, A-kou, and A-chun at different times. Each was destitute, having no place to go and no one to turn to, so he took them in and provided for them, and they begged for him. Cap-sa:-hou was one of his fictive daughters. She had been adopted out as an infant, but her foster parents both died when she was in her early teens, leaving her to fend for herself. She wandered about, seeking a living, but the trauma of her experience was too great, and she became mentally unbalanced. When Tiek-kou met her, she had one child, O-niau, but she had no idea who her natal family was. She knew only that they came from the town in which Liong-hiat was located. Tiek-kou, making inquiries through his acquaintances in the teahouses, was able to find out who her kinsmen (two brothers) were and where they lived. They were unwilling to take any responsibility for her, however, so Tiek-kou arranged for her to live in Liong-hiat, where she has been ever since. A-cui-a and Chun-bieng, both now deceased, were Tiek-kou's other fictive children. A-cui-a was a double amputee whom Tiek-kou supposedly bought from his relatives. Chun-bieng was blind. But the two of them teamed up as entertainer-beggars, she singing and he accompanying her on the *hien-a*. Afterward, Tiek-kou arranged a marriage between them, and they had two children.

Tiek-kou established *khe-* links with his beggar implements in an attempt to soften the otherwise harsh and instrumental nature of the tie, and the relationships between them by and large have been characterized by affection, warmth, and concern. But in only two instances have his *khe-* relations been treated as kinsmen in anything more than a symbolic sense. A-m was regarded by his children as a wet nurse; in fact, she could not have been because she was too old, but when they were younger, they treated her with the respect and affection due a father's mother. Being childless herself, she was especially heartened to be called *A-m*, "Aunt" (father's elder brother's wife). Chun-bieng's relationship with Tiek-kou's family was even closer. When I first interviewed Cieng-a, Tiek-kou's second daughter, she included Chun-bieng as a natural sister and her children as niece and nephew. Moreover, Tiek-kou's family looked after her orphaned children after their guardian, A-iu:, died.

For the most part, however, by 1974, Tiek-kou's *khe-* relations with his beggar implements had lapsed. Some of his former beggar implements, their children having grown up, no longer needed to beg as they once had. Others had died. Tiek-kou himself now makes most of his money from gambling and *tiau-lo-ce*. The affective side of their relationship remains, but the nurturant content is gone, as is its economic raison d'être. The only one who still receives any economic aid from him is A-m, who lives in a room in his house and once in a while receives small sums of money.

There are two others in the community with *khe-* relationships, Pai-kha-e and Gong-a. They are both single males in their fifties and have no children of their own. Their *khe-* ties provide them with special relationships with the children of others. Gong-a is a *tong-hiong* of (i.e., a man from the same county as) A-kim, and he lives with A-kim and his mate, A-tho. He was "given" Iok-lan, the daughter of A-kim and another woman (see page 131) as his fictive daughter. Pai-kha-e is the *khe-* father of Tho-bak-e, Tiek-kou's eldest daughter and A-tan's wife. He rents a room from A-tan, and he spends a lot of time in their guest room playing with A-tan's infant son, acting as if the boy were his real grandson.

Tiek-kou also makes the most frequent use of the sworn brother type of fictive kinship. In 1974, in addition to his many sworn brothers outside, he had seven in Liong-hiat, and these gave him ties to half the middle-aged males (over forty years old) in the community. In addition, he had kinship ties to three others, his sons-in-law A-tan and Niau-chi-hi:, and A-sek-a, a distant cousin (see discussion in chap. 7). Besides Tiek-kou, O-baq-e had two sworn brothers in the community, Be-bin had one who came to stay with him for several months in 1974, and A-kim shared a sworn brother relationship with Gong-a, his housemate. Many of the young men, sons of the Beggars, have also linked themselves in this manner. Others, including some of those I have discussed, also have extensive sworn brother networks outside the community.

The content and intensity of sworn brother relations varied both with the individuals linked and over time. On the surface an expressive relationship, it seemed, particularly among the Liong-hiat adults, more frequently to serve instrumental purposes, especially to expand one's network of politically and economically useful alliances. As one informant expressed it, sworn brotherhood denoted a relationship based on *kau-ce* "social obligations," more than *iu-gi,* "friendship." Thus the strength of the relationship in terms of rights, duties, and obligations varied more or less directly with its utility. As the economic activities of the Liong-hiat community have shifted away from dependence on cooperation and group enterprises, the sworn brother relationships have weakened.

Yet in 1974 there were still expressions of duties and obligations to those linked through sworn brother ties. When Cieng-a started her *he-a* (rotating credit association) to buy an apartment just prior to her marriage, she did not ask A-ieng, whom she disliked, to join. A-ieng wanted to invest in her *he-a,* and he confronted her with the fact that he and her father were sworn brothers. "How can you disregard me like that?" he demanded of her. "I am like your *A-ciek* (father's younger brother)." Whether he could normally have a right to expect this fictive relationship with Tiek-kou to transfer in this manner to his daughter or not, he nonetheless used the moral force of the tie in an effort to influence her. In the case of the sworn brotherhood between A-kim and Gong-a, A-kim's children give Gong-a the respect normally due a father's brother, and he acts toward them as a real *A-peq* would, caring for them, teaching them, and disciplining them.

This same efficacy can also be seen in relationships based on other kinds of fictive ties. We have seen this illustrated in the protection of Kua:-chui by Tiek-kou, Tiek-kou's children's treatment of A-m, Cieng-a's inclusion of Chun-bieng as a sister, and Tiek-kou's family generally seeing that her children were cared for after she died.

While it is true that these are selective examples and that there are also examples of such ties being ignored, it can safely be concluded that fictive kinship has a positive function to the Beggars. Being people without extensive real kinship ties or realistic expectations of as much assistance as they need from their relatives, they have used fictive kinship to increase the number of allies they have and the number of people who have obligations to them. This theme is repeated in the next section, which analyzes the kinship clusters the Beggars have created using links that would be ignored by most Chinese in Taiwan.

Extended Kinship and the Expansion of Kinship Networks

Aside from the fictive ties described above, there were also a number of households in Liong-hiat related by real, though sometimes rather convoluted, kinship ties. In fact in 1974, ten households in the community were related through these kinship clusters, four in one cluster and six in the other. Tiek-kou was the nexus of one of these (see chart 1) related to the households of A-tan and Niau-chi-hi:, his sons-in-law, and to A-sek-a, whose wife is the adopted daughter of Tiek-kou's natural mother's younger brother. A-pui-a was the nexus of the other (see chart 2). Her mother is the wife of Sia-pue, who is thus her stepfather; E-a-cai was a former mate, and he adopted two of her children; Bi-kuan, her oldest daughter, is the wife of Lau-liong, whose mother is the mate of Bok-cong and whose first cousin once removed is O-baq-e. By 1977, four nuclear families could be added to these. In Tiek-kou's cluster, his son, Touq-pi:-a, was married and living with his father, and his daughter, Cieng-a, previously married out, had moved back to her father's household with her husband and children. In A-pui-a's cluster, Lau-liong's

CHART 1
Tiek-kou's Kinship Cluster

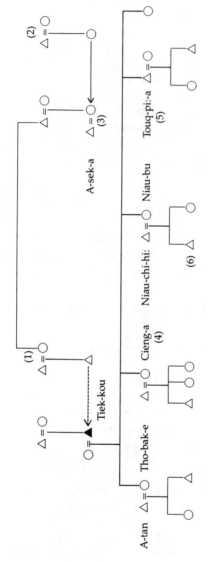

Notes:

1. Tiek-kou's natural parents.
2. A-sek-a's wife's natural parents.
3. A-sek-a's children not shown.
4. Cieng-a was married in May, 1974, and moved out of the community. She had returned by December, 1977.
5. Touq-pi:-a married in 1975.
6. Adopted out to A-iu: but reared by his natural parents.

CHART 2
A-pui-a's Kinship Cluster

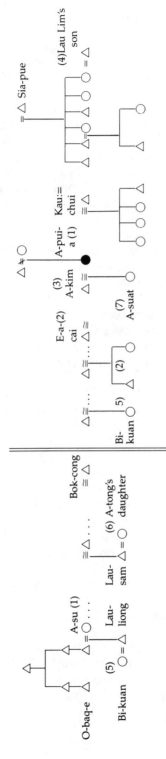

Notes:

1. Not all of either A-su's or A-pui-a's mates are listed. Nor are all of their children listed. A-pui-a had a daughter after Bi-kuan whom she adopted out. A-su had three other sons and one daughter before cohabiting with Bok-cong. She had a son by Bok-cong whom he has adopted.

2. E-a-cai adopted these two of A-pui-a's children by a previous mate, and they live with him.

3. A-kim's relationship with A-pui-a was a casual, sexual one, not a cohabitation.

4. Sia-pue's *sim-pu-a* (adopted daughter-in-law) married into Lau Lim's household.

5. Bi-kuan is pictured twice to facilitate the drawing of this kinship chart.

6. Lau-sam married uxorilocally into A-tong's household.

7. A-suat lived (1974) with Kua:-chui and her mother, A-pui-a.

brother married into A-tong's household to his eldest daughter, and Sia-pue's adopted daughter married into one of the Hokciu families.

The charts are more than just a search by an order-seeking anthropologist looking for possible ties where others do not see them. In 1974 those connected recognized the ties in both word and deed. In A-pui-a's cluster there were especially close ties between those of her children living with her and Kua:-chui, those living with E-a-cai (her eldest daughter, who was married to Lau-liong), and her mother's household. The young children often play together, usually at her mother's house, which is larger and where there is a television set. Li-be, E-a-cai's adopted daughter, often watches over her younger half-siblings and plays with them. Sia-pue, A-pui-a's stepfather, sometimes takes all the grandchildren out to a park or the zoo. And after A-pui-a moved in with Kua:-chui and left E-a-cai without an adult female in his household, he and his children took their meals with Sia-pue and his family. In Tiek-kou's cluster, Tiek-kou subsidized the living expenses of all his children except Cieng-a and has shared the profits from his gambling dens with his son and two sons-in-law. When A-sek-a first came to the Taipei area, Tiek-kou helped him and his family until he found enough work (carpentry) to make his own living.

But not all biological ties are recognized. A-tho's family has a biological and a potentially sociological tie with A-pui-a. It was commonly believed that the genitor of her fourth child, A-suat, was A-kim, A-tho's mate. But no one in A-tho's household recognized any tie with A-suat or with A-pui-a or others in her kinship cluster. Yet in a parallel situation, A-tho's family does recognize Iok-lan, again the daughter of A-kim and another woman; they even rear the girl, and she is known by A-tho's surname, as are A-tho's own children. Other factors may be involved, but some informants explained this anomaly on the basis that A-tho dislikes both A-pui-a and Kua:-chui, her mate, and therefore she does not want to form any sort of link with them. To recognize A-suat as A-kim's child would create at least the potential for such a link, so she has chosen to ignore it.

With regard to kinship networks extending outside the community, a popular misconception about beggars is that they are *bo-chin bo-chiek*, "without kith or kin," that they have no connection with their relatives, having abandoned or lost track of them or having been abandoned by them. Judging from Liong-hiat, this stereotype does not hold. Only three of the 1974 households had no outside kinsmen whom they could contact if they wanted to, and two of these were retired servicemen from mainland China. Of those who have outside kin, only two have no contact at all. One of these is Cap-sa:-hou, whose brothers refuse to recognize her. The other is Tua-kho-e, who has no contact because he is ashamed of the way he has conducted his life. Once, after he had been begging for some time, he went back to the area near his home when he thought his brothers would be attending a festival. He was walking about outside the family home when one brother spotted him and asked, "Aren't you Number Five Brother?" Tua-kho-e hastily denied his identity and hurried off; he has not gone back since.

The majority of Liong-hiat Beggar families not only have contact with their outside, extended kin, however; they have positive contact. They have kept in touch and maintained friendly relations, writing letters, attending life-cycle ceremonies, especially funerals, and sometimes simply visiting for a few days during a festival. In several cases the Beggars' relatives were as poor as they were, but in some others better-off relatives aided their Beggar kinsmen. Some gave money from time to time, and others assisted the children, in one case giving a boy an apprenticeship and in another offering employment in a small factory they owned. Only one Beggar, Be-bin, complained that his relatives looked down on him and that their contact was limited because of this.

The former subdistrict head, in discussing kinship among the Beggars, made the observation that their kinship networks were characterized by what he called indirect (*kan-ciap*) as opposed to direct (*tit-ciap*) links. Direct links were through agnatic ties or close (one or, at most, two degrees removed) affinal or uterine ones, and those related in this way would be widely recognized as kinsmen. Indirect links were somewhat contrived, passing through adoptions and fictive relationships or through a complex series of ties including uterine and affinal ones several degrees removed. Other Chinese, the subdistrict head explained, if they recognized such distantly related people as kin at all, would simply call them "distant relatives" (*oan-chin*) and, having much closer kin, would probably have little to do with them unless there was some obvious reason to. However, the Beggars, hungry for tangible links to others, have not only recognized but have acted upon such ties.

The relationship between Tiek-kou and A-sek-a is a case in point. The latter's wife is the adopted daughter of Tiek-kou's natural mother's younger brother (see chart 1). Besides the number of steps necessary to trace the relationship, what makes this link all the more indirect is that Tiek-kou was adopted out (a *bieng-lieng kia:*). Thus he should have severed his ties with his natal family. But his adoptive parents died when he was twelve, and he returned home. He kept his adopted surname and fulfills his ritual obligations to his adoptive descent line, but he traces his kinsmen through his family of birth. The indirectness of his link with A-sek-a is made even clearer by the fact that several informants, members of the two families, were themselves confused about what the relationship actually was. Informants gave conflicting explanations. It was only after I sat down with A-sek-a and drew out the relationship on paper that it became clear exactly how the two were related.

A further observation by the subdistrict head, that the use of indirect kinship ties was peculiar to the Beggars, was incorrect, however. Aside from the kinship clusters found among the Beggars, there is also one that unites their long-term neighbors, the Hokciulang. This cluster links four households (see chart 3), and curiously, the nexus is not a Hokciulang at all but an old woman from Ch'üanchou called A-cim.

She is called A-ma (grandmother) by the youngest generation in all the linked families. Lau-kho's wife is a cousin. One daughter—all her children are adopted—has married out and lives in Taipei. Another daughter, now deceased, was the first wife of A-liong, an ink maker. Her son was engaged to marry, but he died before the wedding. A-cim then arranged a marriage between her deceased son's fiancée and Lau Lim, another ink maker, who was supposed to marry into A-cim's family and take her surname. But he reneged and set up his own household, keeping his own surname. However, he did agree to place the spirit tablet and a photo of A-cim's deceased son on his domestic altar.

A further tie once existed between the families of Lau Lim and A-liong. The latter had a daughter who, after several years of marriage, was still childless, so Lau Lim, whose wife already had four daughters and two sons, adopted out his next child, son number three, to A-liong's daughter. The child was frequently sick, however, and his natural mother, besides being somewhat apprehensive, had doubts about A-liong's daughter's ability to take care of him. So she asked to have the child back for a while to nurse him back to health, and the adoptive mother agreed. After several weeks, A-liong's daughter got the child back, but again, the child became ill and was returned to his natural mother. Over the next few years the child went back and forth between natural and adoptive mothers several more times, but finally A-liong's daughter decided that she would either keep the child or send him back permanently. An agreement was made

CHART 3
A-cim's Kinship Cluster

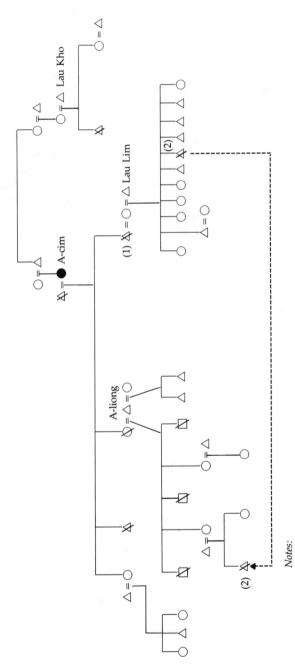

Notes:
1. A-cim's son betrothed before he died but not married.
2. The son adopted out from Lau Lim's family to A-liong's daughter's family.

that she should thereafter keep the child, which she did, but before long the child became ill again, and this time he died. Lau Lim's wife never forgave A-liong's daughter, and the relationship between the two families has been strained every since.

Thus the subdistrict head's idea that the use of indirect ties in forming kinship networks is exclusive to the Beggars is incorrect, but his explanation for it, that it is a result of a need to establish alliances in face of being away from home, kin, and friends, is at least partly accurate. All Hokciulang family heads are migrants to Taiwan and thus are away from home and the location in which a "natural" set of alliances would be found. The other half of the explanation is poverty. The need among the poor to expand one's network is more acute because they have little wealth by which to attract allies, and they are less likely to be able to maintain a "natural" network because they have a higher mortality rate.

CHAPTER SEVEN

Leadership

B Y THIS POINT it should be obvious that Tiek-kou is the central figure in Liong-hiat. As was shown in chapter 4, he created the community, attracting other beggars around him to form a beggar group. When they had to shift locations because of an urban renewal project, he held the group together, even attracting a number of nonbeggar families to it, and found them a new place to live. Before and since, he has been a leader to the beggars as an occupational group and to the entire neighborhood, serving as community head. He has rendered aid and service to the community as a whole and to individual members in it. He is the central figure in Liong-hiat. In the view of Iek-a, the former subdistrict head, it would cease to function as either a social or a beggar group without him. In these accomplishments he has shown himself to be a truly creative, innovative individual.

This chapter will review the roles of Tiek-kou in the community. I will demonstrate how he serves both the community as a whole and individuals in it; then I will discuss his "political style," his bases and exercise of power, and the effects that the illegitimacy of begging in modern Taiwan has had on these.

As community leader, Tiek-kou renders assistance to the community as a whole as well as to individuals in it, Beggars and non-Beggars alike. For example, when Chieng-cui, Sia-Bue's son, wanted to get married, he ran into problems because his intended's parents did not want their daughter to marry a "beggars kid." So Tiek-kou, together with A-ieng, who was assisting him in managing the community's affairs at the time, made appeals to them on Chieng-cui's behalf, telling them that although his parents had begged, his father

145

no longer did so but worked as a cart driver. Moreover, Chieng-cui was not a beggar himself but had a responsible job. His future parents-in-law were finally convinced that Chieng-cui was worthy of their daughter, and they consented. When Cap-sa:-hou's younger daughter, A-hui, was arrested while begging, Tiek-kou went to the police and obtained her release. He also assisted Cap-sa:-hou's entire family in their efforts to get their identity cards from the government. He arranged for A-chun to get on the public welfare rolls, which allowed her to receive small increments to her livelihood. He helped A-m to "adopt" Chai-thau in the hopes that he would look after her in her old age. He arranged for A-chun and A-iu: to become foster parents to children of deceased beggars. When the group moved to Liong-hiat, he concocted a marriage between two single beggars so they could claim a right to public housing then sell this right and reap a profit. When, after a flood, the subdistrict head brought A-cim to Tiek-kou and asked him to see to her care, he did so, getting her a place to live and setting up a small business for her selling snacks, drinks, and cigarettes to others in the area. And when A-sek-a was in financial difficulty because someone defaulted on his rotating credit association and left him deeply in debt to the other members, Tiek-kou helped him arrange to indenture his eldest daughter for a three-year term as a prostitute.[1] Later, when Be-bin, A-tho, and Hiong-a all wanted to indenture their daughters, Tiek-kou found places for each of them and negotiated terms for the parents. Thus a number of people in Liong-hiat are morally indebted to him.

At the community level, he made the arrangements with Lau Ong for those who moved to Liong-hiat to obtain their water supply from his tap, and until A-ieng moved in and assumed this function, he calculated each household's share of the bill and collected the money to pay for it. When someone has died, he has arranged for the funeral and burial and has also conducted the ceremonies at the home and the graveside.

By far his most important functions in the community, however, have been to keep order and to settle disputes. These are essential both to keep the community together and to prevent the attention of outsiders from being focused on it. There is a good deal of illegal gambling in Liong-hiat, and word of disputes and fights not only makes potential customers fearful of going there, but it also draws the attention of the police. Tiek-kou thus has a heavy responsibility. When two people have a dispute, he moves quickly to settle things before they escalate. He first upbraids the disputants for losing their tempers, then he listens to each side. After hearing the differing versions, he tries to reduce, then eliminate, the importance of the events that brought about the conflict. In the words of the subdistrict head, he makes "the big matter become a small matter and the small matter disappear altogether" (*tua-su hua siou-su; siou-su hua bou-su*). He then suggests a compromise solution, which he pressures both sides to accept. After the dispute is settled, that must be the end of it; no one may bring it up again.[2]

I have already explained how Tiek-kou negotiated settlements in the cases of Pai-kha-e's seduction of a neighbor's mate, Be-bin's accusation against Lau-kheq's son, Giok-a's case against the woman with whom her first mate ran off, and E-a-cai's case against Kua:-chui, also for stealing his mate. To prevent or at least minimize future occurrences of such events, Tiek-kou suggested some rules of behavior, one of which forbids mate seduction or stealing. Its not infrequent recurrence demonstrates the need for a leader to deal with the disputes that inevitably follow.

Tiek-kou has also helped settle disputes involving outsiders. A-liong's problem with the Ch'üan-chou people is one example (see chap. 4). Lau-liong's fight at the gambling den during which he hacked A-hong's arm, severing the tendons, is another, and it can serve to illustrate the process of dispute settlement and Tiek-kou's role in it. This dispute was a difficult one for Tiek-kou to resolve, and he had to look for outside assistance, even though A-ieng was already helping him. The problem was that although A-hong was a petty hoodlum (*chit-thou gin-a*), his father was the principal of a primary school. As his position in society was much higher than that of Tiek-kou or A-ieng, they were unable to negotiate with him directly. They needed a "gentleman" (*sin-su*), someone whose social status was equal to or higher than that of A-hong's father, so they sought out Iek-a, the former subdistrict head, who agreed to assist them.

Iek-a also had to represent them to the police. In disputes that remain on the verbal level, the police encourage the parties to settle the matter among themselves, but since A-hong had sustained personal injury, the police wanted to make sure a settlement was reached so the fight did not escalate to a feud. Tiek-kou and A-ieng, because they both had criminal records, were ineligible to act as guarantors, so Iek-a rendered assistance.

The settlement took several months to complete from the time of the incident itself. Before any terms could be agreed to, A-hong's arm had to heal so that damages could be accurately assessed. When the agreement was reached, Lau-liong had to pay NT$40,000 for medical bills and NT$9,000 for recuperation to A-hong; NT$15,000 to A-hong's father for compensation because A-hong lost a bit of mobility in his hand; NT$3,000 to the police involved in the settlement; and an undisclosed amount to Iek-a and his counterpart who represented each side. Finally, Lau-liong had to host a banquet in A-hong's honor, the number of guests and the menu determined by A-hong.

At the banquet, a mediator read the contract containing the terms of settlement. Three copies of this contract, one for each party and an abbreviated one for the police in which the subject of money for compensation was not mentioned, were handed out. No mention was made of the cause of the dispute, only that the parties had had some misunderstanding. At this point, the mediator directed the disputants to toast each other and then to exchange cigarettes. With this gesture the dispute was considered settled, and the two were to remain friends from then on.

Although Tiek-kou was unable to settle this dispute on his own, through his network he was able to find someone, in this case Iek-a, who could help him. Moreover, he played an important economic role in the settlement, raising much of the money Lau-liong needed by increasing the "tax" on the winnings at the gambling dens, and by soliciting donations from his fellow Beggars in the community.

Another service that Tiek-kou performs that is vital to the continued existence of the community is to ensure that all Beggars meet their rotating credit association obligations. The greatest risk in this form of credit and investment is that someone will *tou he-a*, that is, after taking his turn to receive the money, run off and not fulfill his obligations to contribute to the shares of others. Rotating credit associations are virtually the only form of credit available to the Beggars other than pawning and short-term, high-interest loans for gambling. The failure of someone to meet his obligations endangers the whole system; thus it is imperative to make it as reliable and risk-free as possible.[3] The results of Hana defaulting on her obligations have been recounted in chapter 4, but in another case, A-shieng, a beggar from T'aoyüan who had spent some time with the Liong-hiat group, ran out on obligations totaling NT$150,000. Tiek-kou contacted beggar chiefs throughout Taiwan and learned that A-shieng had gone to Hualien. He then arranged with the Hualien chief to allow A-shieng to remain in the beggar community there only if he turned over a certain percentage of his income each week to be sent to Liong-hiat for repayment of his debts.

Aside from being community leader, Tiek-kou is also the beggar chief. As such, his most important functions have been to advise the beggars and to organize begging activities. Through his network, he gathers "intelligence" (*cieng-pou*), finding out when and where funerals and festivals are going to be held. In the event of a funeral, he goes to the family concerned, offering to keep the beggars away in exchange for a sum of money. If he collects, he keeps the money for himself, though he occasionally buys treats for the beggars. If the family does not pay him, he organizes the beggars to *tiau-lo-ce*, and the individual beggars then keep the money they themselves collect. In the case of a festival, Tiek-kou passes the information he gathers on to the beggars so they can take advantage of the lucrative opportunity to beg.

He also gives advice to individual beggars as to where they might go to beg and what places they should avoid, but he does this only on request, not as a matter of course. Although they are not inviolable, there are territorial arrangements between the various dens in the Taipei area, negotiated by the chiefs, and on special occasions such as festivals, Tiek-kou may suggest that beggars go to various spots to take best advantage of the situation. But whether by choice or because he is unable to, he does not assign territories to individuals in his den in the course of normal, everyday begging.

His other activities as beggar chief concern other dens. He has kept in close touch with beggars in other dens and with their chiefs for a variety of reasons. First, beggars sometimes leave one place and go to another. Because Tiek-kou knows the chief in such-and-such an area, he can provide an introduction for the traveler, who will often be able to stay with people in the den. When Ho-a went to Kaohsiung to work as a construction laborer, he was able to stay with the beggars there until he found more permanent accommodations. Second, beggars often travel to another city to take advantage of an important festival there. When they do, they can stay with fellow beggars during their visit because the chiefs in the host dens know they are coming. Third, close relations with the other chiefs are also quite helpful in resolving cases such as A-shieng defaulting on his rotating credit association obligations.

At one time, Tiek-kou thought of organizing all the beggars' dens in northern Taiwan into a beggars' union with monthly dues to support a *ki-kim*, a fund on which anyone affiliated could draw when in need. He discussed the idea with several other chiefs but gradually came to the conclusion that, while such a union might be advantageous in some ways, its net results would be negative. Although illegal, begging is tolerated by the police and officials in many areas, but these same authorities might find a wide-ranging beggar's union potentially more disruptive or threatening than what had previously existed, and they might then take steps against the beggars. Nonetheless, that he came up with such an idea and canvassed other chiefs for support demonstrates his initiative and the range of his imagination.

Tiek-kou's influence within the community and his ability to secure compliance with his directives and courses of action are based on a number of factors, especially the character of his relationships with the community members and the manner in which he leads and advises them. As he has no formal-legal authority—he is not recognized as a beggar chief by the authorities, as beggar chiefs were in traditional times—in order to lead, to influence the behavior of the beggars, or to impose sanctions on individuals, he must rely on the moral authority he can generate from within the group itself.

He creates this moral authority by the way he acts as leader. In stark contrast to the traditional chief, Tiek-kou lives with the Beggars and is most definitely one of them. In his position vis-à-vis the others, he is a down-to-earth figure, not a stern and distant one. Like many others in the community, he is called or referred to by his nickname, or, if one wished to show respect, as Tiek-kou A-peq, "Uncle Tiek-kou." He is also referred to as the "eldest older brother" (*tua-hia:*) of the group, a form of reference common in gangs and groups of sworn brothers. In this sense, he is the primus inter pares but with more emphasis on *pares* than on *primus*. His only title that indicates social distance is that of beggar chief (*khit-ciaq-thau*), and that title is used or imposed more by outsiders than by those in Liong-hiat. A-tan made little of this appellation, saying, "He is called beggar chief only because he helps people." Indeed, he is seen as a helpful, charitable individual, a *hao-hao hsien-sheng* (good and kindly man), in the words of one of the Neighbors.

Many Beggars and others described Tiek-kou as having *gi-khi. Gi-khi* (Mandarin *i-ch'i*) is often translated as "personal loyalty." In classical philosophy the concept is closely associated with the Mohist school with its emphasis on brotherhood and equal treatment of all, of treating, for example, someone else's father as one would one's own. In more concrete terms and as described by informants, it suggests acting in a universalistic manner and doing what is best for all, of being helpful to all with no thought of a return favor, or assisting a friend even when his predicament is of his own making and when one will suffer a loss by helping, or of making a fair and even-handed decision even when one's friends and kin have an interest in the decision.[4] In the minds of informants, Tiek-kou fulfills all these conditions. He has helped people on a number of occasions who had no foreseeable way to repay him—for example when he took in A-cim, or when he fed, clothed, and provided care for the late Cui-shieng-a when he was ill and could not go out to beg. He once saw some beggars drinking beer in a small eatery outside the den, and he told them to buy the beer and bring it home to drink. His reason was that beer is an expensive form of alcohol in Taiwan, and if people noticed beggars drinking it, they might be less inclined to give in the future. Thus he suggested a rule to the group for the good of all. The fact that he has resolved a number of disputes and that people keep coming to him for help in such matters demonstrates his reputation for fairness.

The knowledge that Tiek-kou makes money from the activities of the beggars does not detract from his *gi-khi*. When he assists people in begging or gives them financial advice and then takes his 30 percent commission, he is merely taking what is rightfully his as a beggar chief. This is his job, the way he earns his living. Informants, even non-Beggars, held the same view of his economic relationship with his beggar implements. They were people who, because of age or physical disability, were unable to make a living on their own, and their relatives, for whatever reason, were unable or unwilling to provide for them. Tiek-kou took them in and guaranteed them a living, even when they were unable to contribute toward their upkeep; in exchange they turned over what they earned as beggars to him. In addition, he found a mate for A-cui-a, and the couple had two children; he arranged for A-m to "adopt" Chai-thau; and he located Cap-sa:-hou's natal family. He personally profited from his relationships with these people, but this did not alter informants' opinions of him. To them it was quite natural that he should profit. After all, he took responsibility for them, made it possible for them to beg by making sure there were people to assist them, and helped them out in many ways over and above providing them with a livelihood. Informants viewed him as kind and caring, not as exploitive or cynical.[5] To them it was naïve to believe that someone would perform services that were a part of the way he earned his livelihood with no thought of a return.

Tiek-kou's exercise of leadership, by contrast to that of a traditional chief, is markedly circumscribed. He has acted against people in only two circumstances, and in both, the actions he took were very limited. As I have explained, he has acted against men who violated another's control of a woman's sexuality. To ignore such incidents would have placed the solidarity and even the existence of the community in jeopardy. He has also moved when the actions of some might have endangered the community's economic well-being. In this regard, he has acted to resolve quickly or prevent disputes because they cause friction and attract the attention of the police, which in turn frightens would-be gamblers away from the dens. He has also suggested a few sumptuary rules: beggars may drink beer, but they should buy it and bring it back to the den for consumption; beggars should avoid dressing in nice clothing or wearing jewelry, especially outside of the den; and beggars should not attend or give banquets outside the den. These rules were offered to maintain the image of beggars as impoverished, needy people.

The sanctions available to Tiek-kou to impose on violators of these rules are also very limited. He can impose a fine, more often in the form of a banquet than an exaction of money, and he can expel someone from—more precisely suggest they leave—the community. The latter punishment sounds worse than it is, but it deprives the person only of the company of others in the community, not of his ability to earn a living. There are many free-lance beggars scattered throughout the Taipei area, and there are other dens to which they can go.

Tiek-kou does not use force or threats of force. Although tall, he is not an overly strong man, and he does not use physical force to get his way. On one occasion, after he caught Tua-kho-e peeking under his youngest daughter's dress, he set in motion a train of events that resulted in Tua-kho-e's being beaten. Whether this was his intention was never clear, but, even if it was, he would have been justified, not as community leader, but as the father of the victim. On other occasions he has relied solely on voluntary compliance, backed up by community pressure, to achieve his aims.

There is evidence, in fact, based on a challenge to his position as leader by someone assisting him, A-ieng, that if he resorted to force, he might destroy the community. Although his group is not large, Tiek-kou has often needed an assistant because he is illiterate. In the past, Chai-thau and Cieng-a have helped him, reading documents that came to him as neighborhood head and drafting replies. But late in 1972, A-ieng moved into Liong-hiat, and he became a more or less regular assistant. This coincided with Tiek-kou's gradual move away from begging activities and toward gambling and *tiau-lo-ce* as ways to earn his living. He began to concentrate more on outside matters, leaving the mundane activities of running the community to A-ieng. So A-ieng took over the collection for the water bill. At funerals, he received contributions, gave the return gift to contributors, and made arrangements for food, musicians, and transport to the grave site. Tiek-kou still conducted the rituals at the funeral and the burial, the more prestigious services, however. This division of labor worked for a while, but by the end of 1974, it became clear that A-ieng wanted to push Tiek-kou out of the way, into retirement, and take over the leadership of the group for himself. He was not acceptable to the beggars, however, and he moved away soon afterward.

The main objection to A-ieng, other than that he was an interloper and that no one wanted to get rid of Tiek-kou, was that he was prone to violence in both action and speech. Whereas Tiek-kou would upbraid people for violating rules and everyday manners, A-ieng would curse them, heaping abuse and scorn on them. Moreover, in keeping with his *lo-mua:* background and connections, he was quick-tempered and tended to use his fists or a weapon when he became angry. Informants compared Tiek-kou and A-ieng using the classical *wen-wu* dichotomy: Tiek-kou was *wen*, "smooth, well-mannered, gentlemanly," and A-ieng was *wu*, "fierce, martial." Although he displayed a kind heart in some of the things he did for people in Liong-hiat while he was there, A-ieng was rejected as a potential leader because of his personality and manner of operation. Given the choice between the two, the community remained loyal to Tiek-kou.

Having no formal-legal authority and eschewing physical force, Tiek-kou has relied on the "consent of the governed" in order to lead. This has meant limiting his exercise of leadership to areas and particular situations in which he has popular support and handing down decisions or imposing sanctions that are within accepted definitions of what is fair and proper under the circumstances. Thus, when he suggested a rule, imposed a fine, or expelled someone, he was in effect exercising the will and reflecting the judgment of the majority. For example, when he ordered Pai-kha-e to give a banquet in A-go's honor and then to leave the community, he was transmitting the decision of the community. His order had widespread support, and this, no doubt, made it sufficiently forceful to be obeyed.

Within the community, Tiek-kou has two resources that encourage compliance with his decisions: in material terms, he is a valuable person to have as a leader; and among community members, he has a wide network, encompassing most of the Beggars, of people related to him through real or fictive kinship ties. As an economic resource, he provides a number of services to the beggars such as intelligence and opportunities to beg at funerals and festivals. He also provides aid to those in need, help to those arrested, and income to those who share in the profits of his gambling dens. Through his network outside the community, he has secured favors for Liong-hiat from officials and politicians, and through his network with other beggar chiefs, he can get a place to stay for a traveler. In a material sense, therefore, he is a very valuable person. It is in the material interest of those in Liong-hiat to accept his leadership.

As the center of a kinship and fictive kinship network within Liong-hiat, he is related directly or indirectly to all but three households, those headed by Tua-kho-e, Hana, and Hiong-a. As is shown on chart 4 (see also chap. 6) he is related by kinship ties to the households of his married daughters, Niau-bu and Tho-bak-e, more distantly to A-sek-a, and by fictive ties to his godsons (*gi-kia:*), Siong-a, Kua:-chui, and Ho-a; his goddaughter (*gi-ca-bo-kia:*), O-niau; his fictive son (*khe-kia:*), A-cui-a; his fictive mothers (*khe-ma*), A-m, A-kou, and A-chun; his fictive daughters (*khe-ca-bo-kia:*), Cap-sa:-hou and Chun-bieng; and his sworn brothers (*kiat-pai e hia:-ti*), A-ieng, A-tong, Pai-kha-e, A-iu: (with whom he was a de facto co-husband), A-kim, Be-bin, and Sia-bue. Through Sia-bue, he is connected to and can individually influence Sia-bue's onetime de facto son-in-law, E-a-cai, and his grandson-in-law, Lau-liong. Through Lau-liong, he is linked to O-baq-e and Bok-cong. Thus Tiek-kou is not only the founder of the Beggar group but also its nexus. The ties he has with individuals and households add a moral dimension to the relationships that exist between them, and this serves to strengthen the compliance and support he can expect from them.

His relationships with those outside the Liong-hiat community, people in his outside network with whom he can trade favors, are based on quite a different sort of relationship. With these people—politicians, police, *lo-mua:*, and his teahouse acquaintances—his role is more nearly that of the classical broker, exchanging a good for a good or the implied promise of a future good. From politicians, he has secured a number of benefits for the Liong-hiat community. In exchange, he helps them get votes. He does this in three ways. First, he can deliver the votes of those in Liong-hiat; the community members respect him and see it in their interests to vote for whomever he recommends. Second, because he is known to be a beggar leader and because of the association of begging and poverty in the popular mind, Tiek-kou's endorsement is valuable. The status difference between him and a candidate being what it is, he would certainly not appear on the same rostrum, but on his own he can sing the praises of a candidate, telling people that So-and-so is charitable and mindful of the poor, thus deserving of electoral support. Third, Tiek-kou

CHART 4
Tiek-kou's Ties to the Beggar Community

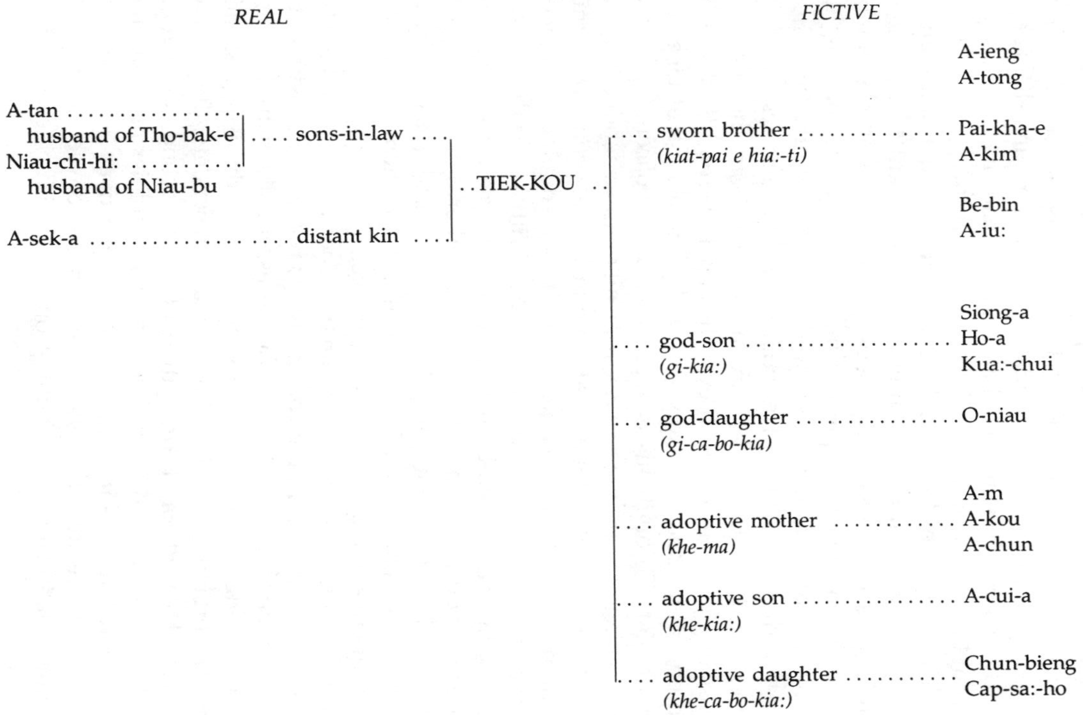

REAL   *FICTIVE*

A-tan ...
  husband of Tho-bak-e .... sons-in-law .... sworn brother .... A-ieng
  Niau-chi-hi: ....   *(kiat-pai e hia:-ti)*   A-tong
  husband of Niau-bu .. ..TIEK-KOU .... Pai-kha-e
        A-kim

A-sek-a .... distant kin ....   Be-bin
        A-iu:

.... god-son ....   Siong-a
  (gi-kia:)   Ho-a
        Kua:-chui

.... god-daughter ....   O-niau
  (gi-ca-bo-kia)

.... adoptive mother ....   A-m
  (khe-ma)   A-kou
        A-chun

.... adoptive son ....   A-cui-a
  (khe-kia:)

.... adoptive daughter ....   Chun-bieng
  (khe-ca-bo-kia:)   Cap-sa:-ho

assists candidates by buying votes. This is a common practice in Taiwan, at least in local-level politics, and with his wide range of acquaintances, Tiek-kou is very effective at it. He is given a certain amount of money by a candidate to purchase votes, and he gives a number of people NT$100 each, the going rate in 1977, for their votes.[6] He also turns a handsome profit for himself. The former subdistrict head estimated that Tiek-kou had made NT$20,000 at a recent local election.

The exchanges between Tiek-kou and both the police and the *lo-mua:* revolve around gambling. The police want to keep gambling under control. Tiek-kou complies, preventing or at least minimizing incidents in which people are injured and those that might draw public attention to the gambling dens and to the fact that the police are not doing their job. The police also "eat red" *(ciaq-ang)*, that is, receive gifts of money at certain holidays from the profits of the gambling dens. In return they either tip Tiek-kou off in the event of an obligatory raid or simply ignore the gambling that takes place in Liong-hiat. Through his acquaintance with policemen, he has also been able to secure the release from jail of apprehended beggars.

The *lo-mua:* also get a small amount of the profits from the gambling dens, and those who do protect Tiek-kou and the others from being preyed upon by other *lo-mua:*. With his teahouse acquaintances, he acts as a go-between, putting people with complementary interests and needs in touch with each other. For his part, he gains the prestige of knowing and being known and accepted by a large number of people, and he also learns from them about weddings and funerals that are about to take place.

These relationships differ from those between him and the Beggars in several ways. First, the content of his relationships with outsiders, while by no means devoid of affect, is essentially instrumental, a mutual exchange of services. Between him and the Beggars, although there is certainly a two-way flow of material benefits, the relationships are moral, based mainly on mutual affection. Second, his relationships with outsiders are dyadic. He deals with politicians, policemen, *lo-mua:*, and others as individuals, not as collectives. With the Beggars, although there are some dyadic transactions between them, his fundamental relationship is with the group, not with a series of disparate individuals.

Tiek-kou is in some ways like the ward-heeler of the urban American political machine. He knows a group of constituents personally, and he secures benefits for them by dealing with those in official positions who control access to and distribution of such benefits. He is unlike the ward-heeler, however, in that his reference group is the constituency, not the politicians and police. He is someone the latter deal with when it is in their interest and when there are favors to be secured or repaid. He is not a part of their unofficial organization, as a ward-heeler is.

A closer comparison is with those in the employ of the factions in local Taiwanese politics (see Jacobs 1979, 1980; Crissman 1981). These are often people with morally based ties to a particular constituency—a village, a workplace, an occupational group, or a section of town—who run errands for and assist the factions, secure votes (often by purchase) for them, and make such other arrangements as are necessary for the mutual benefit of the faction and the constitutency. Again, the critical difference is the focus of reference: Tiek-kou is the leader of the Beggar group, not the servant of the faction.

Tiek-kou does hold one position, that of neighborhood head (*lin-chang*), that integrates him into the formal authority structure of Taiwan society, but his influence in Liong-hiat does not derive from this, nor could it derive from its formal attributes. A neighborhood head is the lowest level in the official organization of a city in Taiwan. The neighborhood consists of thirty to forty households, and its head is basically a messenger who passes information between the citizens or households and the next higher officer, the subdistrict head. A neighborhood head has no authority or power, and he receives no remuneration for his efforts. A wooden plaque hung outside his door identifying him as the head of X Neighborhood, Y Subdistrict (a subdistrict has a name, a neighborhood only a number) is his only badge of office. Those in this position usually serve out of a feeling of public-spiritedness. As a general rule, neighborhood heads are at best slightly larger fish in the smallest of ponds, and they are usually of humble means and status.

Among the neighborhood heads I have known, Tiek-kou is certainly the most active, making the greatest use of his office. He uses his title, either believing or—more likely—pretending to believe that it earns him some respect in his contacts with politicians and the police, when he acts as road guide at a funeral procession, and as an entree to weddings and other social events attended by wealthy and important local figures. Being a neighborhood head and performing a public role also give him a modicum of legitimacy in society, and this is important to a man who grew up in poverty and spent most of his adult life stigmatized as a beggar. He has taken the greatest advantage of this humble position, making it important far beyond its inherent attributes. But his being neighborhood head is important only in dealing and interacting with the outside world. It does not enhance his stature in Liong-hiat. More over, this position is a *result* of his influence in Liong-hiat, not a *source* of it.

Tiek-kou's exercise of leadership and his position within his group and in the wider society can best be illustrated by contrasting him with the beggar chief of premodern China. The latter had a formal-legal position within a corporate group. His authority over those under him was extensive and autocratic and was enforced by at least the threat if not the actual use of physical coercion. Tiek-kou, by contrast, has no formal-legal position other than that of neighborhood head, a status that itself is noncorporate. Tiek-kou is able to exercise leadership not because he coerces or threatens people but because his decisions and advice are seen as just, fair, and wise, and because group members see it as in their best interest to follow him. They have benefited materially from following his advice or when he directly assisted them. More importantly, they have benefited socially in that his leadership has held the community together. The key to the difference in the two leadership types lies in the legal position of the beggars themselves. In premodern times they were, if not welcomed, at least tolerated, and they were legitimate. In present-day Taiwan, if they do not make too much of a nuisance of themselves, they are tolerated in some contexts and some areas of the island, but they are illegal, and they are actively suppressed in more modern areas of the big cities. Thus, whereas the premodern chief had the authority and coercive power of the state behind him, Tiek-kou, since his group is not and cannot be formally constituted, has had to lead by means of moral suasion and the consent of the governed.

A final word about Tiek-kou will highlight and reinforce his creativity and innovativeness as a leader. Because of the very marked differences in the social, economic, and political conditions in present-day Taiwan as compared with China of the past, many of the tactics used by traditional beggar leaders are no longer employable by Tiek-kou. For example, the collection in advance of protection money from shopkeepers, a primary source of income for his counterparts of the past, is closed off to him. But he has responded by finding new or adapting old ways to beg. His role at funerals as the leader of the procession to the grave (*khui-lo-e*) is his own invention, as is his role at weddings, where he shows up self-invited and then hobnobs with politicians, wealthy men, and others of importance. But without doubt his greatest creations are the beggar group itself with him at the head, and the networks which he has built up to support himself and the group and which give him access to power. He epitomizes the success story of a man from the floating population who was able to survive by his wits and rise far above his origins.

CHAPTER EIGHT

Change and Mobility

As I EXPLAINED IN chapter 1, this account of the Liong-hiat community is based on two periods of fieldwork, 1973–74 and 1977–78, plus a few visits in 1980 while I was engaged in field research in another area. Over this period of time, a number of people moved out of the community, and some people dropped or deemphasized methods they formerly used to make money and took up new ones. These changes were often linked with attempts at upward social mobility, and they resulted in significant differences both in the character of the community and in the people making it up. In this chapter I will discuss these changes and analyze the various strategies of mobility open to and employed by the Beggars and their children. I will first outline the trends perceived in 1977–78 and then demonstrate how they continued in 1980–81.

1977–1978

Changes in the Liong-hiat Community

Since its coming together in the late 1940s, Tiek-kou's Beggar group has never been static. Although personnel changes between the early 1950s and 1973 were not numerous, there were a few who died or moved into or out of the group. The most important change in that period, however, was the increasing importance that gambling assumed for some as a means of generating income. Not long after the formation of the community, gangsters suggested that the beggars exploit their image as a poverty-stricken group and their own small-stakes, recreational gambling as a cover to establish larger-stakes gam-

159

bling activities, the gangsters taking a small percentage. This gave Tiek-kou, who ran a gambling den, a source of income not related to begging. He continued to operate gambling dens following the move to Liong-hiat, and, after A-ieng and A-tan were able to enlarge and improve their houses, they, too, established gambling dens. Most of the others in the Beggar group continued to rely on begging as a primary source of income, however.

By late 1977 another set of changes had taken place that altered both the personnel and the economic activities of the Liong-hiat community. In December 1977, eight of the twenty-four households that made up the Beggar group in 1974 were no longer there, and the household heads had left in two others. A-iu: and A-kou, both single, and A-tong had all died, A-tong's family remaining in the community. A-go and his family were expelled shortly before I left in 1974. Kua:-chui took his children and went south in a hurry; he had bought a color television on installments and then pawned it before he had paid for it. Hana left after selling the equity she had left in her house to pay off her gambling and rotating credit association debts. A-ieng moved away after his bid to take over the leadership from Tiek-kou failed. His children had never been happy living in a "beggar's den" anyway and had been urging him to leave for a long time. He did not move far away, but he never visited anyone in Liong-hiat. His mistress occasionally went back to gamble, however, and she also attended A-kou's funeral. O-baq-e, a journeyman mason in the truest sense of the term, simply left. Sia-pue tried to set up a gambling den in his home, but he lost heavily and had to sell his house to pay his debts. He was living outside the area, supporting himself as he had before, hauling goods in the central market in his trishaw. His mate still lived in Liong-hiat with her sons and unmarried daughter. Be-bin left after indenturing his three daughters to a teahouse. He, his mate, and his two sons moved to another part of town.

These changes in personnel are manifestations of the changes in the economic activities of individuals and in the character of the community. By 1977 both begging and gambling had declined in importance as income-producing activities for the community as a whole, and a number of Beggars, some of whom had moved and some of whom still lived there, became independent of or reduced their dependence on them.

Income from gambling declined for three reasons. First, an increasing number of fights, some in which people used knives, frightened customers away. It will be recalled that Tiek-kou often had to contend with such altercations while he was actively leading the community, but after A-ieng took over some of his duties, the violence increased. Customers became fearful not only that they might become involved in the fights themselves but that the violence might attract the attention of the police, and they did not want to be caught in a police raid. Second, in 1976, under pressure from the central government, the police began a campaign to "eliminate the four evils" (ch'u ssu hai), one of which was gambling. With pressure coming from such a high source, the local police had no choice but to crack down, despite the personal and financial relationships some had with the den operators. Third, two of the four persons operating dens in 1974, A-ieng and Kua:-chui, left the community, though, as I explained above, not because of a decline in gambling activities. People in Liong-hiat still gambled, mostly among themselves and for relatively low stakes, and Tiek-kou still imposed a "tax" on the winnings of all games in his house, but he no longer had a formal den, and his income came mainly from other sources. A-tan still hosted mahjong games in his house, but his gambling-derived income had also fallen with the general decline in gambling.

Begging also declined. There were still some who begged regularly: Bok-cong and his mate, Cap-sa:hou, Pai-kha-e, Tua-kho-e, Gong-a, and A-m. But there were a number who had quit completely or significantly reduced the amount they begged. Others stopped street begging but still participated in tiau-lo-ce when the occasion arose. It should be remembered, however, that tiau-lo-ce was considered to be at least semilegitimate work and that participants did not incur the same stigma as they did from street begging.

As with gambling, a number of factors account for this change. Foremost among them is that the offspring of the Beggars, on whom they used to rely to take them out, grew up. As they did so, they became a liability to their beggar parents, reducing rather than increasing the sympathy of passersby. More importantly, they became unwilling themselves to endure the shame of begging, so they refused to take their parents out any longer. In 1973, on Chinese New Year, Sia-pue's mate wanted to go out to beg, but her two daughters absolutely refused to go with her. Being blind, she could not go out alone, and being mentally unbalanced, she began screaming at everyone within earshot and behaving wildly. Finally A-suat, her granddaughter, took her. As her daughters were already in their late teens and were working in a factory, it is not surprising that they refused to accompany her. But even children much younger, such as A-tho's youngest daughters, aged six and eight, refused to accompany adults to beg. A-suat's willingness was exceptional, and comparing her circumstances to those of others may help to explain why. No one in her family had any education. Although they had no physical disabilities that forced them to do so, both her parents begged for a portion of their income, the remainder of which her stepfather, Kua:-chui, got from gambling. Moreover, her parents lived from day to day, spending or gambling what they earned and letting tomorrow take care of itself. A-tho's family relied on begging for many years when her children were growing up, but A-tho was blind, and she had to support the family much of the time because her mate was a morphine addict and spent several periods in jail. But all of A-tho's children received at least six years of education. Moreover, the older ones, at least, were highly motivated, and their mother encouraged them to make a success of themselves. Most families in Liong-hiat were more like A-tho's than like Kua:-chui's.

Children were a factor in reducing the dependency on begging in another way. When they became old enough, many went to work. The wages they earned were often used not to increase the family income but to reduce the amount the parents needed to beg, and if their children's income was sufficient, they ceased to beg altogether. E-a-cai stopped begging when his son opened up a motorcycle repair shop. All of A-tho's children except Ho-a, who was in the military, contributed to the family income, so she no longer needed to beg to support her family. Actually she began to reduce the amount she begged when her eldest son started to work, but she has since stopped altogether. Sia-bue and his mate stopped begging under similar circumstances; as his children grew older and began to earn money, he began to drive a trishaw, and his mate no longer needed to beg. A-tong's family had not stopped begging, but since both daughters were working and one had a married-in (*ciou-sai*) husband, they begged less. Hiong-a's mate had to stop begging after he indentured their daughter. As his mate was physically unable to go out on her own, with his daughter gone, there was no longer anyone to take her. Their younger son, partially crippled, could not, and their older son absolutely refused. Be-bin's mate also stopped begging after he indentured his daughters. In fact, except for one household, those still heavily dependent on begging were single men or widows with no children to support them.

Informants living outside Liong-hiat suggested another reason why they thought there were fewer beggars now. They said that the police had been cracking down on begging, as they had been doing on gambling. This may have been true, but I saw no evidence that it affected any of the Liong-hiat beggars. They were very experienced and had been eluding the police for quite a number of years. None said they were any more fearful of arrest than they had been in the past. Even if this supposed police crackdown were a factor, it was certainly not as important as the earnings of the younger generation or their refusal to accompany adults to go out to beg.

One external factor was quite important, however—the growth of the Taiwan economy and the creation of jobs, especially for unskilled workers. Although one can only infer a connection between the two, the link seems obvious. Moreover, it was seen as significant by people in Liong-hiat itself. Tiek-kou asserted that it was only those with no dependents to support them who still begged. And one informant said that, given the availability of work in Taiwan today, there was no longer an excuse for begging. The work may not have been ideal in terms of pay and career possibilities to many, especially the males, but at least it provided people with income sufficient to meet basic needs, and there was no stigma attached to it.

These changes in personnel and economic activities led to changes in the nature of the community. First, with all the deaths and moves, a number of houses were vacated, and those moving into them were not beggars but tradesmen, clerks, peddlers, and the like. The only dealings they had with the Beggars was the use of a common water supply and the sharing of the bill. They did not associate with the Beggars, nor did many gamble with them. The influence of the beggar element in Liong-hiat had decreased, and it became less and less a beggars' den.

Second, many of those who left or died had been part of the beggar group almost since its inception. It was these men and their mates who lived together, gambled and begged together, and formalized their relationships by forming fictive kin ties. With many of the older generation gone, the strong affective ties (*kam-chieng*) that had characterized the group for so long weakened or disappeared altogether; they had never been so strong anyway between members of the younger generation or between members of the older and the children of their peers.

Actually these bonds had been diminishing for a number of years. As individuals developed their own begging strategies, as other, less stigmatized sources of income became available, and as the younger generation grew up and began to work, people began to see the futures of themselves and their families heading in different directions from those of others. The benefits of cooperation and the shared stigma of begging, factors that had held them together as a united group, were no longer strong enough to maintain the level of cohesion that had once existed.

Even Tiek-kou developed his own personal income strategy and became increasingly concerned with himself and his own, and this affected the cohesion of the community even further. When A-ieng moved into Liong-hiat, Tiek-kou gradually turned more and more of the mundane tasks of leadership over to him, tasks that required realtively constant presence in the area. Meanwhile, Tiek-kou began spending more time outside, pursuing his interests in *tiau-lo-ce*, promoting himself at funerals and weddings, and cultivating his network, especially his ties with politicians. When A-ieng left, Tiek-kou resumed the leadership functions himself, but the way he exercised that role was not the same as before. He still did important things such as collecting for the water bill and prestigious ones such as conducting funerals, and he still let the beggars know about opportunities to *tiau-lo-ce* or beg at a festival. But spending as much time outside as he did, he simply was not as conversant with community affairs as he had previously been. He continued to assist others, but whereas before he was almost as aware of people's problems as they were, he now learned about them only when someone came to him for help. He became a passive leader rather than the active one he had once been.

On the surface this made little difference. There were fewer beggars in Liong-hiat, for instance, and those who still begged were experienced and needed little advice or assistance from him. But there were differences in Tiek-kou's interests in the group, in his relationships with its members and the perceptions others had of these relationships, and in the ramifications this had on the cohesiveness of the group.

According to Chieng-cui, a son of Sia-pue, the *gi-khi* that had once characterized relationships, especially those involving Tiek-kou, was gone. "If you look at those he helps now, they are all his relatives, his close relatives, not his sworn brothers and the like. It does not count as *gi-khi* when those you help are your own people." Chieng-cui was somewhat bitter because a few years earlier, his father had proposed a gambling partnership with Tiek-kou, but Tiek-kou turned him down. "My father's relationship with him goes back a lot farther than does A-tan's or Niau-chi-hi:'s [his sons-in-law], yet he was willing to share his profits with them but not with my father." Chieng-cui's bitterness increased when his father failed in his attempt to set up a gambling den on his own and had to sell his house to pay off the debts that resulted. He felt that Tiek-kou could have helped his father and ensured that he did not fail. Instead, in his own interest, as Chieng-cui saw it, he did not.

Chieng-cui had an ax to grind in his comments about Tiek-kou, but others ageed that the attributes that had made Tiek-kou the leader of the community—his willingness to help people and his magnanimity—were much reduced, and that his attentions were turned toward his own family. According to some, the reason Be-bin moved when he did was that he was increasingly dissatisfied with Tiek-kou's treatment of him, despite their sworn brother relationship. Others complained that although he provided her with free lodgings, Tiek-kou no longer gave adequate financial support to A-m, who had once been one of his beggar implements. One said that if it were not for the leftover food she got from A-tho, she would often go hungry. On strictly formal grounds, people recognized that Tiek-kou owed her nothing; she no longer begged for him, so he had no obligation toward her. But because she had had such a close relationship with his family, having been regarded as and referred to by his children as their wet nurse, some felt she should have been given better treatment. A-m herself was known to be bitter, much as a mother whose children had turned against her would be.

As far as the community as a whole was concerned, it was not that the Beggars had become enemies, that the atmosphere was one of hostility, tension, or rancor, or even that they had become like a more typical urban neighborhood in which people mind their own business and ignore their neighbors. The Beggars were still very friendly with one another, and they still cooperated with and aided one another in such matters as the water supply, rotating credit associations, life crises, and sometimes begging. But the feelings of mutual obligation and the willingness to sacrifice for each other that had previously existed were no longer there, victims, as it were, of the individualization of economic strategies and of Tiek-kou's less active leadership performance.

Mobility among the Liong-hiat Community Members

In the discussion to follow, mobility refers to a decrease in or a cessation of begging as a means to gain a livelihood and the substitution of a socially more acceptable means. In terms of social acceptability, anything is better than street begging, including illegal and dishonorable activities such as gambling, gangster activities, and prostitution. Not only are they often more lucrative, but they are also less visible, and they allow the participant to retain more dignity. Conventional work, while usually not so lucrative, is higher than any of these in terms of social acceptability. Although there is some overlap, it will be helpful to discuss separately the strategies for mobility of the older generation, the beggars themselves, and those of their children, the second generation.

One set of strategies used by the beggars was to substitute a more acceptable for a less acceptable form of begging. Thus those who could entertained while they begged (*be-gi*) rather than simply engage in street begging, the lowest form of mendicancy. Another substitution was to *tiau-lo-ce* rather than to beg on the streets. Tiek-kou has taken this substitution strategy as far as it can be taken. As soon as he was able, he enlisted a group of beggar implements to beg for him. Moreover, he does not even engage in *tiau-lo-ce* himself but instead restricts his role to that of contacting the families of the recently deceased in hopes of receiving payment from them to keep other beggars away from the funeral procession.

Another strategy adopted by some in the first generation was gambling. Two who begged themselves, Kua:-chui and Tiek-kou, have used this, and after Tiek-kou began earning a fair amount of money from running gaming dens, he allowed his relationships with his beggar implements to lapse, removing himself yet another step from begging. Kua:-chui made the bulk of his income from gambling and begged only when he ran out of money.

Yet another strategy used by the older generation was to rely on their children's earnings. As I have explained, several families cut down on begging and then ceased altogether as their children were able to assume an increasing role in supporting them. Some of the children have done this by means of conventional work, but others have been indentured as prostitutes in order that their families might be able to quit begging. In fact, this was a decision that all families with daughters had to make: one could allow daughters to work in factories, where they would not earn very much, and hope that sons would find steady work and at least moderately acceptable wages; or one could indenture one or more daughters into prostitution and achieve a comfortable standard of living independent of begging at one fell swoop. Feelings of individuals in the community were mixed. As one informant put it, "I've thought about pawning one's daughters quite a bit. If one doesn't do this he will be considered a very moral and good father. If he does, he will be thought ill of. But one has to face reality. If one is poor, this may be the only way." Others agreed that it indeed might be, if not the only way, certainly a very strong contender. One person commented that the reason A-tong's family was still so poor was that they "had not yet pawned either of their daughters." Most were also quite certain that Iok-lan, the granddaughter of the T'aoyüan beggar chief, whom A-tho had reared, would become a prostitute as soon as she was old enough. "They're poor," said one informant, matter-of-factly. "They need the money." Adopting this strategy was simply a fact of life.

Only one person who had indentured his daughter showed any remorse for what he had done. When A-sek-a talked about his own case, he did so with his voice trembling and his face downcast. He said he had no recourse. He felt badly toward his daughter, and he also felt a great personal loss of face; what he had done was a clear manifestation that he was inadequate as a provider. He felt this more sharply than others who had done the same thing because he was an able-bodied worker who up to that time had been successful at supporting his family. The others were beggars, and in his eyes his actions lowered him to their level.

On the other hand, Be-bin, who indentured three daughters, felt no remorse at all. In his fifties, he was neither young nor in the best of health, but at the same time, he was regarded as somewhat lazy by several informants, and the fact that he did not even beg himself but lived off the earnings of his mate made him a man of little standing (bin-cu) in the community. Unlike A-sek-a, who was left deeply in debt by the dishonesty of another, Be-bin indentured his daughters mainly because it was an easy way to get money. In doing so, however, he achieved some very important results. With the money he received he bought a house away from Liong-hiat. He then left the community and its gambling dens, where he had lost so much money in the past. His mate stopped begging, so he was able to remove the stigma of "beggar's kid" from his two sons. He also put his sons into a position where they could enter "respectable" society; the elder, who had completed junior middle school, got a job with one of the television networks and was learning to act, and the younger was enrolled in primary school. The cost to his daughters was great, although such sacrifices are not uncommon among the daughters of the poor (see M. Wolf 1972:205–14), but he fulfilled his obligation to his sons and probably assured himself of their filiality and support in his old age.

Some of the beggars tried conventional work as a means to escape beggary, and a few succeeded. Sia-pue drove a trishaw for a number of years, and after leaving Liong-hiat he relied on this for his livelihood. E-a-cai and his daughter began to operate a small store selling snacks, sweets, cold drinks, and cigarettes in Liong-hiat. After moving away, Be-sin set up a pachinko parlor, but the business failed because, according to him, it was in a bad location. "I was near a school," he said, "and a lot of youngsters passed by and played my machines. But they had only a few dollars each in pocket money, not enough to make my business profitable." He still had his shophouse, however, and he lived in the rear with his family while renting out the shop itself to a man who repaired and sold watches. A-iu: at one time bought a pushcart and sold noodles, but he soon gave it up and went back to gambling. A-tan had a similar experience, attempting to make a living selling fruit, but he gave it up after a few months, finding it too demanding. He still talked about starting up a business of one kind or another; in fact it was rumored that he had bought a storefront and was going to start an "old-man's teahouse."[1] But neighbors were convinced that he never would; they said he did well enough at gambling and other activities that he lacked the ambition and drive necessary to try another business venture.

There were some striking differences in the strategies adopted by those in the second generation. Few, if any, had resorted to begging in any form, and few wished to; and most had an equally strong abhorrence of gambling. Some might find prostitution acceptable, as O-niau had, and it is impossible to predict whether those indentured by their parents would continue after their contracts expired. One of them, A-sek-a's daughter, had finished her term and returned home. She was working in a factory, and to look at her—the way she dressed and carried herself and her very sparing use of make-up—one would never have suspected that she had spent three years in a brothel. Indeed, she looked the same as other female factory workers her age. Those still under contract will have to make a decision to quit or continue when their terms expire, and when each does, she will have to consider some powerful pressures to remain a prostitute. First, her parents might want her to stay in the brothel. Legally, the decision is hers, but a filial daughter is expected to be obedient to her parents' wishes. Second, she must make a decision regarding her own future. Given her level of education, her only alternatives are factory work or begging. But the pay would be lower and the working conditions more arduous as a factory worker than as a prostitute, so although it would still be possible for her to help her family, it would be at a greatly decreased level. Moreover, the job would be a dead-end one. She would have very little possibility of advancement, and the only thing she would have to look forward to would be marriage. Begging would be worse yet. She would get less money than as a prostitute, though more than as a factory worker, but she would suffer a greater loss of status. A prostitute does not have to shame herself in public. For a beggar, the only downward step is to fail to survive. Prostitution would be a step up. As Cieng-a put it, "At least as a prostitute you have money. And if you do, no one can look down on you." Thus, for those indentured daughters from Liong-hiat, a career as a prostitute was not such an unattractive alternative, particularly if one had already spent three years in it.

Most of the second-generation females worked in factories. The work was routine and lowly paid, but given their level of education and training, it was one of the very few options open to them. They were able to earn pocket money for themselves and also to make a contribution to their families, but that was about all. They would have little opportunity for advancement because these jobs were not meant as careers but merely as something to do until they married.

Other jobs Liong-hiat females had done were hawking and working as a department store clerk. Only Cieng-a worked at the latter, she alone among the beggars' daughters in her age group having sufficient education to do so, but she gave it up soon after she started. Not only was the pay less than that of a factory worker, but the hours were half again as long, so she had little incentive to stay. After leaving, she held a few factory jobs but was too ambitious to continue for long in that line of work, so she began to work as a hawker. She put in long hours but earned much more than she could have from any other work for which she was qualified. For a long time she hoped to open her own shop, but she admitted that there was little chance that she would ever be able to get sufficient capital to pay her lease, buy her wares, and tide herself over while she was getting started. So she continued to operate as an illegal hawker in a partnership with her husband. A-tho's daughters also hawked, selling flowers on the street in Hsimenting, the entertainment sector of Taipei, but they did so only part-time, to supplement the family income.

One other type of work available to females in Liong-hiat was the putting-out system, assembling or finishing products in one's home on a piecework basis. This work was usually done only by women from poor families who, for reasons of poor health or the need to look after small children, could not leave the house to do other things. The rates of remuneration for such work were scandalously low, but it did provide poor, usually unskilled and poorly educated women with a way marginally to increase a meager family income.

Moreover, it was convenient; one could work at it as much or as little as one pleased and whenever one had spare time.

When the TCS began working in Liong-hiat, its social workers tried to get some of the women there to take up such work, but none would. For such a small return on their time, they preferred to beg, gamble, or even do nothing. In 1977, however, after she had stopped begging, A-tho, assisted by her daughter-in-law, worked at cutting the long yarn ends off factory-made sweaters. For this they were paid NT$0.60 per piece. It took them about two minutes to complete one sweater, but because of the irregularity of both the amount of time she was able to spend and the supply of work from the factory, A-tho was unable to estimate her earnings over a given period. It was not much, however.

Second-generation males had more options open to them, but they also faced more uncertain futures. It was possible for a male to do the same sort of factory work that women did, but few were willing to do it because it paid poorly and there was no future in it. Hiong-a's son worked in a factory at nights for several weeks but quit because he was a student at the time, and his long hours at work interfered with his studies. Chieng-cui also worked in a factory for a time before he got married, but he quit because he could not earn enough to support a wife.

Some young men had also worked as unskilled laborers, usually on construction sites, carrying bricks and mortar to the masons, or in small workshops where they manufactured simple products such as packing crates. The rate of pay for unskilled construction laborers was quite good, particularly for those who worked on a casual basis, but there were also some disadvantages to it. It was a dead-end job with virtually no chance for advancement. Moreover there was no security. Workers went from day to day or job to job. Should they become ill or have an accident, there was no coverage or insurance of any kind to cushion their total loss of income. Finally, the work was extremely arduous. Very few young people, those under thirty-five, took up such work. Only one in Liong-hiat, Lau-sam, did it on a permanent basis.

Unskilled factory work was less taxing physically, but the rate of pay was also somewhat lower. Moreover, in one sense, there was an even greater element of insecurity in it. When an order was filled, there was no guarantee that there would be further work or even that the factory, sometimes simply a room in someone's home, would remain in business. Touq-pi:-a came home one day with the news that the shop where he had been working was folding and that his job would end the next day. But he was luckier than some, who had gone to work in the morning to discover that the "factory," as well as the man who hired them and still owed them several days' wages, had disappeared.

Another strategy, used by both sexes and generations, was to open up a small business. Nine in the first generation had gotten at least to the planning stage of operating a shop, stall, or pushcart at some time in their lives, and it was clear that they saw this strategy as the one with the greatest potential to earn them a living. Given the fact that most had low levels of literacy and skills, they were probably correct. Moreover, the perceived life-style of a small businessman also appealed to many; although the business might operate for many hours each day, the work was not taxing, and it could be shared among several members of a family. Even when one was working, between customers he could chat, rest, or play a game of chess.

However, for various reasons, this strategy was rarely carried out successfully. Some, such as Be-bin and A-iu:, failed to get their businesses going, but many others did not even get past the planning stage. A-tan found gambling too easy a way to earn a living to give it up for business. Chai-thau and A-ieng, who had plans to open a noodle shop together, quarreled, and their plans ended there. Chieng-cui and his wife had thought of operating a fruit stall after he returned from the navy, something he had done for a while before his military service, but his father's unsuccessful attempt to establish a gambling den and subsequent bankruptcy dried up any collateral or funds that might have been available. Cieng-a's plans, too, were curtailed by a lack of capital. Niau-chi-hi: had thought of several business schemes. At one time he was going to set up a shop and manufacture packing crates, but he never did. Early in 1978 he came home one day with three purebred pups, a male and two females, which he and Touq-pi:-a had bought and were planning to breed. Although neither had much education, they seemed to have some knowledge of what they were doing, but I left the field before I could see the result of that venture.

Only two businesses aside from Cieng-a's hawking could be judged a success. Cui-a's motorcycle repair shop did quite well for several years until he became involved with a motorcycle theft ring and the police closed him down for dealing in stolen parts. His father, E-a-cai, was more successful, however, and his small snacks, drinks, and cigarettes shop was doing a respectable business.

Some second-generation males in Liong-hiat had tried driving a taxi to make a living. Touq-pi:-a did so off and on, and both Chieng-cui and his older brother were doing so in 1978. Taxi owners can make a comfortable living in Taipei. An owner will either drive his own cab every day, working ten to twelve hours daily with some rest periods during slack hours, or he will work a twenty-four hour shift every second day and rent the cab to another driver for 40 percent of the gross or a flat fee (NT$500 in December 1977) on his day off. Depending on how hard he wants to work, an owner-driver can clear NT$8,000–12,000 per month, perhaps even more. Even one who rents a cab every other day, if he gets steady work, can make NT$500–600 per day, about NT$8,000 per month (according to Chieng-cui, the minimum he needed to support his family of three adults and two children). The problem was getting steady work with a reliable cab. "Being able to drive is the most common skill in Taiwan," Chieng-cui said. "Choose any ten people, and eight of them will have a driver's licence.[2] There are many people who want to drive a taxi, especially at this time of the year with the New Year approaching. If you have a connection with someone who owns a taxi or works for a taxi company, you have a good chance. I don't." He was able to rent cabs off and on, but he sometimes got one that was not in good working order, and since he rented for a flat fee, on those occasions he ended up not even making his costs.

The solution was to buy his own cab, but that was not easy. The cost of a new auto was in the neighborhood of NT$160,000. Most who buy arrange finance and pay off the loan over three years. But to do this, one needs references and a guarantor, something Chieng-cui felt, with his family background and in his circumstances, he would be unable to get. A more achievable hope was to buy a used car, probably for around NT$40,000 with interest of NT$1,600 per month. He figured that by cutting household expenses to the bare minimum and driving every day he would be able to repay the loan in six months. But he needed half the principal to get a loan for the other half, a sum he did not have and could not see the possibility of borrowing. "I have a poor person's outlook (*san-ciaq lang e sim*)," he said. "I just can't ask people for money." Moreover, because his father had defaulted on his rotating credit association payments and had had to sell his house to pay his debts, Chieng-cui felt he would be unable to organize a rotating credit association himself. His elder brother was planning to buy a taxi at that time, but he was in a much better position to do so. He had been living and working away from home for several years and had contacts and references who could help him get a loan. Moreover, being single, he did not have the financial burden of providing for a family that Chieng-cui had.

Another problem Chieng-cui faced was how to keep a second-hand car in good running order. According to him, one could get by with a used taxi if he were able to do his own minor repairs, but since he knew nothing about auto mechanics he feared he would be unable to make a profit. His situation seemed hopeless. He wanted desperately to get his family out of Liong-hiat and what it represented, but he had no foreseeable way to do so. Still, he kept trying, renting a cab whenever he could and hoping that he might happen onto the right opportunity, one that would allow him to make a steady income and put his family into better circumstances.

A more promising strategy was to receive technical training and learn a skill, a path taken by six second-generation males. Three were in ironworking (*t'ieh-kung*), one had learned motorcycle repair, another had done a medical technology course in a vocational high school, learning to give physical examinations, and one was working days and doing a commercial course at night, also at a technical high school.

Of the first four, all of whom had learned or were learning their trades by serving apprenticeships, one was still undergoing training, one was in the military, and another was about to be inducted; only one, Ang-a, A-tho's eldest son, was working at his trade. His income, with bonuses, was adequate and had kept pace with rises in the cost of living. Moreover, he had a good relationship with his boss, and since he was a senior worker, his job was as secure as the shop in which he worked. But in 1977 he felt some anxiety. The shop was a small operation, employing half a dozen or so workers, depending on how many orders it had. Its business was in taking orders too small to be profitable to larger, better-equipped, more up-to-date factories. Ang-a felt his place of employment was secure as long as Taiwan's economy was healthy, but an economic downturn such as the one in 1974 would imperil its survival. In that event, he was not sure what would happen to him. The other two qualified ironworkers, neither of whom had begun to practice his trade in 1978, saw their futures in a similar fashion. As long as Taiwan's economy remained healthy and they were not replaced by technological advances, they had no worries, but changed economic circumstances could put their careers at risk. Under 1978 conditions, however, they regarded their futures as relatively good.

Cui-a's future as a motorcycle repairman was more open to question. With the growing number of motorcycles in Taiwan, there was no dearth of work for one with his skill. Moreover, his trade was less likely than that of the traditional ironworker to be made obsolete by a machine. But his past brush with the law and its implications on his outlook on life were a cloud hanging over his head. In 1978 he was married and had an infant son, and he was about to be inducted into the armed forces. Both of these, informants felt, would be positive influences on him. They saw marriage as having a settling effect on young men, something that brought home to them the responsibilities of adulthood and the seriousness of life. And although the military was a place where "good boys turned bad" (they picked up habits such as smoking and drinking that they had not practiced before), the discipline it provided often "made bad boys turn good."

The other two young men with skills training regarded their futures as bright. Hiong-a's son had one more hurdle to clear to be certified as a medical technologist, a government examination that, according to him, fewer than half passed. He said he would be aided by the fact that he was serving in the army and practicing his skill, getting on-the-job training, but even if he failed, he still had his high school certificate, and that should qualify him for other types of job, particularly clerical ones. A-tho's third son was better off as well, guaranteed a job with the company for which he worked after he finished his military service. But he planned to look for something better.

The most important factor determining the opportunities for mobility or lack thereof among the second generation was their level of education. Most young people in Taiwan born before 1955, especially those in urban areas, had a minimum of six years of education, and those born afterward had at least nine. These levels of formal education were almost minimum requirements for jobs, and many young persons, especially males, went on for some further skill training, either in school or through an apprenticeship.

Most of the beggars and their children shared the views generally held in Taiwan that education was important in getting ahead and that those who were well educated were worthy of respect. Indeed, the most admired young people in Liong-hiat were those with the most education. Some parents urged their children to study hard so that they would be able to get good jobs. One father hoped that his son, then two years old, would eventually get into medical school, something only the brightest and most diligent of Taiwan's high school graduates could hope to achieve. On a less ambitious level, but nonetheless displaying a consciousness of mobility, was a remark a twelve-year-old girl made to a friend, a few years younger, "You must go beyond junior high school [grade nine]. You must go to high school. Then you will be able to get a job writing characters for someone." By "writing characters" she meant working as a clerk in an office. Despite its low rate of pay, such a job carried more prestige than did factory work, which was manual labor. For a girl of her background, to hold such a job would be a considerable step upward.

Such feelings, sentiments, and hopes were often betrayed by actual performance, however, Table 3 shows the educational attainment by age group of the Beggars' children as of 1978.

In general, the younger a child, the more likely he or she was to go to school, but the table shows that for the older age group, the one about which one can speak meaningfully regarding mobility, a large number were either uneducated or inadequately educated. Only four, two of whom were still in school in 1978, went beyond the pre-1967 compulsory education level of six years.

There are a number of reasons for the gap between ideals and hopes for the children, on one hand, and the children's levels of achievement on the other. First, some parents had difficulty motivating their offspring. Some tried; they urged, encouraged, cajoled, and even ordered their children to study and do homework, but often to no avail. The children simply ignored them and went on playing or watching television. Perhaps it was because the parents, themselves at best poorly educated, lacked the necessary authority in the eyes of their children to make such demands. Perhaps it was because of the home and community atmosphere, in which there was little to reinforce positively the importance of education to a school-age child. Some young people said that, despite the encouragement of their parents and older siblings, they were simply not interested in school at the time they quit. Touq-pi:a, for example, said that his father, Tiek-kou, and his sister, Cieng-a, both encouraged him to continue on to middle school. "My father told me I could go as far as I wanted to. He would make sure the money was there. But I was foolish. I was not interested in studying, so I left school." His regrets seemed sincere. He was lavish in his praise of the two young males who had

TABLE 3
Education of Beggars' Children, 1978

Age Group	In Primary School	Not in Primary School	Not Educated	Less Than 6 Years	6 Years	More Than 6 Years
6–12	9	1	NA	NA	NA	NA
Over 12	NA	NA	13	4	14	4

NA = not applicable.

gone on in school, and he had gone some distance in educating himself. He read quite widely at a popular magazine level and was conversant on a number of subjects. But in terms of job qualifications, he still had only a sixth-grade level of education and had learned no work skill.

Another possible reason for the gap between stated goals and actual achievement was a contradiction in the signals given by parents. Some young people said that their parents did encourage them to study hard and to get as much education as they could, but they also complained frequently about how poor the family was, how much they needed more money, and even how expensive it was to buy books, supplies, and school uniforms. This message was perceived by the children as pressure for them to leave school and go to work as early as possible. Two of Sia-pue's children gave this reason for quitting school, as did A-tho's eldest daughter.

Some females suffered in their education because their parents did not believe it was necessary for girls to go to school. A-tong's elder daughter had no schooling for this reason, and his younger one was ten before one of Tiek-kou's sworn brothers convinced him that she had no future without some education. Sia-pue allowed his natural daughter to go to primary school, but he kept his adopted daughter home to take his mate out to beg. Hiong-a's daughter finished primary school and wanted very much to go on, as had her elder brother, but her father made her stay home, again to take her mother out to beg. However, not all parents discriminated against their daughters in this way. In some families neither sons nor daughters went to school, and in others, daughters went as far as or farther than their brothers did. But if families did discriminate, it was invariably against daughters.

Another reason some gave for quitting school was that their schoolmates learned they were children of beggars and teased them for it. Siong-a left in grade four. His teacher made it a practice to call on the families of her pupils, and after such a visit, perhaps out of naïve idealism, she told the class that Siong-a's parents were beggars and that he should be respected for trying to improve himself. The result was just the opposite. Siong-a's schoolmates teased and ridiculed him as a "beggar's kid," and he decided that education was not worth the price he had to pay for it. Moreover, at that time he felt little support in his home environment to stay in school. Cieng-a quit school in grade seven for the same reasons. She could not stand the teasing of her classmates. Moreover, her mother's cancer had just been diagnosed, and she was pressuring Cieng-a to go to work as a dance hall hostess (*bu-lu*) to earn money for the family. She did not accede to her mother's wishes, but she did quit school and go to work as a department store clerk.

Some Liong-hiat youth did go farther in school, however, and some parents changed their attitudes toward education. During the initial field research period in Liong-hiat, A-sek-a cared only that his children finish grade six. To him that was all the education they needed, and his two older children did quit after primary school. But in 1977 his third child, a daughter, was in grade eight, and he had every intention that the younger two, another daughter and a son, would also go on, at least through junior middle school. Lau Lim, one of the Hokciu family heads, had a similar change of mind. In 1974 he said his younger children would stop at grade six, just as their older siblings had. He complained that his family was poor and needed the money his children could earn. He also objected to the fact that to transfer from a primary to a junior middle school meant a large (for him) outlay of cash for new uniforms, books, and supplies. But in 1977, one son was in grade seven, and he intended that his two younger children should also go to junior middle school. What brought about these changes of mind was an increased understanding that the world was changing, that higher levels of education were required to get jobs, and that for those with more schooling and training, there were real possibilities to improve their economic and social circumstances.

In addition to their insufficiency of training and education, the Beggars' children faced a number of other impediments to upward mobility. One was a lack of patience with the progress they were making or a lack of satisfaction with the types of jobs they could get with their levels of qualifications and the incomes such jobs would bring. They were well aware of the disparity in income received for effort and time expended between begging, gambling, and prostitution, on one hand, and conventional work on the other, and this heightened their impatience and dissatisfaction. In one conversation, a young informant respectfully commented that Mr. Kou, one of the Neighbors, who eked out a living hawking fruit in the summer and cooked sausages in the winter, had pride because he refused to beg for a living. "Yes," replied another, "but look how poorly he feeds his family."

Chieng-cui began an apprenticeship after leaving school, but gave it up before finishing. He explained: "I wasn't making much money as an apprentice, and I knew I would make more working. Besides, those who finished their training and went to work didn't make very much, and I didn't want to be working for two thousand a month for the rest of my life. If only I had kept at it. Wages have increased since then, and I would have been doing fairly well now. But I didn't."

Another impediment was discouragement. Siong-a, Chieng-cui's younger brother, had been moderately ambitious and willing to work throughout most of his teenage years, but early in 1973, when he was eighteen, he lost the middle and index fingers of his right hand in an industrial accident. After that, he entered into an extended period of inactivity, perhaps working a few days a month, but he spent most of his time hanging around home or going out with friends. His father, Sia-bue, defended him in front of outsiders; he once demonstrated how difficult it was to wield a hammer without using the two fingers his son was missing. But he was not at all happy with his son, and the two often quarreled when Siong-a asked for pocket money. This pattern continued throughout the initial fieldwork period. But in 1978 the son had a job in Taichung working for a company that made cassette tapes. He had been working there for some time, and he returned to Liong-hiat only on holidays.

Another problem some young people had was a result of ambition combined with impatience, an inclination that induced some to take risks. The willingness of Chieng-cui and his brother to chance what for them were substantial sums of money on what would quite probably be unreliable taxicabs has already been recounted. Others took risks with the law. The gamblers did this, of course, but so did Cui-a when he joined up with the motorcycle theft ring. Prior to that time his repair shop was providing him with a fair living, but according to one of his age mates, "he thought he could get rich quickly." As a result, he lost his business completely. Since his shop was a squatter structure, it existed at the sufferance of the police. After he was caught, they simply tore it down. All Cui-a salvaged was the wood from the walls, which later made up the walls of his father's shop, but at least he did not go to jail.

In the eyes of the second generation, the most serious impediment to mobility was gambling, and they had seen the damage it did through the experiences of their parents. Gamblers sometimes lost the family food money. They lost so much that they were frequently in debt. They borrowed money to gamble, then they bid it out of a rotating credit association on very unfavorable terms, sometimes as low as NT$48 on the hundred, to repay the loan. They pawned objects and then lost them or paid a high rate of interest until they could redeem them. Gambling impoverished them, so they had to beg to get by. It caused quarrels between spouses, and in one case it even brought about the breakup of a union because the woman sold herself to repay gambling debts. Men stayed away from work in order to gamble, and women became so rapt in their games that they neglected cooking, housework, and children. Fights took place in gambling dens in which people were sometimes seriously injured. The young people suffered not only because they had been deprived of the material goods their parents should have been able to provide and the attention they should have been able to give, but also because they had to take their parents out to beg and in some cases be indentured as prostitutes in order to improve the family income, depleted by the gambling losses of the parents.

The list of evils they attributed to gambling was long, but its worst aspect was its tendency to addict. As Chieng-cui put it, "one gets up in the morning and goes to work. He makes some money, and that night he gambles and wins a day's wages. The next day he decides not to go to work. Why should he? He got money much more easily by gambling. That day, he gambles again, but this time he loses three days' wages. The next morning he wakes up to go to work, but he realizes that by working hard all day, he will recoup only one-third of what he owes. Why bother? He rolls over and goes back to sleep." Although he had not intended it, what he described was a very accurate account of what happened to Ho-a, A-tho's second son. Fortunately, after several years of gambling and running with petty gangsters, he found the resolve to extricate himself from that style of life.

But many of those in the community feared that they would one day lose their resolve not to gamble. They saw what happened to A-sek-a. When he and his wife first came to Liong-hiat, they were both hardworking, "clean-living" people. As time passed, first he, then his wife, began to gamble, and soon they found themselves gambling often and suffering heavy losses. According to his neighbors, had it not been for his gambling losses, he would not have had to indenture his daughter when one of the members defaulted on his rotating credit association. To many young people in Liong-hiat, gambling cost their family the opportunity to move out and establish a life in a better community, and they feared that it would cost them the same.

Many felt that their only hope was to leave, to get themselves and their families away from the destructive influences of the community. This feeling was widespread among them and was reinforced by the example of Be-bin. He was one of the worst of the gamblers, and although his mate brought in a lot of money, he spent any extra they had on gambling. But he was always very strict with his children, and he punished them severely for playing any game that resembled gambling, even billiards. When the opportunity came, he indentured his daughters, bought a house outside of Liong-hiat, and moved away, breaking his gambling habit in the process.

1980–1981

Although I made only a few visits to the Liong-hiat community in this period, I was able to talk to several informants and to learn about changes in their lives as well as in the lives of others and changes in the community as a whole. Moreover, I was able to see the further development of trends already apparent in 1977–78. Gambling, which had declined in importance as a generator of income in the earlier follow-up, had disappeared completely except as an occasional recreational activity by 1980. Begging, too, had declined, although there were a few who still begged. The trend to give young people an education and to let them go farther in school also continued, as did the seeking and finding of means other than begging to earn a living by those in both the younger and the older generations. More deaths and moves further altered the character of the community so that, although there were still a few living there who begged, it could no longer be called a beggar community (*khit-ciaq-liau*). It became like much of the surrounding neighborhood, a squatter settlement, an area of illegal and usually substandard housing inhabited by people tending to be less educated, less skilled, less well off, and less integrated into the urban complex of greater Taipei than those in better neighborhoods.

With regard to individuals, a number experienced an improvement in their situation over the three years between follow-ups. Perhaps the most dramatic example was Ang-a, A-tho's eldest son. Until 1979 he worked in a machine shop as an employee. Then, through a series of circumstances, he quit his job and formed a partnership. That lasted about a year, and then he went into business for himself, purchasing a label-making machine similar to the one he had operated before and renting a small shop to house it. Meanwhile, getting the deposit through loan from his sisters-in-law (they had lived with him for many years after migrating to Taipei), he and his wife bought a flat of their own. His wife was working in a small garment factory to help with the monthly payments. His youngest sister lives with him and is going to school. His mother has left

Liong-hiat and is living with relatives in the Taipei area, and his stepfather has been arrested again for morphine use and is in prison. His eldest sister is still working as a prostitute, but his "adopted" sister, Iok-lan, escaped that fate and is now married. His other sister is working in an electronics factory, and she says she enjoys her job. She is the only one left in Liong-hiat. His first younger brother works in Kaohsiung, and his second younger brother is in the military. Their situations will be discussed later.

A-tan's family situation also improved. Early in 1980, A-tan got a job as a cook in a factory canteen. Responsible for purchasing as well as preparing the food, he works from early morning through the lunch period, takes a rest until mid afternoon, and then prepares the evening meal. For this he receives a slightly above-average salary for semi-skilled work (NT$11,000 per month in 1980) and is able to take food home for his family. His wife has also gone to work, helping her sister, Cieng-a, from time to time. Moreover, both have given up gambling; A-tan no longer runs a mahjong game in his home, and his wife no longer joins card or dice games. Further, he has moved from his own home to a smaller place. He pays rent for his present living quarters but collects rent for his old house, coming out ahead by about one thousand New Taiwan dollars per month in the process.

These changes in his occupational and financial situation have had a marked effect on his physical and mental state. When we talked in 1980, he told me over and over how much better he felt about himself, something already obvious just from observing him. Whereas in the past he had been glum and withdrawn, he was now exhuberant, friendly, and talkative. Previously he had been very guarded about what he said, but on this visit, he was full of information. He wanted to tell me that he—and most others in the area—did not gamble anymore and that he was now working for a living. Before, he had been ashamed of himself and his life, but now, it seemed, he had sufficient "face" to entertain me in his home. He even looked better physically. He still suffered from stomach ulcers from time to time, but otherwise he both appeared and acted as one in high spirits and robust health.

Several members of Tiek-kou's family are also better off. Cieng-a and her husband have done well enough selling apples to buy their own flat and to afford to let her stay home with their three children. Touq-pi:-a, since leaving the military, has found work as a guitarist and singer and now makes his living performing in night clubs. His younger sister works in the same factory as Ang-a's sister. Tiek-kou still makes his living from funerals, either by receiving payment for keeping beggars away or by acting as a road guide, but like A-tan, he has given up gambling completely.

Several other individuals have also done fairly well. O-niau is no longer a call girl but is married to a Japanese and living in Japan with him and her son. They are well enough off for her to afford visits to Taiwan once or twice a year to see her friends and family. A-chun is quite ill with diabetes, but she manages to get enough money from her sons and various welfare agencies that she no longer needs to beg at all. Moreover, she has allowed her foster daughter to finish junior middle school—quite a sacrifice, given A-chun's age, state of health, and financial condition. Bok-cong's son has finished junior middle school and is now doing an apprenticeship, and Hiong-a's eldest son is working in a hospital, doing his last level of on-the-job training before receiving his professional licence.

A number of families and individuals have more or less maintained their living patterns. Lau-sam is still a casual cement worker. Although an arduous job, it is quite rewarding financially, and his earnings, NT$15,000–20,000 per month, put his family above the per capita average income for Taipei. His brother, Lau-liong, could be doing even better were it not for his drinking, but this has given him a reputation as unreliable and has correspondingly decreased his potential income. E-a-cai has expanded both the size of his shop and his range of goods, and he appears to be better off than before. A-sek-a is also prospering as a carpenter, sometimes going as far away as Kaohsiung on a job. He has improved both the structure and the furnishings of his home. He now has, among other things, a telephone,[3] a two-door refrigerator-freezer, and a large display case in which he keeps several bottles of imported scotch, cognac, and sake that he has bought or received from friends as gifts.

Other families and individuals have not fared so well. Tua-kho-e has died, as has Sia-pue. Sia-pue's eldest son has returned to Liong-hiat and lives with his mother and sister. His sister still works in a factory, and he drives a cab. But he works irregularly, taking time off to play cards when he has money to spare. Sia-pue's two other sons, Chieng-cui and Siong-a, have also taken to gambling, but as a profession rather than a pastime. Both work with organized gambling dens as bouncers and as participants in what are said to be crooked card games. As both were doing or trying to do legitimate work in 1978, this is a retrograde step, especially for Chieng-cui, who had spoken of his intense disapproval of and dislike for gambling. But he had already attempted to make his living that way on one occasion, when his father had tried unsuccessfully to establish a gaming den. After that he tried driving a taxi, but, as I have recounted, he could not afford to buy his own cab. He tried to borrow money, at least enough for a deposit, from his parents-in-law, but they refused him because he still owed them money from a previous loan. His determination to escape the poverty-stricken and stigmatized existence he had experienced as a child finally overcame any scruples he had about gambling, the only way to make a sufficient living, short of more serious crime, that he could see open to someone such as himself, one whose levels of education and occupational training were inadequate. In Siong-a's case, he simply lost interest in his job making cassette tapes and returned to Taipei. According to neighbors, he hung about doing nothing for several months before following his brother's lead and taking up professional gambling.

The other family that has fared badly, in one sense at least, is Niau-chi-hi:'s. What began as a stroke of good fortune turned out to be a disaster, at least for his wife, Niau-bu, and his children. Although he grew up in the Beggar community and both his parents begged, his kin group owned some property, previously marginal farm land, in their native village near Taichung. After an uncle died, control of the property passed to Niau-chi-hi: and his cousins. In 1980 they sold some of the land, taking advantage of the infrastructural and industrial development underway in that area, and received a substantial sum of money. Niau-bu urged her husband to use his share, several hundred thousand New Taiwan dollars, to establish a business of some sort. But he would not listen to her. Instead he began to frequent teahouses and dance halls. Soon afterward he abandoned his wife and family and took up with a dance hall hostess. Too old even to contemplate returning to a teahouse herself, Niau-bu was forced, for the first time in her life, to work for a living. She had a job washing dishes but quit because she found the work too hard. However, according to her brother-in-law, A-tan, she would soon have to find another job in order to support herself and her children.

With regard to begging, Gong-a, Bok-cong and his mate A-su, and Pai-kha-e are the only regular beggars still left. A-m still begs but only rarely. For the most part she lives on handouts from her neighbors. Her adopted son, Chai-thau, is still of no use to her. If anything, he drinks more frequently now than before. Of the others who beg, two will likely continue to do so until they die. Neither Pai-kha-e nor Gong-a, both childless and over fifty, have any kinsmen who can or will support them. Habit and physical condition will probably ensure that they spend the rest of their days begging.

It is possible, however, that the other two, Bok-cong and A-su, will be able to stop someday. Their son is now doing an apprenticeship and will soon have a recognized skill. He can then begin to work, but he will receive fairly low pay until he finishes his military obligation, at about twenty-three years of age, and can settle into a long-term job. At that time he will be able to support his parents. Whether they stop begging then will depend on whether they prefer to beg or to live with their son at a lower level of living but devoid of the stigma of begging.

In addition, one former member of the community, Kua:-chui, also continues to beg. He left Liong-hiat with his children and went south after his wife died in 1974. He still comes up for visits, however, so people there know what he is doing. According to A-tan and Ang-a, he takes his children out to rural festivals and has them beg. On one visit to Liong-hiat, someone wrote a "letter of sympathy" (*seng-sim-su*) for him, a document explaining his supposed plight and reason for begging and asking readers to contribute generously to his support. He was later arrested and the letter was confiscated by the police, but he had anticipated such an event and had several photocopies made of the letter for future use. A-tan once asked him why, since he had a taxi licence and was able-bodied, he did not earn a living driving a cab. Kua:-chui simply asked why he should; he made a comfortable living the way things were and with much less effort.

Some members and former members of the community continue to live off prostitution. Although O-niau has now married and A-sek-a's daughter works in a factory, the other beggars' daughters have chosen or consented to remain prostitutes. Both A-tho's and Hiong-a's daughters are now in the free system, but Be-bin has kept his daughters in the unfree system, bound to the teahouse, where he can retain better access to their earnings.

There are a few others about whom little can be said, either because no one knew much about them or because they are not in an even potentially stable situation. Cap-sa:-hou has moved away, and no one seemed to know anything about her or her younger children. Cui-a, E-a-cai's son, had just finished his military obligation and had not yet found a job or a line of work. A-tai, A-tho's youngest son, was still in the military. He has both technical school training and work experience as a customs agent, but there is no future in that as an occupation, so he will look for another job when he is mustered out. Given his background and personality and the influence his brother, Ang-a, has over him, the chances are high that he will do some sort of legitimate work.

The case of his brother, Ho-a, is somewhat less certain. Although he seems to have reformed himself from his period as a gambler and idler, like some others in Liong-hiat he is tempted by get-rich-quick schemes and is thus less stable than his brothers are. He has worked at several jobs since leaving the military, each one supposed to earn him a lot of money in the short term. But he tired of each quickly or found what he thought would be a better line of work, so he has not stayed with anything very long. He even drove a cab for a while, one he purchased by means of a rotating credit association. But, as with his other ventures, he soon moved on to something else, and he took a substantial loss when he sold his cab. In 1981 he was working with his brothers-in-law in Kaohsiung as a plumber-electrician (*shui-tien kung*), a potentially stable and well-remunerated trade if he will stick with it. But given his past, this must be open to question.

What, then, can be concluded about mobility among the Beggars? Of the older generation, there were twenty-four in 1974 who willingly begged for at least a part of their income. Of these, by 1981, twelve—one-half—had stopped. Four did so by indenturing their daughters into prostitution, but the rest have either found other ways to support themselves or retired after their children took jobs and were able to support them. Of the remaining twelve who begged in 1974, three have left the community and their situations are unknown, three died as beggars, and the others still beg for a living.

The picture for the younger generation is much brighter. With the possible exception of Kua:-chui's children, who beg under his guidance and direction, mobility among the beggars' children is total. Whatever else some may do, none begs. Moreover, there is virtually no possibility that any ever will. The older ones have found other ways to make a living, and the younger ones are sufficiently well educated and skilled to be able to find jobs. In Ang-a's opinion, "none of the children will become beggars themselves. They had to beg when they were young, but they won't beg as adults. They can find other ways to earn a living, and they have had more contact with the outside world. They would never allow themselves to become beggars!"

This degree of mobility is much greater than one could have expected as a result of comments made on mobility among beggars by other authors. Of those cited throughout the text who wrote on Chinese beggars, four discussed mobility. Shih Ch'ien, whose actual contact with beggars is most extensive, is very pessimistic. In his book he emphasizes the reasons why those who begin to beg for a living continue to do so. These include age; lack of dependents or kin on whom one can rely for support; state of health or physical condition; impoverishment and loss of one's means of livelihood; having beggar parents; becoming inured to the taunts, derision, and condescension suffered while begging; and finding begging a sufficiently free and materially rewarding way of life that one loses the motivation to change (1925:28–53). He refers to the perceived comfort of the beggar life-style by repeating a saying often quoted by informants, "After three days as a beggar, one is unwilling even to become emperor" (*co sa:-zit khit-ciaq, m-khi co hong-te*). Wang reflects a similar degree of pessimism, reporting that although some beggars are diligent, hardworking, and even frugal, "eight or nine out of ten are satisfied to have enough, to be lazy and sleep, going out [to beg] only when they run out of money" (1974:152). Chan, whose Penang study included Indian and Malay as well as Chinese beggars, feels the same: "They [the beggars] have accepted their situation as such, and it does not occur to them at all to have any future plans" (1973:15). Only Liu Hsü holds out any hope, saying that beggars might be able to do some sort of legitimate work as entertainers. But he also fears that the inundation of Peking by farmers who became impoverished because of rural unrest and natural disasters and who then turned to begging might signal the continued existence of street beggars (1936:176–80).

What may account for the discrepancy between my findings and their observations? One possibility is that the latter were merely comments, not research results, and that they do not present an accurate picture. Only Shih Ch'ien and Chan actually did any sort of field research involving systematic, firsthand contact with beggars, and none of the four writers just mentioned gives any evidence of having any longitudinal data. Their conclusions, then, are most likely based on synchronic observations, and do not reflect the diachronic perspectives, which, as events in Liong-hiat illustrate, can manifest dramatic changes in the fortunes and activities of individuals. Another possibility is that what other authors said does present an accurate picture but that the Liong-hiat beggars are simply different, having a stronger desire to take advantage of an opportunity to leave begging.

A third possibility is that, regardless of the accuracy of the picture painted by the others, differences in social and economic conditions suppressed expressed desires for and actual achievement of mobility in earlier times and other places, whereas they facilitated it in the 1960s and 1970s in Taiwan. Taiwan's economc development in that period has created an enormous number of new jobs, and while not all of them are ideal in terms of wages and conditions, almost anyone who wants to can find a job and expect continued increases in real income. Expansion of education, communication, and the mass media have also been beneficial in that they have served to integrate the Beggars, previously cut off by their relative poverty and by the stigma attached to their activities, into mainstream society.

Not having access to either the communities studied or the raw data collected by the other authors, I cannot further resolve this discrepancy. But what is more important, the Liong-hiat results in themselves demonstrate that, given the opportunity, people will gladly leave begging to take up more socially acceptable means of making a living.

CHAPTER NINE

Conclusions

THIS BOOK HAS EXAMINED begging in the Chinese sociocultural context. It has explored the legal and social status of beggars, their forms of organization, the tactics and appeals they use in getting alms, and the reasons why people give or refuse to give to them. It has analyzed a specific group of beggars living in the Taipei area in Taiwan and has inquired into the community they formed, including the social relations of people in it, how it was led, and how it gradually dissolved; their kinship relationships and behavior; their material life and how they earned money; and how they and their children achieved upward mobility.

Finally, it has shed light on the effects of poverty and stigma on the lives of a small community of poor people, the effects on their marital and kinship relations, their education, their careers, their economic activities, and their personal and social lives. I will now return to themes mentioned in the Introduction and expand on them.

The Definition and Source of Beggars in China

In some sections of this book, in accordance with usage in much of the literature consulted, the terms *beggar* and *begging* have included a number of activities that are well outside the normal semantic range of those words, activities such as extorting, working, and entertaining, which can be much more accurately labeled. Why should such semantic confusion arise?

The answer is not a difference in the range of meaning of Chinese words translated as "beggar" (*khit-ciaq, ch'i-kai, chiao-hua-tzu*)

188

and the English term. Indeed, several native Chinese with whom I discussed this were quite puzzled that people who are, more precisely, ruffians or robbers were called beggars. Moreover, readers will recall from chapter 2 the various notions of what was meant by the designation *beggar* and how they restricted rather than broadened the use of these terms.

Another explanation is that some writers allowed themselves a good deal of poetic license as to whom they called beggars. While this might have been true of some of the missionary authors and those who wrote on a popular or traveler's report level, there are too many examples of serious, analytical writers who also used the terms in the broad sense. The eminent social historian, Hsiao Kungchuan, refers to local bullies, extorters, secret society members, and bandits as beggars even though the Chinese referent is *kuang-kun*, usually translated as "bare sticks" or "local bullies"[1] (1960:454–59). Bodde and Morris cite two law cases in which persons, after failing to extort money from victims, committed arson against them. Both are referred to as beggars (1971:439; 443), perhaps because, in their attempts at extortion, they "begged" for money. Wu To writes of beggars in present-day Shanghai who use coercive tactics to get money. To distinguish them from "normal" beggars, he uses the term *ch'iang-kai* rather than *ch'i-kai* (1981:43). The last character is the same in each, but in the first term, the initial character means, "to rob, force," and denotes the extortive, coercive nature of the act. While this may not be Wu's own coinage, it is not a common term, nor is it used by any of the other authors consulted, all of whom use the conventional *ch'i-kai*. The broad usage by such scholars demonstrates that the idea of begging can be stretched to include violent means of obtaining alms. Perhaps if the person at some point asks for—"begs"—money or substance, he or she can be referred to as a beggar.

It is plausible that this broad usage is basically correct, not semantically but in terms of social reality. This implies that at least some people who begged also robbed, stole, extorted, worked, entertained, and so on, and that there were people who did a variety of things to earn money.

This supposition can be supported by the acceptance of a hypothesis on the source and origin of beggars, that is, the sorts of people who begged, their reasons for begging, and their socioeconomic origins. I propose the following. There existed in premodern China a large category of persons who were rootless and resourceless, without tangible or steady means of livelihood. This category was probably made up of second and third sons whose fathers had insufficient wealth to get each a wife and insufficient land to divide among all heirs and give them each a viable property; peasants who were already poor but who lost their livelihood completely because of illness or accident; persons who suffered a disaster such as a flood, drought, bandit raid, or civil war; persons who lost their property through gambling; and even scholars who did not get a sufficiently high degree or who otherwise failed to secure a post. In short, they were poor and without the means to support themselves. They had to earn a living by whatever means were available to them: working at odd jobs or perhaps as punters on river or canal boats, entertaining if they had a talent, reading and writing letters and documents for people if they were literate, smuggling salt, stealing, swindling—and begging. Those who were physically unable to do anything else and those who found it easy, personally acceptable, and lucrative probably relied entirely on begging, but most did not do any of these things exclusively. They did whatever the circumstances demanded or allowed. They were a category of people whose income-earning activities were mixed and varied rather than one of persons who relied on only one method throughout their lives. Thus someone who begged one day might sing for his supper the next and steal on the third.

Actually there was a sort of homeless lumpen proletariat group in premodern China, referred to as *p'ao-chiang-hu-te* (those who roam the rivers and lakes) or *yu-min* (wandering people). Little is known about them, but they were rootless and resourceless, and they lived by their wits. It is not improbable that they also lived a jack-of-all-trades existence such as the one just described. I have no evidence for this, but it is quite plausible. But simply the existence of this group lends support to my hypothesis, and that hypothesis, if correct, would explain the broad usage of *beggar*.

To test its validity, we can compare the evidence for it and its explanatory power with those of other ideas and hypotheses on the source and origin of beggars in China. Three other explanations have been offered in conversations with informants and in the literature on Chinese beggars. The first is fate. Though this may seem somewhat whimsical, it is the most popular. Folklore and legends are replete with examples of those with a "broken physiognomy" (*phua-siong*)[2] or a "beggar's destiny" (*khit-ciaq-mia:*) who became beggars (Schak 1979:123–26), and there are also many popular sayings that convey a fatalistic attitude toward the unpredictability of life. This explanation was offered by a number of informants, some of whom stated that this fate had been fixed by one's behavior in a previous existence (see also Wang 1974:145; 149). The shopkeeper, who left his young, handicapped son out to beg in a marketplace in suburban Taipei, excused his action on the basis that a fortune-teller had said the boy had a beggar's destiny and must beg for a living (*Chung-kuo Shih-pao*, 3 Dec. 1977:8). While one can certainly understand how this explanation might appeal to people who see some succeed and others fail, seemingly through no fault or special effort of their own, it is not scientific and it tells us little. Moreover, and quite curiously, no one in Liong-hiat offered this as a reason for or a rationalization of their own or anyone else's begging.

Another quite popular explanation is heredity. Matignon differentiates handicapped beggars from those he terms "professional"; the latter choose to beg rather than do manual labor, and they pass this way of life down from parent to child (1900:216). Informants who proffered this explanation pointed to the existence of beggar guilds or groups, to such hereditary outcast groups as the *kai-hu* of Kiangsu and Anhwei, and to a general impression that begging was a hereditary occupation. One can understand how children growing up in a beggar community might themselves become mendicants, especially if they had been maimed by their parents to make them more effective beggars as children.

But there is much evidence to controvert this hypothesis. While it is quite possible, even probable, that traditionally the beggar headship passed from father to son, it is more doubtful that working as a beggar did so. Neither activity had much prestige attached to it, but at least the former was lucrative and offered the holder and his descendants a stable living and authority over others. Simply being a beggar did not, and the stigma attached to that occupation should have acted as a powerful disincentive to continue it if there were alternatives. As to the existence of guilds with hereditary membership, even if beggar groups were actually guilds, they could still have recruited much of their membership from outside. Liu Hsü supports just that proposition in observing that it was the duty of the chief, rather than the parents, to teach the art forms Peking mendicants used in seeking alms (1936:174). Moreover, urban beggar groups, even though they were well organized, existed at least as much at the behest of the authorities as because of the desires of ordinary beggars.

Regarding the *kai-hu*, literally "beggar households," despite the name, they were not actually mendicants. The men earned their living mainly by rendering services at funerals and weddings, and the women worked as hairdressers and *pan-niang*, women who accompanied the bride. Their origin is cloudy, but one theory is that they were descended from a Sung general who surrendered to the Chin and were "humbled" and classified as "mean" (outcasts) by the Sung government (Ch'ü 1961:130–31). Moreover, it is quite possible that the *kai* (beggar) in *kai-hu* was used simply as a pejorative[3] to denote the lowly status of the group rather than as an accurate description of their occupation. Furthermore, whereas the *kai-hu* were an outcast (*chien-min*) group who were not allowed to participate in the official examinations or to marry outsiders, no such restrictions existed for beggars, for whom the possibility of mobility is strongly reflected in folktale and legend.

Finally there is the relatively small number of beggars in Liong-hiat or in the survey done by Shih Ch'ien in Taiwan fifty years earlier whose reasons for becoming mendicants can be explained by heredity. Only eight of the one hundred whom Shih questioned (1925:47) and one in thirty-six in Liong-hiat had parents who begged. If heredity was a primary factor, it should be more strongly reflected in these two samples (the only sources of such data).

A third popular explanation is that people become beggars because of personal factors, flaws in their personalities and character structures. Wang writes of profligate and wasteful persons whose habits finally condemn them a life of mendicancy (1974:146). Shih Ch'ien cites both crime and morphine addiction as causes. Criminals, in order to escape capture or prosecution, forfeit bail and go live with beggars, where the police network does not fully penetrate. After a while they take up begging themselves. Morphine addicts are reduced to begging because their habit impoverishes them. He also mentions laziness. Some young men who do not want to work take up petty crime and gambling but gradually become beggars because it is the easiest route open to them (1925:37–42). Of his one hundred surveyed beggars, Shih claims that eleven begged for such reasons.

Character and personality account for six of the Liong-hiat beggars. Three joined the group because of the incessant gambling there. One of them had been a beggar and a gambler before, and the other two began to beg after joining the group because it was the easiest, quickest, and most lucrative way they knew to get money to support themselves and their passion. Another was a wastrel who had spent his inheritance drinking and whoring and who was ashamed to return home. Yet another was a morphine addict, and a third was described by his neighbors simply as lazy—able-bodied and young but choosing to beg rather than to work. For another three the main cause might be put down to environment, although personality and character are also factors. They all had spouses who begged, and after living in Liong-hiat for a while, they became beggars too.

On the other hand, there is considerable support for the "rootless person" hypothesis. In terms of numbers, Shih Ch'ien attributed the cause of begging to sickness in twenty-five cases, blindness in twenty-four, being crippled or injured in sixteen, and being mentally deficient in six (1925:47). He also states that sickness need not be serious, chronic, or crippling and cites a Japanese scholar, Kagama Toyohiko, who said that people lived such a marginal existence that as little as three days' illness in a year could ruin their chances of survival (ibid.:31; see also Wang 1974:146). Shih Ch'ien further notes that some mentally retarded persons were abandoned by their families and left to their own devices (1925:36). Of the Liong-hiat beggars, a poor state of health and a physical handicap were the most common precipitating factors. Fourteen had physical problems: six were blind, three were disabled, three had serious chronic illnesses, one was the victim of an industrial accident, and one was mentally unbalanced. In five other cases, poor health was a contributing cause.

Another important factor was poverty. Two women in Liong-hiat, both illiterate and unskilled, began to beg after their conjugal relationships broke up, leaving each to support herself and, in one case, her children as well. Additionally, four males for whom I do not know the events immediately preceding their beginning to beg were unskilled and illiterate and came from economically depressed areas of Taiwan. Poverty was also a contributing factor in a number of other cases. Two of those who began to beg after contracting serious illnesses, for example, did so because they had no resources and no one who could support them; they begged in order to survive.[4]

Accounts of begging in premodern China, while they do not provide numbers, do lend support to this hypothesis. The role played by disasters in leading to a loss of livelihood, thence to begging, is cited by many. Martin states that in "seasons of drought . . . the city was infested by beggars" (1900:77). Huc gives an account of peasants in Chekiang who, after fighting successive floods to save their lands, finally had to abandon them and turn to begging (1856ii:310–11). Loewe writes that "the number of such displaced persons [the peasantry] who wandered around seeking a living by beggary or other means was increased considerably at times of natural disaster" (1968:165). Liu Hsü, echoing this statement, notes that it was farmers who had lost their livelihoods who swelled the ranks of Peking beggars

(1936:170, 178; see also Wang 1974:146; Huntington 1945:188–89; Ti 1974:382; Shih Ch'ien 1925:35–40). This proposition can be further supported by comparing the numbers of beggars in Peking, located in the center of much of the economic and sociopolitical turmoil in the century preceding 1950, and Taiwan, where in the period 1900–1937 there was stability and relative prosperity. Burgess and Gamble give a figure of 20,000 "naked beggars" in Peking in 1875 (1921:275), and Matignon, for the same city, reports an estimate of 100,000 beggars—about one-sixth of its population (1900:236). By contrast, Wang says that in 1906, Taipei (population 300,000) had eleven dens with a total of 55 beggars (1974:153). Shih Ch'ien, referring to a time twenty years later, gives a "rough estimate" of 100–200 beggars for Taipei and 800 for Taiwan (population 3,500,000) as a whole (1925:7–8). One can appreciate the size of the displaced population in mainland China by noting Moise's estimate that, because of net downward mobility in the period between the Opium War and 1950, about 10 percent of the population were too poor to marry and failed to reproduce themselves (1977). For all those who died, there must have been some, albeit a smaller number, who survived.

Thus there can be little doubt that economic disaster, whether in the form of bandit raids, floods, or illness, pushed people into begging. There is also indirect evidence that the cohort of rootless persons I have referred to lived a jack-of-all-trades existence, that they did a number of different things and none of them exclusively. Loewe, commenting on the impoverished lot of the Han peasantry, writes, "Small wonder that many of the peasants were forced by economic stress to take to a life of the wilds, living as vagabonds or beggars, as starvelings or robbers" (1968:60). Hsiao, quoting Frank Binkley, gives a number of occupations—"petty bread-earning positions"—that failed scholars engaged in, including begging and several activities often associated with begging such as entertaining (raconteurs) and fortune-telling (1960:479). Moule (1902:123) and Huc (1856ii:310–11) observe that peasants who lose their livelihood and have to beg to survive turn to violence if they do not receive sufficient alms or help from the local gentry and the magistrates. Moreover there are too many accounts in the literature (see chap. 3) of "beggars" who entertained, robbed, stole, extorted, and worked not to accept this proposition. This is further supported by the activities of the Liong-hiat beggars, who, besides beseeching alms, also gambled, worked, entertained, sold products, and performed "services" at funerals.

Comparing the four explanations, fate aside, none is without value. No doubt some people did beg because they found it easier and more lucrative than anything else they could or were willing to do. One need only look to Liong-hiat for examples—Kua:-chui, able-bodied but lazy, or Hiong-a, who begged and had his mate beg in order to support his gambling habit. Nor is it difficult to believe that some beggar children followed in their parents' footsteps. But the available evidence indicates that the majority of those who begged dis so because they were victims of disaster or poverty, were in a poor physical condition, or lacked opportunity; they had to, at least part of the time, in order to survive. This hypothesis of the origin and source of beggars is not incongruent with other aspects of pre-modern Chinese society, and it explains the broad use of the terms *beggar* and *begging* in the literature on Chinese mendicancy. This usage simply reflected social reality; a broad range of persons begged, and those who sometimes begged did a lot of other things as well.

The Beggars, Poverty, and Theories of Poverty

The Liong-hiat beggars have made a number of adaptations in their social behavior, notably in the economic and kinship spheres of life, as a response to their poverty and the stigma attached to their occupations.

Many of these adaptations are very similar to those found among the urban poor in other societies. Their explanation is essentially ecological: the position of the beggars in Taiwan's socioeconomic system. For some others, the explanation must be at least in part a cultural one; they are a response to poverty, but they are also re-sponses by the beggars as Chinese.

First, looking at economic adaptations, we have already examined (see chap. 5) the ways the Beggars economized—eating inexpensive food, wearing inexpensive clothing, and living in squatter houses, all of which were built by members of the community, usually by or with the assistance of the owner. Other adaptions can be found in their income-generating activities. There we see a group of poorly educated, lowly skilled (except for a few of the younger generation) persons who have little to offer other than their raw labor. Those who find jobs work at either physically demanding or mundane and repetitive tasks. Their alternatives are illegal or dishonorable—begging, gambling, prostitu-tion, petty crime, or hawking. All of these are high-risk activities. Those who break the law can find themselves in trouble with the police and facing fines or incarceration. Those with low-skill jobs are less secure than people with more education and training. Fortunately, Taiwan's economy has proved strong over the past two decades, even when it had to absorb the impact of the 1973 oil crisis, and unemployment rates have been very low. Nevertheless, in an economy so dependent on the health of its trading partners, given the place of the lowly skilled in the employment structure, such persons must live with the danger of job loss in the event of an economic downturn.

A second characteristic of their income-generating activities is that the most lucrative ones are also illict. Even the least effective of the beggars on a bad day can make over NT$100, and that is more than a female factory worker can make even with overtime and normal bonuses added in. Pai-kha-e, Ti-bu-a, Tua-kho-e, and several others can make as much in half a day (NT$300) as a skilled construction worker can in a full one. O-niau and Tiek-kou each make as much in one day (NT$2,000) as an unskilled laborer does in ten. Of those who work in the conventional sense of the word, Cieng-a earns most, perhaps NT$15,000 per month after fines and lost time owing to police activities to control illegal hawkers, but she works very long hours and rarely has a day off. Thus those who work at a conventional job do so at a considerable material cost to themselves.

A third characteristic is the high participation rate in income-generating activities. Most families have two or more members bringing in income, and some have as many as five. Of those who would be officially considered part of the potential work force by the government—those between fifteen and sixty, not in school, and with no small children to look after—the only noncontributors are three adult males, one of whom assists his wife in her begging by watching out for the police, and several teen-age males who work only from time to time. Even those who are officially underage contribute; infants and young children accompany their parents to beg to enhance their *kho-lian-iu:*; and slightly older children who can get around on their own take their disabled mothers out to beg.

Children can contribute to the family income in another way; they can be sold. A-suat's stepfather, Kua:-chui, considered selling her after her mother, his mate, died. Nine years old at the time, she was already an accomplished beggar, and she could easily have fetched more than NT$10,000 from a beggar family in the south. It was only pressure on Kua:-chui from her uterine relatives that saved her from being sold. They pointed out that without his mate, he needed her to take care of his younger children, the oldest of whom was five at the time. But several other children from the community, especially infants, have been sold. A-tong, for example, had four children, two of whom were males, when a third son was born. He was⁵ sold to a family with no natural son for NT$5,000. A-pui-a also sold an infant. And several have indentured postpubescent daughters into prostitution.

In this respect, the Beggars are certainly similar to the world's urban poor, but they are also similar, though with a significant difference, to most Chinese as well. Traditionally it was to his or her children that a Chinese looked for support and security in both old age and after death. Thus children, especially sons, were a vital future economic resource, an investment that should bring returns just when they were most needed. This relationship is described in the concept of *fan-pu*, *pu* referring to a mother bird feeding her young by disgorging food into their mouths, and *fan* denoting a reversal of the process, in other words, children feeding their dependent parents. To the beggars, however, and to others who are poor and desperate, children can be an economic resource at a much younger age in that they can be sold to families who want children (or in the past, servants) or to brothels. But the beggars are unique in one respect; it is only they whose children, by accompanying their parents when begging, can make a direct economic contribution even as infants.

The fourth comparable characteristic of the Beggars' economic life is their use of informal credit devices. In the case of Liong-hiat, this means *he-a* (rotating credit associations) and, to a lesser extent, pawning. The high degree of participation in *he-a*, many people being in several at one time, has alrady been recounted. But this is not unique to the Beggars or even to low-income persons in Taiwan. Many middle-class and even wealthy people participate in *he-a*, and there is a variant form practiced in rural areas in which interest paid or earned is determined by fluctuations in the price of rice. In fact, the only sector of society in which *he-a* are not found is the very poor—because no one would want a penniless person in a *he-a* he organized or would be willing to invest in the *he-a* of a person with no job, money, or resources. As for pawning, it is found in Liong-hiat, but it is not nearly so common as Eames and Goode imply in their survey of coping responses of the poor (1973:164–65). Once in a while someone pawns an object, usually to gamble, but more frequently, if he is in a "live" *he-a* (*huat-he-a*),⁵ he will bid out his money rather than pawn something. Moreover, if he has money to save or invest, rather than buying an object that can later be pawned if he needs cash, he is more likely to join a *he-a*. In Liong-hiat, many of these are short-term, meeting several times each month, giving one a fair degree of liquidity or at least the ability to borrow against a potential withdrawal. Furthermore, this form of saving gives one an opportunity, if he can hold out long enough, to earn interest and increase his capital.

In the kinship sphere, the Beggars have also made some obvious adjustments to poverty. Most notable is the high proportion of consensual unions. This has been noted as a characteristic of the poor in a number of cultures in the world (for a summary see Eames and Goode 1973:172–81). However, the reasons for it appear somewhat different in Liong-hiat. It is certainly not a rejection of marriage. As I noted in chapter 6, several in the first generation who originally formed consensual unions later legitimated them as marriages, and those in the younger generation who formed unions very consciously married before they set up housekeeping together. Nor is the difficulty of divorce a factor. In premodern times divorce was strictly a male option, and it was rare for several reasons: A woman's conjugal family needed her labor and reproductive powers. Marriage was very costly, half a year's to a year's income, thus making a second marriage impossible for most. A divorced woman could not return to her natal family and had nowhere else to go; thus divorcing her would be very cruel. Sexual outlets outside marriage—concubinage or prostitution—were readily available for men. Finally, harmony was highly valued, and since divorce was evidence of disharmony, it would cause the husband's family to lose face. Today divorce carries with it a very heavy stigma, especially for the woman, but there are no legal or religious barriers to it. Still, there is no indication that anyone would cohabit rather than marry for fear that a divorce, should it be desired, would be difficult to obtain. And as for the Liong-hiat women, those who have wanted to leave one relationship for another have done so whether married or not.

The number of consensual unions there can best be explained by the cost of marriage. In Chinese marriage there is no public ritual such as that performed in front of a judge or a minister of religion in the West to signify that a couple is married. However, it is traditional that a feast be given for kin, friends, fellow villagers, and so forth, to demonstrate to a public of significant others that a marriage has taken place. Such a feast is costly, and sometimes urban couples will begin by cohabitating until they can afford to invite guests, at which time they will marry. For some, including several couples from Liong-hiat, that time never comes, and the relationship is never transformed into a marriage. Consensual unions, then, are a result of the exigencies of the moment and of subsequent chronic poverty.

The number of endogamous marriages (half) among the second

generation in Liong-hiat can also be explained on the basis of poverty and stigma. I observed earlier that many beggar children left school early. They did so because of a lack of encouragement and direction on the part of their parents, to help their parents beg, and because they could not endure the taunts of "beggar's kid" from their schoolmates. This not only affected the amount of schooling they received but also denied them the opportunity to mix with and adjust to the outside world and to develop self-confidence in dealing with outsiders. Lacking ego strength, when it came time to find marriage partners, it was much easier for them to do so among their neighbors, with whom they grew up and who shared their stigmatized background.

Another adaptation of the Liong-hiat Beggars is in their kinship networks. Traditionally in China persons were filiated into agnatic descent lines, although matrilineal and affinal kin were also potentially important. The agnatic group formed one's first line of allies, but it was localized around one or a few rural villages. Moreover, its strength and ability to aid and protect its members depended on its wealth. Most of the Beggars were losers on both counts: they had migrated away from their native areas; and they were from poor kin groups. Although the Beggar community itself was, in terms of cooperation and mutual assistance, the functional equivalent of a village, in order to increase the number and range of people upon whom they could call for aid, they utilized all available kinship links—matrilateral and affinal ties, ties several degrees removed, and ties created through adoptions. These last two types would normally be ignored by most Chinese or recognized only as "distant kin," but the Beggars actively cultivated them and frequently mentally reduced the distance. In this sense, they "created" kinship ties. They further expanded their networks by establishing fictive kin relations of the appropriate sort with peers, seniors, and juniors. Far from being weakened by poverty and urban living (see Eames and Goode 1973: 190–93), kinship as an idiom and as a basis for a social bond is still quite strong in Liong-hiat.

In the context of comparisons with poor people elsewhere in the world, two other aspects of the Beggars' kinship relationships deserve mention. First is adoption. This is found in Liong-hiat, but it is by no means unique to the residents there. The transfer of the filiation of children is probably age-old in China. Moreover, it is found among wealthy as well as poor people. Nonetheless, it is quite common in Liong-hiat, and it serves a number of functions: to get heirs; to get children; to get a daughter-in-law; to provide for orphans; and to get rid of surplus children. However, in contrast to what one finds among the poor in some other societies (Eames and Goode 1973:185), it is not common there to "farm out" children. With the exception of orphans brought up by foster parents and the sons of O-niau and Cieng-a, who were reared in their early years by Tiek-kou's relatives until their mothers married, children are brought up by those by whom they are filiated. They do not pass through a series of households.

The other aspect is conspicuous by its absence: the syndrome associated with the matricentric household. The abandonment of wives or mates is a characteristic of that structure commonly mentioned in the literature on poverty, and while it does exist in Liong-hiat (and in Taiwan as a whole), it is rare. One case occurred in Liong-hiat, and there was another of male-initiated divorce. On the other hand, there were at least three cases, and probably several more, of females initiating breakups with male partners. Moreover, there is other evidence that it is females who are more likely to abandon males than vice versa. In data from twenty-seven welfare-recipient households in Taipei, there were three cases of abandoned husbands and one of a widow abandoning her children but none of abandoned wives. According to informants, this is the pattern that would be found throughout the housing estate in which they lived. Furthermore, in most Taiwan newspapers there is a section in the personal ads carrying notices of husbands calling for the return of their wives; there is no comparable section for wives calling back their husbands.

Only preliminary reasons can be given for this at present, but it appears that the most important is the strength of patrilineality among the Chinese. Not only do all legitimate children stay with their agnates in the case of a breakup (or the death of the father), but the responsibility of bringing children and heirs into the kinship group is exclusively male (although it is possible for a female to accomplish this through a uxorilocal marriage). A further contributing factor is the scarcity of females. Higher female mortality rates in China combined with a practice of hypergamy leave poor males with a shortage of females and give the female the option of staying in a relationship or moving on to a more advantageous one.

Moreover, the pressures against the family that exist in many countries—discrimination against the male job-seeker in the employment system and against the presence of an able-bodied male in the family in the welfare system—do not exist in Taiwan. The several frequently unemployed teenage males in Liong-hiat lack the skills to get jobs they would like and the willingness to do demanding physical labor to get the jobs available to them. Adult males have no trouble finding work if they want to look for it. As for the welfare system, benefits are so meager that no one who can exist without it would choose to live at the level it provides. The situation that is said to exist in the United States regarding AFDC (Aid to Families with Dependent Children) families who can maintain an albeit meager livelihood by relying on welfare payments and who might choose to do that rather than to work has no equivalent in Taiwan. Moreover, welfare benefits are given in Taiwan to any family without an able-bodied worker to support it regardless of its composition.

The beggars have also displayed a great deal of innovativeness and ingenuity in the adaptations they have made in begging tactics and organization. Because of the lack of detailed, comparative, or longitudinal data, adaptations in tactics in response to changes in the socioeconomic environment are more difficult to establish for the premodern period. Some regional differences probably reflect variations in local customs. For example, beggars in the Minnan area sang the *khuan-se-kua*, while those in the northern provinces sang the *shu-lai-pao* and the *lien-hua-lo*. The former is mournful, exhortative, and pleading; the latter are lively, comical, and upbeat. There seems to be no functional reason for this difference, and in the absence of firm data on their origins, it is best to explain them as two distinct art forms, each developing in a different linguistic area.

However, some tactics appear to have been designed to take advantage of the immediate environment—the invocation of the name of Buddha near temples, *tiau-lo-ce* and disruptions of the burial at funerals, and the preying upon those in a vulnerable position such as shopkeepers, people celebrating family occasions or festivals, and much more recently, young lovers spooning (*t'an lien-ai*) in public parks in Shanghai (Wu To 1981:43). Moreover the many songs, dances, and other performances, some general, others centered on holidays, and even some of the more gruesome tactics of self-mutilation show a great deal of creativity and innovation.

In terms of organization, only one example can be cited, given the available data, but it is indicative of the entrepreneurial spirit that such resourceless people must have displayed in order to survive in a society with the sort of pressure on total production that was the case in premodern China. Most descriptions of the organization of beggars show it to be permitted by but subordinate to the local authorities. But data from late nineteenth-century Peking paint a different picture. There the authorities are shown to have had little control over beggar groups and activities. While it is possible that this is merely a difference in local custom, that is highly improbable since Peking was the imperial capital. It is far more likely the result of the loss of social control in the last days of a waning dynasty, the fall of which was long overdue. The beggars, or more likely their leaders, seized upon the power vacuum and increased their sway in the city to the degree that, according to Matignon, while not a state within the state, the beggars were certainly a force to be reckoned with, and access to the Peking chief was gained only through his protector, one of the eight Manchu "Iron-hat" princes[6] (1900:218; 237). With the failure of the Boxer Rebellion and the takeover of local affairs by foreign forces, there was some restoration of order, one of the results of which was the banning of begging within the city limits. The beggars could not counter this. Many moved outside the city gates, and those who remained inside had to beg in a much more restrained, unobtrusive manner (Gamble and Burgess 1921:275–76). Beggars later had to make a similar adjustment in the foreign-controlled sector of Shanghai (F. Liu 1936:99–100).

As I explained in chapter 5 they have had to do the same in present-day Taipei, where mendicancy is proscribed, and the proscription is quite stringently enforced. They have to beg around temples and in the less modern sectors of the city. Except on public holidays, when a more tolerant atmosphere prevails, they have to keep out of the more desirable crowded, downtown areas and avoid begging in one spot. Most beg in the predominantly Taiwanese suburban areas because it is safer there. Those who regularly venture into Taipei go to markets and temples in the old sector of the city.

Since it is illegal to beg, a beggar group is also illegal. Yet one existed for several decades, and it dissolved not in the face of pressure from authorities but because it no longer served the changing interests of its members. Its leader, Tiek-kou, had to develop a compliance base that did not rely on the coercive force of the state that his premodern counterparts enjoyed or extensive resources that he could dispense in order to indemnify community members and obligate them to follow him. He overcame these disadvantages by his reesourcefulness and talents. He gained knowledge that was valuable to the beggars. He displayed good management and organizational skills. He exercised influence judiciously, never overstepping the bounds of locally accepted moral behavior or sanctions, and he acted in a friendly, caring, and unpretentious manner toward those in the community.

His leadership was certainly crucial to the cohesiveness that characterized the Liong-hiat community, but another factor also played a role, the stigma of begging. This did not force the beggars to live together—there are free-lance mendicants in the Taipei area—but it certainly added to the attraction of community life. In their home neighborhood, at least, they could avoid the condescension of the outside world.

This tightly knit, mutually supportive community served the Beggars well for many years until another change in the socioeconomic environment began to be felt. When the group came together in the early 1950s, the Taiwan economy was in bad straits. The previous decade had seen World War II, the emergence from colonial status, and the addition of about two million refugees from mainland China, most of them coming in 1948–49. In the early 1950s the country was poor, and jobs were not easy to get. But by the 1970s, Taiwan had industrialized, and there was a shortage rather than a surfeit of labor. A new opportunity structure existed, even to those at the bottom of society. This more or less coincided with the coming of age of the children of the Beggars, and most of them took advantage of it to find conventional jobs. The same stigma, which had under the earlier set of conditions produced cohesion, under the new set stimulated those who could to leave the community and assimilate into orthodox society.

When one takes all of this into account, what can be said about the various theories of poverty mentioned in chapter 1? First, with regard to Lewis, while my study does not disprove the theory of the culture of poverty,[7] it certainly casts doubt on its validity. Although Lewis made the point that not all those in poverty had a culture of poverty, the Beggars, with their stigmatized, socially pathological life-style and their low level of education would have to be prime candidates. Yet with all their disadvantages, a fair number of adults and most of the younger generation have escaped that life-style to become solid members of the working and in a few cases the lower middle classes. Although in some cases one can see a connection between their background and the fact that some, especially younger-generation males, lacked the perseverance or patience to follow an orthodox life-style, nothing in their "culture" prevented them from attempting to grasp opportunities they perceived in their desire to achieve a better life. Second, of those who did not escape—who still beg or who died as beggars—only one had any offspring. Thus, while these individuals were failures at upward mobility, in only one case (Kua:-chui) might this result in the perpetuation of mendicancy in the next generation.[8]

With regard to culturalist positions in general, I cannot say whether the unorthodox behavior of the Beggars resulted from a different cognitive structure and value system from that of the mainstream or whether it was simply a function of their poverty. But the research does show quite clearly that behavior patterns can change, and that they need form no barrier to mobility if other conditions allow it. Thus, while I would not claim that there are no cultural differences between the poor and the dominant classes in a society— indeed Waxman had marshaled evidence from several studies to show that there are (1977:62–65)—I will say that they make no difference. In a culturally pluralist society there are at least several different responses one can make in a situation. And although one may be constrained for material or other reasons in one's choice, this does not mean that a different choice might not be made under other circumstances. Quite obviously, as less stigmatized ways to earn a living opened up to the beggars, they took advantage of them. Nor do I believe that responses to questions put by researchers to informants regarding such matters as ambitions or plans for the future are a very reliable guide to future action. My informants, at least, were typically very noncommittal to any question that put them in a "perform or lose face/self-regard" situation. Their lives went forward one step at a time, and although they made discernible progress over the course of several years, no one, least of all the informants themselves, would have been able to predict such accomplishments at the earlier date. In short, I am saying that human beings are not locked into any pattern of behavior that typified one point in their lives but are active maximizers, waiting to take advantage of any opportunities they perceive. This position, which is supported by the research presented in this book, lies closest to that taken by the structuralists. The structuralist perspective is further supported by the facts that those in Liong-hiat who took the plunge into begging did so at a time when the Taiwan economy was at a nadir, and they climbed out after the economic boom was well underway—in other words, their descent into and ascent out of begging coincided with economic conditions quite external to themselves.

How does the stigma hypothesis fare when tested against the data I have presented? In general, being a beggar in Chinese society is about as low as one can be without being an outcast, and, as I have shown, there can be no question that the Liong-hiat beggars were severely stigmatized and that this stigma extended to others in the area. Moreover, nothing happened that magically lifted the stigma from them prior to their finding ways out of begging and out of the life-style associated with the community. But what were the consequences of the stigma? It certainly caused a great deal of discomfort, shame, and even trauma to many in the community, not only to children in school but also to adults in their dealings with outsiders. During the greater part of the history of the community, the stigma acted as a centripetal force, strengthening the ties people had with one another, but as people began to find ways out of begging, it acted not as deterrent but as a stimulus. Far from hindering mobility, the stigma quickened it.

With regard to the existence of an underclass, this research shows that even people at the bottom of the barrel can achieve mobility if conditions—in Taiwan, strong growth in a labor-intensive economy with a high demand for unskilled workers—are favorable. In the United States, despite the existence of large numbers of poor people in the nineteenth and early twentieth centuries, no underclass formed until two to three decades ago. Also, even in the face of levels of unemployment of more than 10 percent, the new Asian immigrants appear to be finding a place in the work force there. These two facts, in combination with the mobility achieved by the beggars, lend support to the thesis that there is something different about the experience, outlooks, and attitudes of today's underclass (see Auletta 1982; Hacker 1982).

In general I agree with Auletta that poverty and the reactions of various persons to it are both complex and often highly individualized. In Liong-hiat, for example, the contrast between Cieng-a and her younger sister, Niau-bu, is striking. Both were pressured by their mother to become prostitutes, but the former, fiercely ambitious and competitive, refused, while the latter, basically lazy, complied. This is not an isolated example; such contrasts within families were commonplace.

Two factors that appear to have contributed to the mobility of those in Liong-hiat may be worth considering in future studies of poor and underclass groups. First, although Liong-hiat was widely known to be a beggars' den, it was quite small in size and occupied a small area in a larger squatter settlement. However, neither Liong-hiat nor the surrounding area formed a physical barrier to contact with the outside. By contrast to squatter areas sometimes described in the literature, neither was geographically large or isolated by any physical barrier such as a river. In fact one could, and Liong-hiat residents daily did, walk to large main streets, shops, and public buildings in a matter of a few minutes. This ease of access to the outside world may have contributed to the integration of the younger generation into the wider society and to their making friends and other contacts outside their immediate environment. A second factor is that the begging in Liong-hiat lasted only one generation. Only one person (A-pui-a) who begged as an adult had a parent who did.

Most were from poor families, but that poverty was rural poverty, and it existed at a time when Taiwan was generally quite poor. When those in the younger generation found opportunities for advancement, they took advantage of them. Both factors, the limited generational depth of mendicancy and the lack of geographical isolation, should be worth investigating as independent variables in future studies.

Finally, one further issue. The 1960s and 1970s saw a large number of books published discussing poverty. For the most part, the authors were highly critical of the culture of poverty, condemnatory of any social system that allowed the existence of manifest poverty, and sympathetic toward the poor. Often this sympathy extended to a defense of the integrity of the life-style of the poor, but it also implied a belief that poverty was a permanent condition, that, although the subject of mobility was rarely directly addressed, once poor, always poor. Yet this was not necessarily the case. Waxman notes that the average welfare recipient family in the United States stays on the rolls for twenty-three months (1977:90). Thernstrom, working from tax records and other materials from the nineteenth and early twentieth centuries, demonstrates that a substantial number of poor, unskilled workers in Boston and Newburyport, despite rather unstable economic conditions and the absence of social welfare safety nets, managed to become home owners and solid members of the working class. He also shows that there was a high degree of mobility among the children of such workers to skilled labor or to white-collar jobs (1969). Plotnick and Skidmore demonstrate that the War on Poverty and assorted Office of Economic Opportunity programs yielded positive results in the United States between 1965 and 1974, lifting many out of absolute if not relative poverty (1975:81–85, 111–24). Thus a number of studies, including the present one, that have taken a diachronic approach have recorded that poverty is not necessarily permanent and that a good number of the poor are able to improve their situations. One problem in studies that give the impression that poverty is forever might be that they are synchronic. Even though the period of fieldwork may have been two years or more, that is not sufficient to record or observe social mobility.

Work is now in progress on a long-range study of welfare recipient families in Taipei, a more typical poverty population. That study contains a larger sample and, begun at the same time as the present one, has been underway for ten years now. In it I will explore more fully some of the issues raised in this one: the extent of social mobility among the destitute in Taipei and the factors that hinder or facilitate it; the strategies used by the poor and their points of entry into the mainstream of the economy; the roles of economic growth and of the particular type of welfare system found in Taiwan; the question of whether there exists a significantly different worldview and value system among the poor; and the sorts of kin networks and relations among low-income people there. It will, I hope, yield firmer, more broadly based conclusions.

Appendixes

Notes

References Cited

Index

Appendix A

Below is an alphabetical list of those named in the book. Household heads are described in full together with others in their families as they were in 1974. Other people are simply identified. Beggar household heads are italicized.

A-chun   After twenty years of marriage as a *sim-pu-a* (little daughter-in-law) and six sons, she was divorced by her husband. She now lives off begging, welfare, gambling, and infrequent handouts from her sons ("They are all very poor") with the daughter of a deceased beggar of whom she is guardian.

A-cim   Old widow; member of the Hokciu group.

A-cui-a   Deceased; former beggar implement of Tiek-kou.

A-go   Also related to Lau-liong, he is a wandering beggar. He and his mate came to Liong-hiat early in 1974 with their four children, but they were expelled after a few months, their children too unruly for others to put up with. They had lived in Liong-hiat on earlier occasions, staying for a few months before wandering off to another place.

A-hong   Petty gangster; friend of many in Liong-hiat.

A-hui   Second daughter of Cap-sa:-hou.

A-ieng   He is not a beggar but a former gangster (*lo-mua:*) who still has connections with the gang he used to run with in the area of Taipei from which he came. He came to Liong-hiat in 1972 both to gamble and with an eye toward taking over the leadership of the Beggars from Tiek-kou. He set up a gambling den in his house, and for a while he performed a number of the leadership roles in the community. In 1974 he lived with his mistress and two of his three children.

A-iu: A single male, sixty-three years old in 1973, he rents a room in Tiek-kou's house and lives with the two children he is fostering. A former commando from Swatow, he is one of the three mainland Chinese in the group. He gambles for his living, but he has never begged.

A-kim   Mate of A-tho; member of the Beggar group

A-kou A divorcée in her fifties, she left her husband to live with the Beggars because she loves to gamble. She has a married daughter who lives in Taipei but who often comes out to visit her and to gamble. A-kou lives alone in a room rented from Tiek-kou, supported by occasional begging and gifts from her daughter.

A-liong   Member of the Hokciu group.

A-m An old widow, blind for many years, she is frequently taken out by some of the adult females to beg with them. She was childless in her marriage, but Tiek-kou arranged for her to "adopt" Chai-thau, a male, with the idea that he would support her in her old age. In his mid thirties in 1974, Chai-thau neither works nor begs. Instead, he is supported by the begging earnings of A-m and by handouts from Tiek-kou.

A-pui-a   Stepdaughter of Sia-pue; mate of Kua:-chui; died in 1974.

A-sek-a He is a carpenter and lives with his wife and five children. His father-in-law, who died early in 1974, had also lived with the family. A-sek-a has never begged, but his father-in-law was a beggar until A-sek-a and his daughter married.

A-shieng   Son of the T'aoyüan beggar leader; a sometime resident of Liong-hiat.

A-su   Mate of Bok-cong; mother of Lau-liong; member of the Beggar group.

A-suat   Daughter of A-pui-a.

A-tai   Son of A-kim and A-tho.

A-tan Like A-iu:, he is a former Swatow commando. He is married to Tho-bak-e, Tiek-kou's eldest daughter, and because he is sterile, they have adopted a daughter and a son. After remodeling his house in 1973, he set up a gambling den in one room where customers paid him for the privilege of playing mahjong. He has never begged.

A-tho Blind from childhood, she begged for many years playing the *hien-a,* a three-stringed Chinese guitar, and singing with a male companion. She lives with her six children and a seventh, Iok-lan, fathered by her second mate with another woman. Her mate, A-kim, is a morphine addict and was in prison during most of the initial field research period. Her three sons are named Ang-a, Ho-a, and A-tai. Ang-a's wife, sisters-in-law, and two children live in the household, as does an adult male, Gong-a.

A-tong Although in ill health (tuberculosis) and not very strong, he makes an attempt at making a living buying and selling scrap metal and refuse. He also begs off and on, but for the most part he relies on the begging income of his blind mate. Like A-tho, she also plays the *hien-a* and sings while she begs. Neither of his two daughters have much education, having been kept at home to lead his mate out to beg. One son is in primary school, and they plan to send the youngest child to school also as soon as he is old enough.

Ai-khun   Cart driver; paramour of Hana.

Ang-a   Eldest son of A-tho.

Be-bin   He and his mate, Ti-bu-a, live with three daughters, two of them his, and two sons. Ti-bu-a begs. In the morning she takes her youngest son, five years old and a polio victim, out to the gates of a primary school, and in the evening, she takes several of her children out to the front of a movie theater. Be-bin does not beg himself but lives off her earnings.

Bi-kuan   Daughter of A-pui-a; wife of Lau-liong; member of the Beggar group.

Bok-cong   The third of the three mainland Chinese, also a former soldier, he is in ill health, and he and his mate, A-su, both beg for a living. They live with their son and her daughter by another man. One of A-su's sons by a former union, Lau-sam, also stays with them from time to time.

Cap-sa:-hou   Although capable of everyday tasks, she is mentally deficient, a result of traumas suffered in her early life, according to her neighbors. She lives with an ink maker who does not mix at all with others in Liong-hiat, her second daughter, A-hui, and her son. Her eldest daughter, O-niau, is a call girl who lives outside but comes back frequently to visit her family and friends.

Chai-thau   The "adopted" son of A-m: member of the Beggar group.

Chieng-cui   Second son of Sia-pue.

Chun-bieng   Deceased; former beggar implement of Tiek-kou; mate of A-cui-a.

Cieng-a   Second daughter of Tiek-kou.

Cui-a   Son of A-pui-a; adopted by E-a-cai.

E-a-cai   A victim of an industrial accident as a young man, he lost one arm and badly damaged the other. Since then he has begged, sold glass figurines from a pushcart, helped his adopted son in the latter's motorcycle repair shop, and managed a small shop of his own. E-a-cai had a union with A-pui-a, the daughter of Sia-pue's mate and another man, but she left him for Kua:-chui. The two children she brought into the union from a prior one stayed with him, and he has since formally adopted them. He now lives with his adopted son and daughter, Cui-a and Li-be.

Giok-khim   A Neighbor woman.

Gong-a   Beggar male from the same county as and housemate of A-kim and A-tho.

Hana She was a divorcée who came to Liong-hiat in 1973 so she could be close to her passion, gambling. She lives with her paramour, Ai-khun. She does not beg.

Hiong-a He had polio as a child, although it only slightly crippled him. He repaired sofas for a living for a number of years, but then he gave it up to move to Liong-hiat to gamble. He begs from time to time himself, but for the most part he relies on the begging income of his mate, a pitiful woman horribly crippled with muscular dystrophy. His sons are both in school, but his daughter had to drop out after completing the sixth grade to carry her mother, piggy-back, out to beg.

Ho-a Son of A-kim and A-tho.

Iek-a Former subdistrict head and friend of the Beggars.

Iok-lan Daughter of A-kim; reared in A-tho's household.

Khe-o Deceased; former beggar implement of Tiek-kou.

Kua:-chui An "adopted" son of Tiek-kou, he lives with his mate, A-pui-a, and five of her children, four of them also his. By all appearances, he is a healthy, able-bodied man, but his income is derived from gambling and, to a lesser extent, begging. According to his neighbors, he begs because it is easy and because he is lazy. A-pui-a began begging as a child with her mother, and she continued it in her adult life.

Lau-kheq A Neighbor male.

Lau Kho A pig farmer; member of the Hokciu group.

Lau Lim An ink maker; member of the Hokciu group.

Lau-liong The eldest son of A-su, he is a mason and a contractor. He married Bi-kuan, the eldest child of A-pui-a, and they have two children. Neither he nor Bi-kuan beg (1974), but both had to as children, accompanying their parents.

Lau Ong A Neighbor male and pig farmer.

Lau-sam Son of A-su; married-in husband of A-tong's daughter; member of the Beggar group.

Li-be Daughter of A-pui-a; adopted by E-a-cai.

Ng Family A Neighbor family.

Niau-bu Third daughter of Tiek-kou; wife of Niau-chi-hi:.

Niau-chi-hi: He came to the Beggar group as a young child with his parents. His father died several years afterward, and his mother went off with another man. He married Niau-bu, Tiek-kou's third daughter, and had one child in 1974. He is not a beggar, but he spends a lot of time in the company of *chit-thou gin-a*, petty gangsters. He was in the military during most of the initial study, his wife and child supported by his father-in-law.

O-baq-e A carpenter, not a beggar, he nonetheless wandered in and out of the community. He and Lau-liong are affines, and Lau-liong calls him *A-ciek* (father's younger brother). He is a divorcé and has children living with his former wife.

O-niau   A prostitute; daughter of Cap-sa:-hou.

Pai-kha-e   A single man, he has begged for many years. Around 1970 he developed bone cancer and had to have one leg amputated above the knee. He now has to use crutches, but his handicap has made him a very effective beggar. He lives alone in a room rented from A-tan.

Sia-pue   A contemporary of Tiek-kou, he began begging during World War II. He was reared in a remote mountain area but became ill. In getting himself to where his sister was living, he lost his identity card; thus, when he recovered, he was unable to work. He later took up with a blind beggar woman, and although he stopped begging several years before to drive a cart in the central market, she still begs occasionally. They live with two of their three sons, Chieng-cui and Siong-a, Chieng-cui's wife and son, and their two daughters.

Siong-a   Third son of Sia-pue.

Thi-thau-a   Father of Niau-chi-hi:.

Tho-bak-e   Oldest daughter of Tiek-kou; wife of A-tan.

Ti-bu-a   Beggar woman; wife of Be-bin.

Tiek-kou   The *khit-ciaq-thau* or beggar chief. He founded the Beggar group and later led them to Liong-hiat. His personal history and leadership roles are described at length in chapter 7. He lives with his unmarried son and daughter and a married daughter whose husband is in the military. His wife died in the early 1960s. Members of his family include Tho-bak-e, married to A-tan, Cieng-a, married out in 1974, Niau-bu, married to Niau-chi-hi:, and Touq-pi:-a, a son.

Touq-pi:-a   Son of Tiek-kou.

Tua-kho-e   The son of a wealthy Taipei family, he was a wastrel and spent his share of his father's fortune on wine and prostitutes. He contracted syphilis but failed to seek treatment until the disease was well advanced. He lost one eye (he wears a patch), and the rest of his face is badly scarred. He lives alone in Liong-hiat, begging for a living. Drinking and women are his pastimes.

Appendix B

216

bou kang-cok lieng-liek (H)   無 工 作 能 力

bu-lu (H)   舞 女

ch'iang-kai (M)   強 丐

ch'i-kai (M)   乞 丐

ch'i-kai-liao (M)   乞 丐 寮

Ch'ing-ming (M)   清 明

chi-kuan (M)   籍 貫

chi-te (M)   積 德

chiao (M)   醮

chiao-hua-tzu (M)   叫 化 子

chien-min (M)   賤 民

chien-tzu-hang (M)   揀 子 行

chit-thou gin-a (H)   迌 迌 囝 仔

chou-ch'ang (M)   粥 廠

ch'ü (M)   區

ch'ü-kung-so (M)   區 公 所

ch'u-ssu-hai (M)   除 四 害

chui-bi (H)   碎 米

Chung-ch'iu (M)   中 秋

Chung-yüan (M)   中 元

ciaq-ang (H)   吃 紅

ciaq nng-png (H)   吃 軟 飯

cieng-pou (H)   情 報

ciou-sai (H)   招 婿

cit-giap (H)   職 業

co-sa:-zit khit-ciaq: m-khi co hong-te (H)   做 三 日 乞 丐 不 去 做 皇 帝

cu-iu (H)   自 由

cu-png-e (H)   做 飯 的

di-fong (Soochow)   地 方

erh-chi p'in-hu (M)   二 級 貧 戶

fa-ts'ai (M)   發 財

fan-pu (M)   反 哺

fang-piao (Soochow)   放　鏢

fang-sheng (M)   放　生

feng-shui (M)   風　水

gi (H)   義

gi-bu (H)   義　務

gi-ca-bo-kia: (H)   義　查某囝

gi-khi (H)   義　氣

gi-khit (H)   藝　乞

gi-kia: (H)   義　囝

gi-pe (H)   義　父

giok-lan-hue (H)   玉　蘭　花

gua hit-e cha-pe (H)   我　那　個　柴　子

guan (H)   阮

guan-li (H)   權力

Hakka (?)   客家

hao-hao hsien-sheng (M)   好　好　先　生

he-a (H)   會　仔

he-kha (H)   會　腳

he-thau (H)   會　頭

hien-a (H)   弦　仔

Hokciu (H)   福州

Hokciulang (H)   福　州　人

Hokkien (H)   福　建

hong-siok sip-kuan (H)   風　俗　習　慣

hou hia:-ti (H)   好　兄　弟

hsi (M)   喜

hsien (M)   仙

hsien (M)   縣

hsien-jen-t'iao (M)   仙　人　跳

hsien shang-ch'e; hou pu-p'iao (M)   先　上　車　後　補　票

hsiu-shen (M)   修　身

hu-ch'in (M)   胡　琴

khe-ca-bo-kia: (H) 契查某囝

khe-kia: (H) 契囝

khe-ma (H) 契媽

kheq (H) 客

kheq-thia: (H) 客廳

khi-hu khit-ciaq e sue le (H) 欺負乞食會衰了

khi-phian chiu-tua: (H) 欺騙手段

khit-ciaq (H) 乞食

khit-ciaq e ke-si (H) 乞食的傢俬

khit-ciaq he-siu: (H) 乞食和尚

khit-ciaq-kia: (H) 乞食囝

khit-ciaq-liau (H) 乞食寮

khit-ciaq lo-mua: (H) 乞食流氓

khit-ciaq-mia: (H) 乞食命

khit-ciaq-thau (H) 乞食頭

khit-e (H) 乞的

kho-lian (H) 可憐

kho-lian-iu: (H) 可憐樣

khuan-se-kua (H) 勸世歌

khui-lo-e (H) 開路的

khui-lo-sin (H) 開路神

ki-kim (H) 基金

kia-ku (H) 寄居

kiat-hun (H) 結婚

kiat-pai e hia:-ti (H) 結拜的兄弟

kiau-tiu: (H) 賭場

kiong-hi (H) 恭喜

kiu (H) 求

kua-tzu (M) 卦子

kuang-kun (M) 光棍

kung-hsi (M) 恭喜

kung-jen (M) 工人

kuo-t'i (M) 國 體

lao-erh (M) 老 二

lao-jen ch'a-shih (M) 老人茶室

lao-san (M) 老 三

lao-ta (M) 老 大

lao-yeh (M) 老 爺

lau-ziat (H) 鬧 熱

li (H/M) 禮

Li Thiq-kuai (H) 李鉄柺

Li T'ieh-kuai (M) 李鉄柺

li-tiu: (H) 里長

liam-kieng (H) 唸經

lien-hua-lo (M) 蓮花落

lieng-bu (H) 乳母

lin (H/M) 鄰

lin-tiu: (H) 鄰長

lo-mua: (H) 流氓

lu-kang (H) 女工

Lu-k'o yü Tao-k'o (M) 路客與刀客

Lu Tung-pin (M) 呂洞賓

luan (M) 亂

mai-lai-te (M) 買来的

mai-tung (M) 賣冬

men tang hu tui (M) 門當户對

mi-tiam-a (H) 米店仔

mien-tzu (M) 面子

Minnan (M) 閩南

o-cu-a (H) 烏珠仔

O-iu-a (H) 烏窯仔

oan-chin (H) 遠親

oan-chin pu lu kin-lin (H) 遠親不如近鄰

ong-si (H) 枉死

ouq-phai (H) 學歹

pa-to-khit-ciaq (H) 霸道乞食

pai-ni (H) 拜年

pai-pai (H/M) 拜拜

pan-niang (M) 伴娘

p'ao chiang-hu te (M) 跑江湖的

phia-cui-lau (H) 避水樓

phin-hiet (H) 貪血

phok-su (H) 博士

phua-siong (H) 破相

p'i-p'a (M) 琵琶

pian-tong (H) 便當

p'in-hu (M) 貪戶

p'in-min (M) 貪民

p'ing (M) 坪

pou-piou (H) 保鏢

pun-ci: (H) 分錢

pun-png (H) 分飯

san-ciaq-lang e sim (H) 竊亦人的心

san-hsien (M) 三弦

san-tao (M) 三刀

sang (M) 喪

seng-sim-su (H) 誠心書

she-ch'u (M) 社區

shen (M) 神

shen-fen-cheng (M) 身份證

shen-tzu (M) 嬸子

shu-lai-pao (M) 數來寶

shuang-shan tsuan-tung (M) 双鱔鑽洞

shui-tien-kung (M) 水電工

si-he-a (H) 死會仔

sian-liong (H) 賢良

sim-pu-a (H) 媳婦仔

sin-su (H) 紳士

sin-su khit-ciaq (H) 紳士乞食

sit-pat-a (H) 十八仔（骰子）

su-siek-phai (H) 四色牌

sui-pian (H) 隨便

ta-a (H) 攤仔

ta-ch'i-hsiang (M) 打七響

ta-chin (M) 打金

ta-po-khi-khai (H) 唐夫氣慨

ta-shu (M) 大叔

Taipan (Cantonese) 大班

t'ai-pao (M) 太保

t'ai-t'ai (M) 太太

T'ai-wan Chi-tu-chiao Fu-li-hui (M) 台灣基督教福利會

tan (M) 蛋

tan-bi (H) 陳米

t'an lien-ai (M) 談戀愛

tang-ki (H) 童乩

tang-sng (H) 凍霜

Tanka (Cantonese) 蛋家

t'ao-ch'ien (M) 討錢

t'ao-ch'ien-te (M) 討錢的

t'ao-fan (M) 討飯

t'ao-fan-hui (M) 討飯會

t'ao-fan-te (M) 討飯的

te-pua (H) 地盤

thau (H) 偷

thau-ke (H) 頭家

thuan-kiat (H) 團結

thiq-kang (H) 鐵工

tho-cui-kang (H) 土水工

ti-pao (M)　地　保

t'iao-pao (M)　跳　寶

tiau-lo-ce (H)　吊　路　祭

t'ieh-kung (M)　鐵　工

tit-ciap (H)　直　接

tng (H)　當

tng-kang (H)　長　工

to-liong-tua-e (H)　肚　量　大　的

to-min (M)　惰　民

to-su (H)　道　士

tong-hiong (H)　同　鄉

tong-ku (H)　同　居

tou-he-a (H)　倒　會　仔

tsing-siao-zoo (Soochow)　青　小　蛇

tua-chua (H)　大　嬰

tua-hia: (H)　大　兄

Tuan-wu (M)　端　午

t'ung-hsiang (M)　同　鄉

tu-su hua siou-su; siou-su hua bou-su (H)　大事化小事,小事化無事

tzu-chu-ts'an (M)　自　助　餐

ui-ciong-kian-tiok (H)　違　章　建　築

wan-hun (H)　冤　魂

wen (M)　文

wu (M)　武

wu-hsia (M)　武　俠

wu-hsia hsiao-shuo (M)　武　俠　小　說

wu-kuan pu tuan-cheng (M)　五　官　不　端

ya-sui-ch'ien (M)　壓　歲　錢

yamen (M)　衙　門

yao-ch'ien (M)　要　錢

yao-ch'ien-shu (M)　搖　錢　樹

yao-ch'ien te (M)　要　錢　的

Notes

CHAPTER 1
Introduction

1. Urban neighborhoods are divided in Taiwan into *lin*, *li*, and *ch'ü*, which I have translated as neighborhood, subdistrict, and district on the suggestion of J. Bruce Jacobs. The *lin* is the smallest of the three, comprising thirty to forty households. The *li* is next, made up of about twenty *lin*, and the *ch'ü* is the largest.

2. These figures and others given in this chapter are for November 1973, when I began research into the community. Figures representing other periods will be so designated.

3. Adult status is based on a combination of age, marital status or its functional equivalent, and economic role.

4. According to Chinese custom, still very much followed in Taiwan, identification of native place goes through one's father. Thus the child of a father whose native place (*chi-kuan*) is Foochow and a mother whose native place is Taiwan (or anywhere else) is considered to be a Hokciulang.

5. This last craft is called, in Mandarin, *ta-chin*. Other traditional Foochow crafts in Taiwan are the *san-tao*, the "three knives," butchering, tailoring, and barbering. Supposedly the immigrant Hokciulang took up such occupations because, when they arrived in Taiwan, they were unable to speak or understand the local languages, and in these jobs they could get by with a minimum of verbal communication.

6. The formation, make-up, and interrelationships within the community are discussed at length in chapter 4.

7. See note 2.

CHAPTER 2
Institutional Aspects

1. In Taiwan, the term *good brethern* (*hou hia:-ti*) refers to souls who have no descendants to make sacrifices to them (hungry ghosts). To my knowledge, beggars there do not refer to themselves in that way.

2. A cash (*wen*), a round coin with a square hole in the center, was the smallest denomination of currency in premodern China. Its worth was very small, and one often reads of payment in "strings of cash," one hundred cash tied together on a string.

3. I found no mention of a deity for beggar groups per se except for those in Taiwan. It is a safe assumption, however, that Li Thiq-kuai (Mandarin, Li T'ieh-kuai) was also the patron deity for mainland Chinese groups. In folklore he often appears as a supernatural being who helps beggars (see Schak 1979).

4. In Mandarin, the words I heard most commonly for "begging" were *yao-fan* or *t'ao fan* for food, and *yao-ch'ien* or *t'ao-ch'ien* for money.

5. *Khit-ciaq* was the only word I heard for "beggar" in Hokkien, but in Mandarin, a number of words were commonly in use: *ch'i-kai, yao-fan-te, t'ao-fan-te,* and, by northerners, *chiao-hua-tzu.* To my knowledge, they are equivalent in meaning.

6. A Chinese acquaintance in the United States related how her father, who had been the dean of one of the larger tertiary institutions in Taipei, was frequently deluged with invitations to weddings of former students. "My father never met most of these students personally," she said, "but they attempted to use the tie of being at the same school to get a gift from him." This, to her, was a form of begging. Another informant described wedding invitations as *hung-se cha-tan,* "red bombs." They were red in color, and they obligated the receiver to send or bring a gift, usually a few hundred New Taiwan dollars, to the couple.

6. A more complete account of the status of beggars in literary, folklore, and ethnographic sources is found in Schak 1979.

7. For the most part, this is a gross misconception, at least with regard to the Beggars I knew. They had homes and families, though not always orthodox ones, and they appeared to eat and cook at home as frequently as anyone else did. Paradoxically, however, only a few days after my informant made this statement, the son of the Beggar chief told me, "Our family usually eats out or buys prepared food to eat at home. We are too busy to prepare and cook food ourselves."

8. According to Bodde and Morris, there were certain groups, the "beggars" (*kai-hu*) of Anhwei and Kiangsu and the "lazy people" (*to-min*) of Chekiang, government runners, prostitutes, entertainers, and servants in private employ of officials, who were *chien-min* and could neither take the civil service examinations nor purchase office (1971:172). Ch'ü, however, states that these "beggars" were not really beggars but hereditary groups

whose function or niche was to perform certain services at weddings and funerals (1961:131n). Wang also states that, although looked down upon because of their occupation, beggars were not *chien-min* (1974:145).

9. In 1973–74, US$1.00 = NT$40.00. By 1977 the exchange rate had dropped to US$1.00 = NT$38.00.

CHAPTER 3
Appeals and Tactics

1. Thanks to Stevan Harrell for this reference.

2. Matignon gives no reason for wetting the streets, but I suspect that it was to dampen down the dust. In Taiwan during the hot season, people often splash water onto floors and onto the sidewalk outside their doors in the belief that the evaporating water will have a cooling effect.

3. This act is called *fang-sheng*, "to release and give life to."

4. Pork liver is considered the most nutritious of all cuts of meat and is therefore the most prized.

5. The same style of singing and accompaniment is used to tell stories, from bawdy folktales to the "Twenty-Four Filial Youths."

6. Doolittle reports having heard the *lien-hua-lo* and the *shu-lai-pao* in the Foochow area sung in both the local dialect and Mandarin (1865ii:260), but informants in Taiwan had never heard of these musical styles.

7. Hsiao uses the Chinese term *kuang-kun*, usually translated as "rogue," "local bully," or "bachelor," but he renders it as "beggar."

CHAPTER 4
The Structure and Character of the Liong-hiat Community

1. A significant sum in those days. According to Tiek-kou, ¥1 was worth about twenty-four catties of rice, and the total sum would have been the equivalent of about NT$30,000 in 1977 values.

2. I have made repeated attempts to find a translation for this disease, even asking Taiwanese doctors, but so far have been unsuccessful. Middle- and upper-class Taiwanese I have asked have often never heard of it, at least by that name. Those from peasant villages who were born before 1940 have, however, and they said it was quite common in the period immediately following World War II, although it is rarely heard of now.

3. It seems that this was an institutionalized method employed by the poor and weak to seek redress from the wealthy and powerful, to embarrass them publicly and make a nuisance of themselves. Episodes in stories and scenes in films frequently depict the poor person outside the door of, for example, the landlord who has dispossessed him. The poor person stays outside the door or gate, shouting, to all who will listen, about the evils of

the rich man. Beggars used tactics similar to this to exact alms from reluctant shopkeepers in premodern times.

4. Floods bringing a meter or so of water into the homes of Liong-hiat residents were common in the event of a heavy or sustained rainfall or a typhoon, and on several occasions the water has been even higher.

5. The rotating credit association is an institution found in peasant societies in many parts of the world. There may be variations from culture to culture, but the purpose is essentially the same, to provide an informal means of borrowing and saving among people without access to more formal institutions. In Taiwan, one person, *he-thau*, the head or organizer, gets a number of friends and acquaintances each to loan him a set sum of money. Let us say that Li Ssu needs $100. He gets ten persons each to loan him $10. He calls a meeting at which each *he-kha* gives him the money. They also agree to meet again ten more times, at set intervals, until each *he-kha* has been repaid, one person at each meeting. Before each meeting, those who are yet unpaid make a bid, the amount of their share they are willing to receive at that meeting. The one who puts in the lowest bid—call him Chang San—is repaid at that meeting. Li Ssu pays $10, since he has already enjoyed the loan, and the others split the difference to make up the amount that has been bid. Before the next meeting, another round of bids is made, from which Li Ssu and Chang San are excluded, and another successful *he-kha*, Wang Erh, is selected to be repaid. This time both Li Ssu and Chang San pay $10 each, and the others, excluding Wang Erh, of course, make up the difference. This process continues until all members have been repaid, after which the organization ceases to function.

Two characteristics should be noted. First, the *he-thau* receives an interest-free loan. In return, he shoulders the responsibility of ensuring that none of the members *tou-he-a* (default) after receiving payment. Should this occur, he is morally responsible for repaying all remaining unpaid members from his own pocket. Second, those who bid out their money early end up paying interest—I cite cases of gamblers bidding out at as low as 40 percent of the original amount. Those who endure to the end, however, earn interest, receiving up to 30 percent above what they paid in.

6. This is all the more the case in an urban community such as Liong-hiat, where there are no ties to the land to hinder mobility.

CHAPTER 5
Economic Activities

1. As table 1 shows, there were sixteen households that depended to one degree or another on begging for a living in 1974. The total number of adult individuals who willingly begged at that time was twenty-four. In addition, I have data on six more adults who lived or had lived there and who had begged.

2. I have been told by academic friends that police round up beggars in September, prior to the national holidays in October, a time that sees the return of many thousands of Overseas Chinese. The beggars are taken to some of the more remote areas in southern Taiwan where the visitors are unlikely to go.

3. I can verify the existence of this boy because I saw him with his parents at a funeral in Liong-hiat. I cannot vouch for his efficacy as a beggar, however. I have also seen young, handicapped children, such as the one described here, sent out to beg in markets.

4. In fact, there was a bit of fakery involved in this incident. What had caught the attention of people was that the boy was deposited early each morning and picked up in the evenings by a man in an automobile. The same man also came around periodically to empty out the alms bowl. It turned out that he was the father of the boy and was a shopkeeper. He tried to defend himself by saying that a visit to a fortune-teller had revealed that the boy had a bad fate and that he must be a beggar if he was to survive. The reporter was very suspicious of his story, and informants who commented on it said that even if the father's claim was true, the boy could have become a beggar in a symbolic fashion, perhaps by "begging" from a few of the father's friends on one occasion, just to fulfill his "fate."

5. One of the terms for brothel, iu-a, also glosses as "kiln," and beggars have often made abandoned brick kilns temporary or permanent shelters. In fact, one of the beggars' dens in the Taipei area is called O-iu-a, "Black Kiln."

6. These daughters were all indentured between the two periods of fieldwork I did in Liong-hiat. None of the women had entered brothels when I left in 1974. When I returned in 1977, one had already returned home and another worked in a local teahouse. The others were still in brothels.

7. All children in Taiwan were required to go to school through grade six—grade nine after 1967—and although this law was generally enforced rigorously, at least in the Taipei area, a good number of the beggars' children had no education at all or did not complete the number of years required by law. None of the boys was completely uneducated, however, whereas nine of the girls either had no education or were of school age but not in school.

8. This and other income figures in this chapter are for 1974.

9. I also found this phenomenon among small shopkeepers and artisans in Taipei. Even though they ran businesses, either selling or repairing things, and even though they were much better educated, more sophisticated in business methods, and more able to keep records than were the beggars, they still did not keep accounts or even separate operating capital from money spent on household and personal expenses. A wife, going out to shop for food, simply took some money from the till. These people could give me estimates of how much they earned each month, but they were only

estimates, not exact figures. Like the beggars, they measured their income in terms of whether it was sufficient to meet expenses.

10. The amount won in gambling is less than the amount spent because of the fees imposed by the "house." The house did not have a hand in games but took its cut from per hand fees and percentages of the winnings.

11. For a broader discussion of working conditions and remuneration rates of Taipei workers, see Nickum and Schak 1979:35–39.

12. The official identity card (*shen-fen-cheng*) is essential in Taiwan to do anything where the government or government regulations are involved. It is also an integral part of the population registration system. Not having one, under martial law conditions, leaves one open to arrest as a spy. O-niau's case is discussed in chapter 6.

13. The TCS did not give out income supplements to anyone, although they did give occasional grants to various households for special purposes. People who received welfare income supplements got them from the government, and though there was some cooperation between the TCS and the local government, one had to apply through established official channels to qualify for government assistance.

14. These were not festive meals to which I was invited well in advance, but normal, everyday meals to which I was invited on the spur of the moment, simply because I happened to be visiting the household late in the morning or afternoon, when the meal was being prepared.

15. I refer here not to Western middle-class ideas of privacy—being able to be alone—but to the provision of separate sleeping quarters for parents, male children, and female children.

16. In 1974 there was an active scavenging trade in Taiwan. Some "rag and bone" men called out as they drove pedicarts through the streets buying such things as used bottles and scrap metal from households. Others simply rummaged through household refuse put out to be collected by the sanitation department.

CHAPTER 6
Kinship Relations

1. This is the correct romanization according to the Bodman/Wu system, which I have used. It may be seen as *sim-pua* in the works of Arthur and Margery Wolf.

2. See chap. 5, n. 12.

3. Several households in Liong-hiat had two or even three ancestral tablets. In such cases there was more than one line of ancestors to worship because of adoptions (worship of both natural and adoptive parents) or a cohabitation relationship (worship of the father's as well as the mother's line).

4. Touq-pi:-a's remark reflects what Hsu has reported from West Town

(1948:57, 109, 253): that the purpose of sex is procreation, not recreation. Since his son had extended the line two generations beyond him, there was no longer any need for Tiek-kou to seek out a new sexual partner.

5. The case is based on the belief that semen is a limited good necessary to sustain life itself, and that the only proper reasons for a male to have coitus is to procreate and have sons and to strengthen his vitality by absorbing the female's *yin* essence. Evidence for the former belief can be found in novels. For example, in *Hung Lou Meng* both Chia Ju and Chin Chung die of sexual excess; in the end they have no more semen left, and they ejaculate only blood. Hsi-men Ch'ing, the hero of *Chin P'ing Mei*, meets a similar fate. (See also Eberhard 1967:80). Evidence for the latter belief can be found in Gulik 1951:7. (See also n. 4, reference to Hsu).

6. Cf. Matignon, who states that "polyandry" was common among Peking beggars, and that "females are the property of all" (1900:243). I think he exaggerates.

7. *Pachinko* is a Japanese form of pinball.

8. *Khit-e* means literally "begged," but, when speaking Mandarin, the Beggars and other Hokkien speakers used the term *mai-lai-te*, literally "bought."

9. This is illegal but not uncommon. A subdistrict head said that he was frequently asked to have records changed to show adopted children as natural children. Doctors and midwives also received such requests. They officiate at births and so are in a position to effect such a change.

10. The Ai-ai Report gives an example of a beggar who left over 10,000 *yüan* when he died to find a godson to make sacrifices and libations at his grave.

11. This is money given by adults to children in the Chinese New Year period with the idea that it brings luck. It is known in Mandarin as *ya-sui-ch'ien*, but Hokkien speakers simply refer to it by the red envelope in which the money is given.

CHAPTER 7
Leadership

1. To some readers, Tiek-kou's actions in this regard may appear reprehensible. To most of the Beggars, too, the indenturing of a daughter is an event of great magnitude and is done out of what is perceived as sheer necessity. Only Be-bin felt no remorse or sorrow for it. However, the practice is by no means specific to Beggars but exists among many other poor people in Taiwan as well. See, e.g., M. Wolf 1972:205–14.

2. This made it more difficult to gather data on disputes and dispute settlement. When I asked Tiek-kou for details about his role, he absolutely refused to discuss the matter, even when I told him I was interested not in who did what to whom but in disputes in general and what he did to bring

about a resolution. He replied that these events were things of the past, and they were best forgotten. From his position in the community, he is correct. It is difficult enough to keep the community together, despite the good feelings that generally exist between community members. Burying past squabbles is essential to prevent them from resurfacing.

3. The rotating credit association is by no means restricted to beggars; peasants, shopkeepers, and even quite wealthy people also use it. But the Beggars and other people tend to use it exclusively because they do not have access to other forms of credit.

4. One obvious exception here appears to be Tiek-kou's favorable treatment of Kua:-chui. However, no informant mentioned it in our discussions of gi-khi.

5. They expressed a similar view of A-ieng when he helped out at the death and funeral of A-sek-a's father-in-law and took a percentage of the contributions for himself. People said he had earned the money; he had performed a service that had to be performed and could not be done by those in the family of the deceased, and he had performed it well. He deserved something for his effort.

6. For a detailed discussion of vote buying, see Jacobs 1980.

CHAPTER 8
Change and Mobility

1. An "old-man's teahouse" (*lao-jen ch'a-shih*) is different from a "flowery teahouse" (*hua ch'a-shih*). In the former, one goes to chat, drink tea, eat snacks, watch television, or listen to storytellers. In the latter, one goes to eat and drink accompanied by hostesses, who will also have sex with customers.

2. I have no idea what the exact situation was, but I am told that this figure is a gross exaggeration.

3. The cost of installing a telephone is NT$16,000, a month's income for A-sek-a.

CHAPTER 9
Conclusions

1. I also translated this in earlier chapters as "bachelor." This is a more modern gloss. The literal meaning is "bare stick," which refers to the unmarried, therefore socially unstable, character of the individual.

2. *Phua-siong* refers to an accident or other unforeseen event that alters the configuration of the facial features (*siong*). Just as the geomancy (*feng-shui*) of a piece of land can be changed by the building of a road, the erection of a building, even the growth of a tree, and can affect the flow of geomantic currents and the fortunes of those who inhabit the land, so, too,

can a change in the alignment of the parts of one's face affect one's fate.

3. Other possible examples of this pejorative use are the Tanka (boat people) of Hong Kong and the *to-min* of Chekiang, both outcast groups. In the former, *tan* is "egg," which was frequently used in a negative fashion in Chinese, and in the latter, *to* means "lazy."

4. In the case of Liong-hiat, the total number of causes of begging exceeds thirty, the number of beggars on whom I have data. This is because some people fit into a number of categories. For example several who gamble are also disabled. Since it was impossible in all cases to assess which was the primary reason for their begging, I have included them wherever they fit.

5. A "live" rotating credit association (*huat-he-a*) is one from which one has not yet bid out money. After one bids out, it becomes "dead," a *si-he-a*.

6. These were princes whose titles were perpetually inherited, hence their crowns were "iron," connoting "absolute, sure." They were the descendants of princely houses that assisted in the conquest of northern China (Mayers 1970:4; 6).

7. There is a small question on the testability of the culture of poverty in a Chinese cultural setting. Among a number of conditions that Lewis said generated the culture of poverty, one was a bilateral rather than a unilateral kinship system. He never explained why this was important, but I suspect it is because of the greater corporateness of unilineal systems. As for the Liong-hiat residents, none belong to corporate lineages, however small. And although they filiate children into domestic groups according to the unilineal principle, as a practical matter they recognize all kin as kin. Grateful for any allies they can find, it is of no discernible difference to them whether someone is related to them agnatically or affinally, biologically or fictively.

In fact, I believe this is generally true of urban residents, certainly those in the lower income brackets, in Taiwan as a whole. Not only are the cities filled with rural migrants, but there is also a large population of mainlanders who, separated from their own biological kin groups by the Taiwan Straits and the state of relations between the governments of the Republic of China and the People's Republic of China, have had to improvise new networks. I will address this issue in greater detail in future publications.

8. I seriously doubt that Kua:-chui's children will become beggars either. I suspect that he will sell his four daughters into prostitution when they become old enough, since they will be of little use to him as beggars then anyway. His son is another question. If he receives no education he will probably be condemned to a life of poverty or one of crime and imprisonment.

References Cited

Ahern, Emily M. 1975. "The Power and Pollution of Chinese Women." In *Women in Chinese Society,* ed. M. Wolf and R. Witke. Stanford: Stanford University Press, pp. 193–214.

Ai-ai Report. N.d. *"Ch'i-kai Wen-t'i chih Yen-t'ao"* (An analytical discussion of the beggar question). Mimeo.

Auletta, Ken. 1982. *The Underclass.* New York: Basic Books.

Banfield, Edward C. 1968. *The Unheavenly City: The Nature and Future of Our Urban Crisis.* Boston: Little, Brown.

Bennett, James W. 1931. "China's Perennially Unemployed." *Asia* 31:215–19, 268–69.

Bernstein, Basil. 1964. "Social Class, Speech Systems, and Psychotherapy." In *Mental Health and the Poor,* ed. F. Reissman et al. New York: Free Press, pp. 194–204.

Bodde, Derk, and Clarence Morris. 1971. *Law in Imperial China: Exemplifed by 190 Ch'ing Cases.* Cambridge: Harvard University Press.

Burgess, John Stewart. 1926. *The Guilds of Peking.* New York: Columbia University, Faculty of Political Science.

Chan Lean-heng. 1973. *The Wayside Loners: Beggars in Penang, Malaysia.* Penang: Universiti Sains Malaysia, School of Comparative Social Sciences.

Ch'en Meng-lei, ed. 1726. *Ku-chin T'u-shu Chi-ch'eng.* No publisher.

Chiang Hsiao-mei. 1954a, b. *T'ai-wan Ku-shih* (Stories from Taiwan), vols. I and II. Taipei: Orient Cultural Service.

———. 1955a, b. *T'ai-wan Ku-shih* (Stories from Taiwan), vols. I and II. Taipei: Orient Cultural Service.

Chung-kuo Shih-pao. China Times (newspaper).

Chu P'o. 1974. *Pei-ching Kuo-ch'ü te Chiao-hua-t'ou yü Ch'i-kai Tsu-chih* (The beggar chief and beggar organization in old Peking). Ch'un-ch'iu Tsa-chih no. 41 (8/16):27–28.

Ch'ü T'ung-tsu. 1961. *Law and Society in Traditional China.* Paris and The Hague: Mouton.

———— 1962. *Local Government in China under the Ch'ing.* Stanford: Stanford University Press.

Coltman, Robert, Jr. 1891. *The Chinese, Their Present & Future: Medical, Political and Social.* Philadelphia and London: F. A. Davis.

Crissman, Lawrence W. 1981. "The Structure of Local and Regional Systems." In *The Anthropology of Taiwanese Society,* ed. E. Ahern and H. Gates. Stanford: Stanford University Press, pp. 89–124.

Doolittle, Justus. 1865. *Social Life of the Chinese,* vols. I and II. New York: Harper & Row.

Eames, Edwin, and Judith Granich Goode. 1973. *Urban Poverty in a Cross-cultural Context.* New York: Free Press.

Eberhard, Wolfram, ed. and trans. 1965. *Folktales of China.* Chicago: University of Chicago Press.

————. 1967. *Guilt and Sin in Traditional China.* Berkeley and Los Angeles: University of California Press.

Fortune, Robert. 1857. *A Residence among the Chinese: Inland, on the Coast, and at Sea.* London: John Murray.

Foster, George M. 1965. "Cultural Responses to Expressions of Envy in Tzintzuntzan."*Southwestern Journal of Anthropology* 21:24–35.

————. 1972. "The Anatomy of Envy: A Study in Symbolic Behavior." *Current Anthropology* 13:165–202.

Freedman, Maurice. 1958. *Lineage Organization in Southeastern China.* London: Athlone Press.

Gamble, Sidney David, and John Stewart Burgess. 1921. *Peking: A Social Survey.* London: Oxford University Press.

Gee, Nathaniel Gist. 1925. *A Class of Social Outcasts: Notes on the Beggars in China.* Peking Leader Reprints, no. 1. Peking: Peking Leader Press.

Gernet, Jacques. 1962. *Daily Life in China on the Eve of the Mongol Invasion, 1250–1276.* Stanford: Stanford University Press.

Goffman, Erving. 1963. *Stigma: Notes on the Management of Spoiled Identity.* Englewood Cliffs, N.J.: Prentice-Hall.

Gray, John Henry. 1878. *China: A History of the Laws, Manners, and Customs of the People,* vols. I and II. London: Macmillan.

Gulik, Robert H. van. 1951. *Erotic Colour Prints of the Ming Period: With an Essay on Chinese Sex Life from the Han to the Ch'ing Dynasty,* B.C. 206–A.D. 1644. Tokyo: privately published.

Hacker, Andrew. 1982. "The Lower Depths." *New York Reivew of Books* 24(14):15–20.

Hannerz, Ulf. 1969. *Soulside: Inquiries into Ghetto Culture and Community.* New York: Columbia University Press.

Harrell, Stevan. 1982. *Ploughshare Village: Culture and Context in Taiwan.* Seattle: University of Washington Press.

Hsiao Kung-chuan. 1960. *Rural China: Imperial Control in the Nineteenth Century*. Seattle: University of Washington Press.

Hsu, Frances, L. K. 1948. *Under the Ancestor's Shadow: Kinship, Personality, and Social Mobility in Village China*. Garden City, N.Y.: Doubleday-Anchor.

Hsü Fang. 1954. "Ch'i-che Wang Weng Chuan" (The story of Wang Weng the beggar). In *Yu-ch'u Hsin Chih*, comp. Chang Ch'ao. Peking: Wen-hsüeh ku-chi K'an-hsing-she, pp. 77–78.

Hsü I-t'ang. 1956. "Social Relief during the T'ang Dynasty." In *Chinese Social History: Translations of Selected Studies*, ed. E. Sun and J. DeFrancis. New York: American Council of Learned Societies, pp. 207–15.

Hu Hsien-chin. 1944. "The Chinese Concepts of 'Face.' " *American Anthropologist 46:45–64*.

Huc, Evariste-Régis. 1856. *A Journey Through the Chinese Empire*, vols. I and II. New York: Harper & Bros.

Hung Jo-kao. 1954. "Chi-hsien Chi" (Record of divining the immortal). In *Yu-ch'u Hsin-chih*, comp. Chang Ch'ao. Peking: Wen-hsüeh Ku-chi K'an-hsing-she, p. 227.

Huntington, Ellsworth. 1945. *Mainsprings of Civilization*. New York: Mentor Books.

Jacobs, J. Bruce. 1979. "A Preliminary Model of Particularistic Ties in Chinese Political Alliances: Kan-ch'ing and Kuan-hsi in a Rural Taiwanese Township." *China Quarterly* (London) 78:237–75.

———. 1980. *Local Politics in a Rural Chinese Cultural Setting: A Field of Study of Mazu Township, Taiwan*. Canberra: Australian National University, Contemporary China Centre.

Kulp, Daniel Harrison, II. 1925. *Country Life in South China: The Sociology of Familism*. New York: Columbia University, Teacher's College, Bureau of Publications.

Leach, Edmund. 1958. "Magical Hair." *Journal of the Royal Anthropological Institute* 88(2):147–64.

Leacock, Elanor. 1971. Introduction. In *The Culture of Poverty: A Critique*, ed. E. Leacock. New York: Simon & Schuster, pp. 9–37.

Leeds, Anthony. 1971. "The Concept of the 'Culture of Poverty': Conceptual, Logical, and Emperical Problems with Perspectives from Brazil and Peru." In *The Culture of Poverty: A Critique*, ed. E. Leacock. New York: Simon & Schuster, pp. 226–84.

Lewis, Oscar. 1959. *Five Families: Mexican Case Studies in the Culture of Poverty*. New York: Basic Books.

———. 1965. *La Vida: A Puerto Rican Family in the Culture of Poverty—San Juan and New York*. New York: Vintage Books.

———. 1968. *A Study of Slum Culture: Backgrounds for La Vida*. New York: Random House.

Liebow, Elliot. 1967. *Tally's Corner: A Study of Negro Streetcorner Men*. Boston: Little, Brown & Company.

Liu, Frances W.   1936. "Woman's Fight against Beggary." *The China Quarterly* (Shanghai) 1(4):99–103.

Liu Hsü.   1936. *"Pei-p'ing te Ch'i-Kai Sheng-huo"* (Beggar life in Peiping). In *Pei-p'ing I Ku*, comp. T'ao Hang-te. Shanghai: Yü-chou Feng-she.

Loewe, Michael.   1968. *Everyday Life in Early Imperial China: During the Han Period 202B.C.–A.D.220.* New York: Harper & Row, Perennial Library.

MacGowan, D. J.   1859. "On the Banishment of Criminals in China." *Journal of the North China Branch of the Royal Asiatic Society* 3:293–301.

Macgowan, J.   1912. *Men and Manners of Modern China.* London: T. Fisher Unwin.

Martin, W. A. P.   1900. *A Cycle of Cathay or China, North and South,* 3d ed. New York, Chicago & Toronto: Fleming H. Revell.

Matignon, J. J.   1900. *Superstition, Crime et Misère en Chine,* 2d ed. Lyon: A. Storck & Co. Paris: Masson & Cie.

Mayers, William Frederick.   1970. *The Chinese Government: A Manual of Chinese Titles Categorically Arranged and Explained.* Taipei: Ch'eng-wen. Originally published 1897, Shanghai: Kelly & Walsh.

Merton, Robert K.   1968. *Social Theory and Social Structure.* Enlarged Edition. New York: Free Press.

Miller, Walter B.   1958. "Lower-Class Culture as a Generating Milieu of Gang Delinquency." *Journal of Social Issues* 14(1):5–19.

Moise, Edwin E.   1977. "Downward Social Mobility in Pre-Revolutionary China." *Modern China* 3(1):3–32.

Morse, Hosea Ballou.   1909. *The Gilds of China: With an Account of the Gild Merchant or Co-hong of Canton.* London: Longmans, Green.

Moule, Arthur E.   1902. *New China and Old: Personal Recollections and Observations of Thirty Years.* London: Seeley & Co., Ltd.

Nickum, James E, and David C. Schak.   1979. "Living Standards and Economic Development in Shanghai and Taiwan." *China Quarterly* 75:26–49.

Pitcher, Philip William.   1912. *In and About Amoy.* Shanghai and Foochow: Methodist Publishing House.

Plotnik, Robert D. and Felicity Skidmore.   1975. *Progress against Poverty: A Review of the 1964–1974 Decade.* New York: Academic Press.

Pruitt, Ida.   1945. *A Daughter of Han: The Autobiography of a Chinese Working Woman.* New Haven: Yale University Press.

Rainwater, Lee.   1960. *And the Poor Get Children: Sex, Contraception, and Family Planning in the Working Class.* Assisted by Karol and Kane Weinstein. Chicago: Quadrangle Books.

Rodman, Hyman.   1971. *Lower-Class Families: The Culture of Poverty in Negro Trinidad.* New York: Oxford University Press.

Schak, David C.   1979. "Images of Beggars in Chinese Culture." In *Legend, Lore, and Religion in China: Essays in Honor of Wolfram Eberhard on His Seventieth Birthday,* ed. S. Allan and A. Cohen. San Francisco: Chinese Materials Center, pp. 109–33.

Shih Ch'ien.   1925. *Kojiki Shakai no Seikatsu.* Taipei: Ai-ai Liao.

Shih Nai-an. 1963. *Water Margin*, vols. I and II, trans. J. Jackson. Hong Kong: Commercial Press.

Smith, Arthur H. 1890. *Chinese Characteristics*. New York, Chicago & Toronto: Fleming H. Revell Co.

———. 1900. *Village Life in China: A Study in Sociology*. Edinburgh & London: Oliphant, Anderson & Ferrier.

Solomon, Richard H. 1971. *Mao's Revolution and the Chinese Political Culture*. Berkeley and Los Angeles: University of California Press.

Sowell, Thomas. 1974. *Race and Economics*. New York: Mckay.

Stack, Carol B. 1974. *All Our Kin: Strategies for Survival in a Black Community*. New York: Harper Colophon.

Stott, Amelia O. 1927. "Chinese Knights of the Open Palm." *Asia* 27(10): 930–33.

Strong, Dexter K. 1967. "Hair: The Long and Short of It." *Seattle Magazine* 4:44–48, 59.

Taipei Shih. 1974. *T'ai-pei Shih Chia-t'ing Shou-chih Tiao-ch'a Pao-kao* (Investigation report of household expenditures in Taipei Municipality), no. 24.

Thernstorm, Stephan. 1969. "Poverty in Historical Perspective." In *On Understanding Poverty*, ed. D. Moynihan. New York: Basic Books, pp. 160–86.

Thomson, John Stuart. 1909. *The Chinese*. Indianapolis: Bobbs-Merrill.

Ti Yü-kuei. 1974. "Ch'i-kai Hsien-hsiang Mu-tu-chi" (An eyewitness account of the beggar phenomenon). *Chung-hua Yüeh-pao* 706:375–82; 707: 487–93.

Tuan Yi-fu. 1979. *Landscapes of Fear*. Minneapolis: University of Minnesota Press. New York: Pantheon Books.

Valentine, Charles. 1968. *Culture and Poverty: Critique and Counterproposals*. Chicago: University of Chicago Press.

Wang Shih-lang. 1974. *T'ai-wan She-hui Sheng-huo* (Social life in Taiwan). Taipei: Orient Cultural Service.

Watson, James L. 1975. *Migration and the Chinese Lineage: The Mans in Hong Kong and London*. Berkeley and Los Angeles: University of California Press.

Waxman, Chaim I. 1977. *The Stigma of Poverty: A Critique of Poverty Theories and Policies*. New York: Pergamon Press.

Wolf, Arthur P. 1974a. "Gods, Ghosts and Ancestors." In *Religion and Ritual in Chinese Society*. ed. A. Wolf. Stanford: Stanford University Press, pp. 131–82.

———. 1974b. "Marriage and Adoption in Northern Taiwan." In *Social Organization and the Applications of Anthropology*, ed. R. Smith. Ithaca: Cornell University Press, pp. 128–60.

Wolf, Arthur P., and Chieh-shan Huang. 1980. *Marriage and Adoption in China, 1845–1945*. Stanford: Stanford University Press.

Wolf, Margery. 1972. *Women and the Family in Rural Taiwan*. Stanford: Stanford University Press.

Wu Chia-ch'ing, ed. 1971. *Wu-chin Min-chien Ku-shih* (Folktales of Wu-chin). Taipei: Commercial Press.

Wu Tao-ying.   1969. *T'ai-wan Min-su* (Folk customs of Taiwan). Taipei: Chin-
    hsüeh Shu-chü.
Wu To.   1981. *"Tang-ch'ien Shang-hai Shih-ch'ü Ch'i-t'ao Hsien-hsiang Shih-hsi"*
    (A tentative analysis of today's beggary in the municipality of Shanghai).
    Society 1:42–45.
Yang, Martin M. C.   1945. *A Chinese Village: Taitou, Shantung Province.* New
    York: Columbia University Press.

Index

Abandonment of spouses. *See* Marriage

Adoption, 65, 116, 128, 129, 196–97, 199; forms of, 129, 130; money exchanged in, 131–32. *See also* Fostering

Alcohol: and conflicts, 74–75; use of, 106, 119

Alms-giving: ambiguities of, 41–43, 61–66; amounts of, 44; negative reasons for, 40–41; positive reasons for, 26, 32, 39, 40; and those most likely to give, 43–44

Bachelors, 118–20. *See also* Marriage; Sexual relationships

Beggar chief: duties of, 23–24, 60; power of, 20, 22, 24; in premodern China, 20, 22, 23, 60, 158; relation to the state of, 20, 21, 22, 23. *See also* Tiek-kou

Beggars. *See also* Liong-hiat, begging in
———appeals and tactics of: in Liong-hiat, 47, 50–51, 85, 87, 93; in premodern times, 19, 20, 32–33, ch. 3. *See also* Alms-giving; *Tiau-lo-ce*
———concept and image of, 17, 25, 31–42
———definition of, 3–6, 25–30, 49–50, 76, 188–89, 194–95
———education among, 108, 175–76
———in folklore, 31, 37, 45
———*gik-hi* (personal loyalty) among, 150–51, 164–65
———living standards of, 105–08

———organization of: in Liong-hiat, 4–5; in premodern China, 24, 25. *See also* Leadership; Liong-hiat; Tiek-kou
———in the People's Republic of China, 28, 56, 201
———as poor people, 3, 4, 195–202
———reasons for becoming: "fate," 38, 190–91, 231n4; heredity, 37, 191–92, 228n8; physical factors, 66, 87–89, 119, 193–95; weakness of character, 192–93
———relations with the state of, 4, 5, 17, 19, 20, 38, 85, 86, 91, 92–93, 158, 321n2
———role of, at weddings, 51, 58
———status of: inferiority of, 30; compared to *chien-min* (mean people), 37; compared to prostitutes, 32, 35. *See also* Stigma
———and territoriality, 21, 149
———types of: as entertainers, 29, 52–53; as "gentry," 26–28, 228n6; as knights-errant, 29, 36; as monks, 26; as refugees, 28; as tyrants 28–29, 57

Buddhism, 26, 29, 36, 46, 49, 50

Charity, 39, 55, 58, 59, 91. *See also* Relief

Chinese language, romanization of, 15

Cohusband relationships. *See* Marriage; Sexual relationships

Conflicts, 73, 74–76, 78, 80, 83; resolution of, 46–48; role of alcohol in, 74–75; role of gambling in, 75–76. *See also* Tiek-kou

243